**Ethics for the
Practice of Psychology
in Canada**

Ethics for the Practice of Psychology in Canada

Revised and Expanded Edition

Derek Truscott
Kenneth H. Crook

PICA
PICA
PRESS

An Imprint of The University of Alberta Press

Published by

The University of Alberta Press
Ring House 2
Edmonton, Alberta, Canada T6G 2E1
www.uap.ualberta.ca

LIBRARY AND ARCHIVES CANADA CATALOGUING IN PUBLICATION

Truscott, Derek, 1959–
Ethics for the practice of psychology in Canada / Derek Truscott, Kenneth H. Crook. —
Rev. and expanded ed.

Includes bibliographical references and index.
Issued also in electronic formats.
ISBN 978-0-88864-652-1

1. Psychologists—Professional ethics—Canada. 2. Psychology—Moral and ethical aspects—
Canada. I. Crook, Kenneth H., 1960– II. Title.

BF76.4.T78 2013   174'.915   C2013-901859-X

First edition, third printing, 2018.
Printed and bound in Canada by Houghton Boston Printers, Saskatoon, Saskatchewan.
Copyediting and proofreading by Joanne Muzak.
Indexing by Elizabeth Macfie.

The University of Alberta Press is committed to protecting our natural environment. As part of our
efforts, this book is printed on Enviro Paper: it contains 100% post-consumer recycled fibres and is
acid- and chlorine-free.

The University of Alberta Press gratefully acknowledges the support received for its publishing
program from The Canada Council for the Arts. The University of Alberta Press also gratefully
acknowledges the financial support of the Government of Canada through the Canada Book Fund
(CBF) and the Government of Alberta through the Alberta Multimedia Development Fund (AMDF)
for its publishing activities.

Dedicated with love to Alexandra and Sara

Contents

Preface

I approach the writing of this edition with deeply mixed emotions. Delight that the first was well-received and that the wonderful University of Alberta Press agreed to publish a second. Sadness that my dearest friend Ken Crook is no longer alive to write it with me.

Born with haemophilia, Ken was precociously aware of his mortality. My awakening occurred one spring day as we sat together in my convertible sports car quaffing root beer at our local drive-in restaurant. While I was worrying about how best to squander an idle summer, Ken turned and said, "I've exceeded my life expectancy." He was seventeen. Even after learning how the blood product that had extended his life would end it by infecting him HIV and hepatitis C, he persisted in living deliberately and well. When his declining health made it impossible to continue a brilliant legal career, he applied himself to collaborating with me on the first edition of this book. Having fully lived his forty-seven years, Ken died at home in Victoria, British Columbia on March 9, 2008.

Ken is an indelible part of this book. I have retained that which remains relevant from what we wrote together and only made changes to update and extend the first edition.

Changes From the First Edition

The Canadian Psychological Association's Canadian Code of Ethics for Psychologists remains unchanged, reflecting an absence of pressing issues. There have been no significant legal decisions affecting psychologists either, although those of importance have been incorporated into this edition. The federal Agreement on Internal Trade has necessitated changes to provincial and territorial entrance requirements to make it easier for psychologists registered in one jurisdiction to practice in another, however, and I have therefore made extensive revisions to the chapter on professional standards (Chapter 2). The agreement also articulates core competencies in ethics, which include research ethics—something not covered in the first edition—so I have added a chapter on the topic (Chapter 11).

During this period of relative calm, I continued to teach, practice, and study professional ethics. Wanting *Ethics for the Practice of Psychology in Canada, Revised and Expanded Edition* to reflect how ethics is actually taught, I reviewed all of the syllabi of all of the graduate programs in Canada. Many included objectives for students to gain awareness of their personal motives and biases. To learn how to facilitate such ethical self-knowledge, I went to the literature on moral development, where I discovered that professional training (medicine, law, education, etc.) tends to be associated with a deterioration toward being more rule-bound (Rest & Narváez, 1994). With this unsettling information rattling around in my brain, I carried on serving as an expert and consultant in matters of professional ethics and misconduct. There I came to appreciate that unethical actions rarely result from ignorance of our duties or of the likely consequences of our actions. I also learned that efforts to prevent or resolve unethical actions are largely ineffective without consideration of the psychologist's motivation and the interpersonal circumstances of the situation.

The line formed by these realizations pointed me toward the person of the psychologist and the important role of nonrational reasoning. In response, I have made some rather significant additions to this edition. Specifically, I have supplemented the previous edition's ethics of duty (deontology) and consequence (teleology) with the ethics of motivation (virtue) and circumstance (relational). They are discussed at length in the substantially revised and expanded chapters on ethical systems (Chapter 1) and ethical decision making (Chapter 4), and the other chapters are now organized around these four ethical systems.

Additional ethical case studies have also been included in each chapter. This was done because exposure to ethical dilemmas is the only pedagogical intervention that has been demonstrated to facilitate moral development. Finally, each chapter now has a reflective journal task to provide an opportunity for gaining awareness of personal motives and biases relevant to being ethical.

The appendices provided in the first edition are not included in this edition because all of that information is now easily accessible online. The Canadian Code of Ethics for Psychologists and professional guidelines are available directly from the Canadian Psychological Association (www.cpa.ca) and the rest (provincial and territorial standards and guidelines) are available via www.DerekTruscott.com.

Aims of This Edition

Ethics for the Practice of Psychology in Canada, Revised and Expanded Edition is written primarily for students in professional psychology graduate programs. The thorough grounding in ethical systems, professional standards, legal expectations, and ethical decision making, as well as comprehensive coverage of the issues that present psychologists with ethical challenges—consent, confidentiality, competence, boundaries, cultures, social justice, and research—makes it ideal for use as the main text for courses in professional ethics or professional issues, as well as for anyone preparing to practice in Canada. This edition will also serve more experienced psychologists seeking to maintain or enhance their ethical practice.

Being an ethical psychologist requires ethical awareness and knowledge, the ability to reason ethically, and the motivation and courage to act ethically. The aims of this book, therefore, are to:

- increase knowledge of ethical, legal, and professional expectations of psychologists;
- raise awareness of ethical issues in psychological practice;
- promote ethical decision-making skills and the ability to resolve ethical dilemmas; and
- foster development of a professional ethical identity.

It is my intention that *Ethics for the Practice of Psychology in Canada* be useful to you in becoming or in helping others to be an ethical psychologist. I welcome any comments you might want to share about this book and your experience of being ethical or teaching ethics. I promise to consider them thoughtfully and to incorporate any constructive feedback that I can if I have the opportunity to write a third edition. You are invited to visit my website at www.DerekTruscott.com where you can find my contact information as well as Internet links to additional ethical and regulatory information.

Acknowledgements

Derek thanks the many students for sharing their ethical challenges, questions, and answers, and Jacqueline Leighton for providing a scholarly environment conducive to teaching and learning. To Jim Evans and Steve Knish he owes a debt of gratitude he can never repay for the countless hours of good talk—this book is a testament to their support. Ken's thanks continue to the partners at Alexander, Holburn, Beaudin and Lang, and in particular to Michael P. Ragona, QC, Jo Ann Carmichael, QC, and Terry Vos, and to their law librarian Susan Daly. As do his thanks to Drs. W.E. Cooper and J. Vortel, without whose very different contributions this book would not have been possible.

Linda Cameron, Peter Midgley, Mary Lou Roy, Alan Brownoff, and Cathie Crooks of the University of Alberta Press provided much-needed and much-appreciated encouragement, guidance, and talent. Joanne Muzak, copyeditor extraordinaire, is responsible for making this book better (and not for any of its faults). Beth Macfie deserves thanks for the thankless job of indexing. Kevin Zak produced an engaging design that, as well as being beautiful, actually helps readers make sense of the information contained in this book. Finally, Diane Zanier has earned heartfelt gratitude for serving as a critical, compassionate and indefatigable reader of innumerable drafts of the manuscript.

We are indebted to Alexandra Kinkaide and Stan Whitsett for providing much of the material in "Anatomy of a Complaint," Chapter 2.

Introduction

While the vast majority of psychologists enter the profession because they want to help people and would therefore not intentionally harm those they come into contact with, such good intentions are not sufficient to navigate the myriad of ethical challenges inherent in professional practice. Psychologists can be ignorant of the ethical standards of the profession; be unaware of the existence of an ethical quandary; not know what to do despite adequate knowledge and awareness; lack the fortitude to do what they know is right; and even resist doing what they know they should. It is for these reasons that proficiency in professional ethics is a core competency for the practice of psychology in all jurisdictions across Canada. And it is also why this book was written.

Defining Ethics

Ethics is the analysis and determination of how people ought to act when judged against a system of *values*. Values are concepts of what is good—such as honesty and generosity—that are affirmed, and what is bad—such as greed and cruelty—that are repudiated in both thought and action. Values do not prescribe specific behaviours or outcomes. As such, ethics are fundamentally *aspirational* in nature and focus on the highest ideals of human awareness, intentions, reasoning, and behaviour. The field of professional ethics deals with clarifying the core set of related values of the profession, applying them to the resolution of problematic issues, and demarcating acceptable and unacceptable professional behaviour.

Ethics differ from *morality*, which is vaguely defined in its common use. Philosophers use morality to refer to an assessment of whether a person's actions are right or wrong when judged against a system of ethics. Ironically, the common usage of the concept of morality is almost the complete opposite of how philosophers use it. In common parlance, morality is used to refer to whether or not a person has firm personal convictions of right and wrong, often grounded in religious dogma. Some standards, such as "behave with integrity," are almost universally shared across individuals who are referred to as highly moral, but how these standards are interpreted and acted upon tends to vary considerably. For our purposes, we will refer to morality when an individual's personal sense of right and wrong is at issue, and we will refer to ethics when discussing professional standards and expectations of right and wrong.

Ethics are enacted via ethical systems, which ought to have four main features: 1) they are based on *principles* that are valued by individuals; 2) the principles have *universality* in that they are applicable to all individuals under similar circumstances; 3) appropriate actions can be deduced by individuals from the principles by *reasoning*; and 4) the resulting actions are likely to produce *outcomes* desired by all individuals. Two important facts are worth noting at this point. First, no system of ethics yet developed perfectly embodies all four of these features. Second, no code of professional ethics represents a pure ethical system. All existing codes are some combination of ethics, professional standards, and legal expectations. Thus, professional psychologists are operating from an imperfect system for guiding their decisions and actions. Despite these imperfections, psychologists' code of ethics can provide useful guidance for professional behaviour when supplemented by a thorough grounding in professional ethics.

DESCRIPTIVE VERSUS PRESCRIPTIVE ETHICS

Ethics can be *descriptive* of what members of a group *actually* do and believe, and they can be *prescriptive* of what those members *ought* to do and believe. Most codes of professional ethics attempt to strike a balance between description and prescription so that they represent the shared values of the profession while also upholding high ethical standards. Such a balance, however, is not an easy one to make, and the development and revision of a code of ethics can be quite problematic. If a professional body attempts to align its codes of ethics too closely with its practitioners' majority opinion, it may simply not be ethical enough. That is, many professionals may be acting in ways that would not be considered ethical when judged against any known system of ethics. Also, purely descriptive codes of ethics would have to be updated with some regularity, not necessarily in response to the ethical development of practitioners, but because of changing societal and professional attitudes. The uncertainty resulting from such fluctuations would also make knowing what to do as professionals much more difficult, and do nothing to help individual psychologists be more ethical.

If, on the other hand, a professional code of ethics is too prescriptive, it must, by design, reflect the opinion of a minority. Given the politics of writing and revising ethics codes, this minority is typically the most vociferous or influential members of the profession and not necessarily the most ethical (See Pope, 2011a, for an example from the US context). Such a code—whether ethically well-informed or not—risks reflecting values so discrepant from those of the typical professional that it will be ignored or rejected. Also, proponents of an overly prescriptive professional code can become so committed to their own assumptions about what is valued that any opposing views are suppressed, resulting in a code of ethics that inspires fear rather than allegiance. None of these circumstances are in the best interest of furthering ethical behaviour.

ETHICS VERSUS PRACTICE STANDARDS VERSUS LAW

While codes of ethics for psychologists typically contain statements prescribing and proscribing particular conduct, these do not properly belong in an ethical code (see Chapter 1). Such statements belong in professional standards and law. *Practice standards* (see Chapter 2) attempt to codify ethical values in the form of behavioural criteria that are consistent with legal expectations (see Chapter 3). Ideally, all practice standards should be consistent with and indeed follow from the Code of Ethics. Practice standards contain descriptions of minimally acceptable behaviour on the part of professionals and are intended to function as enforceable rules of conduct. The rules are definitive, prescriptive and proscriptive. They are the standards against which are judged a psychologist's actions (or failure to act) in such settings as disciplinary hearings.

From time to time, professional psychology groups develop *practice guidelines*. These usually address specialty areas of practice or circumstances that present particular challenges to ethical behaviour. As such, they also tend to exist within an historical context and can become dated or even irrelevant with the passage of time. Guidelines attempt to integrate specialized knowledge in the area of practice into common professional awareness and bridge the gap between the Code of Ethics and standards of practice. They are therefore typically a combination of prescriptive standards and aspirational values.

The *law* deals with minimum acceptable standards of behaviour for members of a society—the "dos and don'ts" of civilized life. Laws relating to professionals deal primarily with regulatory matters, principally around standards for admission into the profession. All Canadian jurisdictions (with the exception of the Yukon) have enacted legislation that identifies professional ethical codes and standards as delineating what society can reasonably expect of a psychologist (see Chapter 2). This statutory recognition, in turn, tends to be closely followed by the courts when making legal decisions in particular cases. More will be said about this in Chapter 3.

Since ethical codes and practice standards are developed by the profession, and legal expectations represent the values of a larger group (i.e., Canadian society), there will be times when professional ethics and standards are not completely congruent with the law. While such situations are rare, they can be particularly vexatious. Fortunately, with regard to most professional activities the law assumes that professional ethics codes and practice standards are appropriate and sufficient, and the courts are therefore very reluctant to contradict them. That is, the law generally attempts to follow psychologists' ethics, and this is where we should turn first for guidance. In fact, any amendments to professional codes and standards in the form of "except where required by law" have the effect of diluting their force and should normally be avoided. This is especially true with regard to case law that are very dependent on circumstances of the case in question and may not generalize to how psychologists (or anyone else) ought to behave in general or in other circumstances.

Being Ethical

The subject of professional ethics is often perceived by the layperson as a set of behavioural rules dealing with what to do and what not to do under certain circumstances. Knowledge of these rules, combined with knowledge of the general laws pertaining to the area should be enough to prevent the practitioner from going astray. Under this view, a book consisting of the Codes of Ethics, standards of practice, and Canadian law relating to the profession of psychology would be sufficient. While such a book could be a worthwhile contribution, it would be of use only if ethics were a static subject that could be reduced to the application of rules delineating what is right and what is wrong for all of the ethical challenges that psychologists face. It is not, however—ethical standards and expectations evolve and change. The ethical psychologist must be willing to do likewise.

KNOWLEDGE AND SKILLS

The uniqueness of each encounter between psychologist and client can be described in a vast—essentially infinite—number of ways. Taking a strictly rule-based approach to ethics would entail consideration of so many different combinations of variables that the number of required rules would be bewildering. Each professional circumstance, even if described by only a few possible attributes, becomes effectively unique. Even if it was possible to develop a system of categorizing relevant ethical variables, it would create an impractical situation for professionals who would have to learn almost as many ethical rules as there are professional situations. Fortunately, rules can serve a useful function in professional ethics. Ethical, professional, and legal rules can guide us in those commonly encountered situations where a consensus exists for how to act, such as avoiding exploitive relationships with clients (see Chapter 8).

In consideration of the fact that codes of ethics and standards of practice cannot account for every circumstance, a considerable amount of latitude is left to the judgement of the professional. This is as it should be because ethical behaviour is the product of decisions made by psychologists acting within the complexity of the context of professional practice. A model for ethical decision making is therefore presented in Chapter 4 that provides you with the skills for ethical reasoning to arrive at a justifiable course of action. An important aspect of these skills is the ability to articulate how a decision was reached. With this we move from merely knowing the difference between what is right and what is wrong to being able to convey the path of reason used to arrive at a decision.

AWARENESS AND CHARACTER

In addition to knowledge and skills, psychologists are expected to be aware of ethically challenging situations. This is so that we can anticipate that ethical reasoning is required and are thereby at least somewhat prepared. Knowing that situations involving consent, confidentiality, and professional boundaries, among others, are prone to be ethically troublesome helps us to be alert to potential problems and forearmed with possible solutions.

Ultimately, no degree of awareness can substitute for the active process of behaving ethically. We must be willing to engage in the struggle of unique circumstances, conflicting motivations, multiple responsibilities, and dire consequences that our profession entails. Psychologists can actually get away with many unethical and even illegal practices if they choose to do so—the risk of being caught and prosecuted is quite minimal. Doing so, however, would be inconsistent with a truly professional identity. Having chosen to enter a profession, and upon being admitted to it, one becomes the recipient of the privileges, status, and prestige that the profession affords. This creates a responsibility that is ethical in nature. It is, in very important ways, greater than the ethical responsibility incurred by someone who sells a product, for example, because what psychologists provide cannot be touched, weighed, or measured. This additional level of responsibility manifests itself in requiring us as professionals to have the courage to do what is right, even—and especially—when it is difficult to do so.

These attributes are very personal in nature and are not acquired in the same way that knowledge and skills are. Self-reflection, focusing on our character, is the best way to foster such attributes. In particular, attention should be devoted to developing self-awareness of personal motives that promote or interfere with ethical behaviour.

Getting the Most Out of This Book

To obtain maximum benefit from this book, I invite you to seek to be 1) sceptical without becoming cynical—rejecting no fact or opinion impetuously because it might be enlightening, and 2) open without becoming gullible—accepting no fact or opinion uncritically because it might be misleading. Above all, I encourage you to develop informed opinions, even if you're unsure of your ideas. This requires that you actively engage in the process of learning.

Learning occurs when you take in information, think about it, and make sense of it in light of what you already know. This may involve assimilating new information into existing knowledge, rejecting it for good reason and thereby confirming already established knowledge, or changing held beliefs in the face of compelling facts or arguments. Learning also involves seeing how, where, and when to apply new information. At its best, learning transforms who we are and how we relate to the world around us.

DISCUSSION QUESTIONS

Discussion questions are included at the end of each chapter primarily for classroom use and can, of course, also be used as prompts for personal consideration. They are not designed to have a right or wrong answer. They are opportunities for you to rehearse what you have learned, argue different points of view, and generally integrate new learning with your existing knowledge. By actively striving to form your own informed opinion, you will learn the material in a manner that supplements what can be achieved through passively reading. Here are a few questions for you to consider now:

1. Do you think that ethics can be taught? Or is it a matter of how you were raised and the experiences you had? Explain.
2. Are people fundamentally good, or evil? Asked another way, do we need to be kept in check through external controls, or provided opportunities to express our virtuous nature?

REFLECTIVE JOURNALING

At the end of each chapter you are invited to add to your own reflective journal. Reflective journaling is an opportunity to facilitate your development as an ethical psychologist. The intent is to challenge you to think about your personal values and motives that may interfere with or promote ethical reasoning and action. You can use journaling to make explicit your implicit beliefs on a range of ethical matters. It can be an opportunity to tease out your assumptions and critically examine them. This is a crucial aspect of your ethical self. To truly be an ethical psychologist requires a deep and thorough processing of the information presented in the pages of this book and how it relates to your personal and professional life. Reflective journaling allows you an opportunity to process the experiences, thoughts, questions, ideas, and conclusions central to your ethical development.

If you find writing to be rather difficult or unappealing, you may choose to create an audio or video journal, or some other method for recording your process. Whatever you choose, find a way that works for you. You might also want to keep a pen and paper or other recording medium at the ready while you are reading this book so that you can record your impressions while they are fresh, particularly with regard to the ethical case studies (discussed below). Your immediate reactions can be a good source of information about your ethical self, and so making a note of them before they are lost is a good strategy. You can later incorporate these impressions in your journaling.

Most people find that where they write affects the quality of their reflective journaling. It is probably best to choose a place with minimal distractions and where you feel at ease. Some like silence; some like quiet music. Many find that it helps to get words flowing by doing their journaling outside—experiencing something greater than ourselves often seems to open our hearts and minds. Journaling during certain times of the day might also work well for you. Some write every morning as the sun rises, while others pull out paper and pen while dinner bubbles on the stove (or "nukes" in the microwave). Regardless of when you do it, most people find that setting aside a regular time is important to help establish a habit. If you're not sure what's right for you, experiment until you find a routine that works.

There is no correct way to begin a reflective journal—just write as you are thinking. It seems to work best to not be in a hurry. Setting aside at least twenty minutes is preferable because it can take a while to settle into a flow of writing. Don't worry if words are misspelled or if it doesn't look neat—this has no bearing on facilitating your development. Our thoughts are usually a non-linear jumble of impressions, words, feelings, and images, so if we write honestly, our writing will not be particularly logical. Indeed, the process of putting our subjective experience into a linear, grammatical form is an important part of what makes journaling so effective.

By way of introduction, begin your journal with recording an autobiographical sketch of your moral development. Who are or were the people in your life who most influenced your values and beliefs about right and wrong? What is the nature of their influence? For most of us, our parents and early family environment was very important, although often in ways of which we are not completely conscious. To what extent can you readily articulate your core moral values? For others, the moral beliefs of our families were quite explicit; perhaps a parent was a judge or an educator, or professed deeply held religious beliefs, for example. Even in these instances, the expressed views of these individuals were often not completely congruent with their behaviours. If this is the case for you, how has it influenced your moral beliefs? To what extent do you find that your values are congruent with your actions? Have there been pivotal events in your life that have influenced your sense of right and wrong? What important choices have you made, for instance, and how do they reflect your moral values? Are there trends in your actions and values, or a few (or even one) that stands out? What overall tendencies do you discern? How easy or difficult have you found this exercise, and what does this tell you about your moral development? Take as much time as you need to write down your responses to these and any other questions that occur to you.

ETHICAL CASE STUDIES

At the beginning and end of each chapter you will find ethical case studies dealing with issues related to that chapter. They are included to provide you with opportunities for enhancing your ethical awareness and practicing ethical decision making. These cases are derived from real events and disguised as necessary to protect the identity of those involved. As such, they do not represent any actual person or situation and any resemblance is purely coincidental. The only exceptions are legal cases distilled from public documents. The case studies therefore represent realistic, complex, and sometimes confusing situations that psychologists encounter in their practice. They tend not to have simple answers, nor necessarily be completely resolvable. In fact, they are chosen for precisely these qualities. While they do not embody all of the ethical issues discussed in the chapter in which they appear, they are intended to stimulate your ethical development by prompting you to struggle with ethical dilemmas that are not easily resolved. As Arthur Schlesinger Jr. (1949) wrote, "Problems will always torment us, because all important problems are insoluble: that is why they are important. The good comes from the continuing struggle to try and solve them, not from the vain hope of their solution" (p. 254).

To enhance the benefit to be gained by struggling to try and solve the cases, you are encouraged to place yourself in the role of the protagonist. That is, rather than saying, "The psychologist should do this and not do that," try, "I think I would do this and not do that." By thoughtfully and earnestly grappling with the challenge the cases present, you will maximize your learning and development.

You should try not to worry too much about how little you may know about the ethics, laws, and professional standards applicable to each case. You will learn more and remember it better if you first try to come to a decision based on whatever knowledge you already possess, and then search for the relevant standards and expectations. This is especially true with ethics because so few situations in real life will be resolved by resorting to the application of one simple rule—you will often have to apply imperfect rules to complex circumstances where you don't have time to look up the answers. So get as much practice as you can here when the stakes are low.

As an introduction, consider the following ethical case study and the questions that follow it. It is one of the original ethical dilemmas presented to the sample of psychologists who informed the development of the Canadian Code of Ethics for Psychologists (see Chapter 1).

Case Study

Compromised Consultant

You have been hired as a consultant to a daycare centre. Part of the contract involves a guarantee of confidentiality. Although privately owned, the daycare centre is licensed by the municipality and receives a subsidy for 20 per cent of its spaces. Shortly after beginning to consult to the daycare centre, it becomes clear that programming for the children is well below existing standards. Staff are underpaid, turnover is high, children are shifted from one group to another depending on who has shown up for work that day, staff complain that consumable supplies are replaced only at inspection time, children are handled roughly by discouraged staff, and distressed children are rarely comforted. Attempts to implement changes are undermined by the owner. After working for the centre for six months and having almost no impact, you come to the realization that consultation was requested because the owner thought that having a consultant would "look good." You can see no basis on which to continue the contract, but have serious concerns about the welfare of the children at the daycare centre. Reporting the centre to municipal authorities would represent a breach of contract.

Questions for consideration

1. Who do you think you need to consider in arriving at a solution to this situation?

2. What rights and responsibilities do you think are owed to the people who should be considered in this situation?

3. What choices of action might you consider to resolve this situation? Why?

4. What feelings are aroused in you by this situation? How might these feelings affect your decision about what to do?

Source: Adapted from *Companion Manual to the Canadian Code of Ethics for Psychologists*, 3rd ed. (Sinclair & Pettifor, 2001).

RECOMMENDED READING

Each chapter concludes with a list of recommended readings. These lists are provided as opportunities for you to go further into the literature on professional ethics. It is not absolutely necessary for you to read all of the recommended texts. Cultivating a willingness to try to be as informed as possible about ethical issues will make you a more ethical psychologist, though. Articles published in journals usually deal with specific, emerging topics, while books (such as this one) tend to deal with material that is broad and established. As such, reading articles can help you develop an appreciation for where the field of professional ethics is heading. Articles are almost always a response to other writers, so you'll better appreciate the issues that ethics scholars are grappling with if you understand who they are speaking to. Therefore, pay particular attention to points where the authors tell you they are disagreeing with someone else. Here are a few readings to get you started that you can find in most libraries and online.

Berry, J.W. (2013). Achieving a global psychology. *Canadian Psychology, 54,* 55–61.

Handelsman, M.M., Gottlieb, M.C., & Knapp, S. (2005). Training ethical psychologists: An acculturation model. *Professional Psychology: Research and Practice, 36,* 59–65.

1

Understanding Ethical Systems

Case Study

A Client in Need

You have been seeing a client for psychotherapy who had agreed to your standard fee. The client was experiencing severe distress due to an abusive marriage and had elected for individual therapy because her husband refused marital therapy. After attending four sessions, she missed the next two. You then receive a telephone call from her and she says that she and her husband have separated. She reluctantly tells you that her bank accounts have been frozen, she has no access to money, and has no family or friends to whom she can turn. If she doesn't soon pay her rent she will be evicted from her apartment. She would like to continue in therapy, but can't drive, and rather than paying for bus fare, has been buying food with what little cash she has.

Questions for consideration

1. *What individuals and/or groups would you consider in arriving at a solution to this dilemma?*

2. *What considerations is each individual/group owed? Why?*

3. *What is your choice of action? Why?*

4. *What alternative choice(s) of action(s) did you consider? Why did you not choose them?*

Our ethics serve to define us as professionals. To be recognized as a profession means that a group of practitioners has been granted a monopoly over the use of its knowledge base, the right to considerable autonomy in practice, and the privilege of regulating its members. Professional status is only bestowed on an occupation that makes a commitment to the public good, however (see Chapter 2). This social contract is enacted through a profession adopting and following a code of ethics.

In order to honour and sustain this interdependence, a professional code of ethics ought not contain anything that is discordant with the values of society at large. That is, the societal recognition of a profession does not signify that unique ethical principles apply to that occupation. Rather, it acknowledges the distinct expertise that members of the profession possess and the difficult situations that they are expected to deal with. A professional code of ethics should therefore represent the application of generally accepted ethical principles to activities characteristic of or idiosyncratic to the profession.

A code of ethics also should be based upon a coherent ethical system so that we might be able to put it to use. This system must be specific enough that we know what to do, while being general enough that we know how to be ethical in novel situations. And it must guide us to actions and outcomes acceptable to the society we serve. There is no system of ethics that manages to fulfill these functions perfectly. Each has its strengths and its weaknesses, and each has something to contribute to being an ethical psychologist. This is why an understanding of ethical systems is necessary for the professional psychologist.

There is another very important purpose for learning about ethical systems. Most of our actions are shaped by beliefs we have about the nature of the human condition. These beliefs serve as a filter by which we selectively attend to all of the potential information available to us as we try to understand the world around us and how best to live our lives (Koltko-Rivera, 2004; Unger, Draper, & Pendergrass, 1986) and they shape our personal moral system (Bendixen, Schraw, & Dunkle, 1998).

Our actions can be incongruent with our personal moral beliefs, however, and when they are, the likelihood that we will behave immorally increases. Also, if our personal moral beliefs are too discrepant with those embodied within our professional code of ethics, we will find it extremely difficult to reliably meet our professional ethical responsibilities. Thus, an understanding of ethical systems can help you bring your professional behaviour into harmony with your personal morals and with the code of ethics of our profession so that you might be more consistently an ethical psychologist.

Four Foundational Ethical Systems

History's greatest philosophers have been particularly concerned with what constitutes an ethical life. You have probably noticed that your moral sense has much in common with that of many other people and is at odds with that of some others. Similarly, philosophers have been debating which system of ethics is best for thousands of years. While there is no one completely uncontroversial ethical system, it is generally accepted that the most important attempts in Western philosophy to understand the nature of human ethics are represented by four foundational systems: teleology, deontology, virtue, and relational.

Each of these systems is based on a philosophical worldview that is valid and useful to a point, without quite managing to be complete. The allegorical tale of "the blind men and the elephant" probably describes this situation best, whereby each touched a part of the elephant and believed that he understood it entirely. The blind man who held the ear declared that an elephant is a fan, he who touched the belly that it is a wall, the trunk that it is a snake, the leg a pillar, and the tail a rope. Each had only a limited grasp of the whole and was thus only partially correct. We are all similarly blind in that no human being can comprehend the entirety of the human condition. Each philosophy describes only part of the whole. Fortunately for us, we are not expected to resolve this millennia-old problem. Instead, we can understand each system as a contribution to an unknowable whole. One way to conceptualize the relationship between the parts and the whole of ethics is presented in Figure 1.1.

The four foundational ethical systems can be usefully mapped along two dimensions: analytic versus experiential and social versus personal. An analytic approach to ethics favours rational analysis while an experiential approach privileges participation in real-world processes. Along the other dimension, a social approach honours publicly observable phenomenon whereas a personal approach values introspection. By organizing ethical systems in this way we can see some of the similarities and differences among them—and glimpse one possible way that they might form a whole.

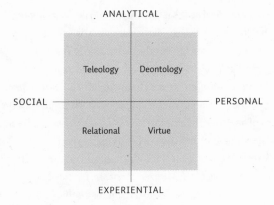

Figure 1.1 Relationship between four ethical systems

TELEOLOGY

Teleology (from the Greek *telos*, meaning "end" and *logia*, meaning "reason"—therefore "reasoning from ends") is an analytic and social approach to ethics. The teleological system operates from the perspective that right actions are those that produce desired outcomes. Teleology is described as *consequentialistic* in that it is concerned with the consequences of our actions. There are a number of different variants of teleology, with by far the most established being *utilitarianism* as articulated by Jeremy Bentham (1748–1832) and John Stuart Mill (1806–1873). Its basic premise is: *an act is right if, all other things being equal, it produces or is likely to produce the greatest amount of good for the greatest number of people.* What constitutes a "good" outcome is typically either the happiness or preferences of the persons involved or affected. A pure utilitarian approach for psychologists would require that our code of ethics contain only one principle: consider the utility of each possible outcome for each action appropriate to each situation we face.

A more practical variant of utilitarianism is *rule utilitarianism*, which can be stated as: *we should behave in accordance with rules that, all other things being equal, produce or are likely to produce the greatest amount of good for the greatest number of people in most circumstances.* Such a system has the advantage of allowing a profession to codify rules of ethics, and each professional then only has to know which rule to apply to a given situation.

DEONTOLOGY

Deontology (from the Greek *deont*, meaning "duty" and *logia*, meaning "reason"—therefore "reasoning from duty") was first articulated by the classical Greek philosopher Plato (429–347 BCE) and honed to a fine edge by Immanuel Kant

(1724–1804). Deontological ethics is an analytic and personal approach that urges us to reflect inward when solving a particular ethical dilemma in order to establish obligatory principles to guide future ethical reasoning. The deontological system calls upon us to *act as if the rationale that underlies our action were to become a universal duty*. It is therefore often referred to as *duty* ethics. From a deontological point of view, neither the intention to bring about good results nor the actual consequences of an act are relevant to assessing ethical worth. Deontology posits that the rightness of an action depends upon whether we perform it in accordance with, and out of respect for, absolute and universal ethical principles. These principles, because of their universal nature, create obligations. For example, suppose a psychologist decided to prolong services beyond their usefulness in order to keep receiving payment from a client. The rationale embodied in such an act is, "it is acceptable to gain money at another's expense," and the duty would be something like, "advance your own interests." Because no one would consent to being so treated, the deontological argument goes, no rational being would accept such a duty as universally obligating. The obligatory principles that are considered to apply to the profession of psychology are: respect for autonomy; nonmaleficence (doing no harm); beneficence (helping others); fidelity (honesty and integrity); and justice (fairness and equitableness).

VIRTUE

Virtue ethics has it roots in the work of another great ancient Greek philosopher, Aristotle (384–322 BCE) and was the dominant approach in Western ethics until the eighteenth century when reason came to be honoured over authority (especially religious authority, which had incorporated Aristotelian principles). Interest arose again in the late 1950s, fueled by a growing dissatisfaction with deontology and teleology as neglecting the subjective experience of the person who is striving to be ethical. Virtue ethics place the *character* of the individual in the central role of ethical considerations. Virtue ethics focus on the ideal rather than the obligatory and on the intentions of the actor rather than the consequences of actions. The rightness of an action does not depend upon its consequences nor its correspondence with principles, but rather depends upon its having the right motive. What is considered ethical is unique to the individual and cannot be completely explained by logic. Where teleology and deontology address *what* is ethical, virtue deals with *who* is ethical. When considering the ethics of a situation, therefore, virtue thus encourages us to ask: *How will my actions embody the type of person I want to be?* Thus, it is not the act that is appraised, but the character of the person who acts. Virtue ethics orients professionals to think ethically at all times rather than only when confronted with an ethical dilemma. Virtue ethics call upon us to aspire to develop traits of character that will naturally result in meeting our ethical expectations. As such, ethical rules and principles are not seen as unimportant, merely insufficient.

RELATIONAL
Relational ethics focus on our experience of others in the social world. Founded in the feminist thought of Carol Gilligan (1936–) and Nel Noddings (1929–) and developed by Vangie Bergum (1939–) and John Dossetor (1925–), relational ethics highlights how relationships are innate and fundamental to the human condition. Based on the premise that ethical actions always take place in relation to at least one other person, relational ethics requires us to ask: *How will my actions manifest consideration of and my concern for others?* Ethical knowledge, reasoning, and action are understood as being imbedded within a complex, never completely predictable, relational context (Bergum & Dossetor, 2005). Behaving ethically is thus not a personal, analytic exercise—it is experiential and social. That is, being ethical entails action in real relationship with real consequences. As such, relational ethics is concerned with how we treat each other rather than the why of a particular ethical decision. What is considered ethical is thereby also open to change and reconsideration as the context of our actions change in response to new relationships and events. This highlights how ethical actions are reciprocal in that professional and client both act and react. Misplaced trust, unfairness in gains and losses, and a whole suite of human relational issues inevitably emerge. These can cause strains in the relational ties that bind people together socially, and relational ethicists point out that we must be willing to continually negotiate new and revised relationships as we seek to be ethical.

ETHICAL SYSTEMS APPRAISED
The major strength of teleology—that it provides us with a calculative framework that allows ethical decisions to be implemented in a logical, objective fashion—is also its fundamental weakness. By focusing on the greatest amount of good for the greatest number of people, teleology allows for the sacrifice of the individual in the name of the common good. Such an "ends justifying the means" approach tends to stand against the basic value that Canadian society places on the innate worth of the individual. It was also the rationale given by most of those who were tried for war crimes associated with cruel medical experimentation perpetrated

by the Nazis during the Second World War (see Chapter 11). The greatest practical difficulty associated with teleology is that it leaves unanswered the question of what counts as a "good" outcome. Some argue that what is good is *hedonistic* or pleasurable. Others argue that what is good is what is *ideal* such as honesty, justice, or beneficence, while others argue that it is some mixture of these.

The inherent difficulties with a deontological approach to ethics come from two sources. First, similar to the problem with teleology, there is no consensus as to which ethical principles are universal and absolute. Second, situations arise whereby principles are at odds with one another. So one might argue that the principle of beneficence requires that we lie to persons dying of an incurable disease in order that they maintain their hope in the future, while another would argue that the principle of autonomy requires that we not withhold information that they might use to make decisions about how to live what remains of their lives. The most pressing practical difficulty arising from deontology is that, with its emphasis on the analytic application of duties without reference to the consequences, it tends to encourage students in professional programs to make ethical judgements primarily in reference to the laws of society, rather than being based on principles grounded in social contracts. This tendency is also associated with a decline in moral reasoning from admission to graduation (Rest & Narváez, 1994).

As with deontology, virtue ethics struggles from a lack of consensus as to which virtues are universal and absolute. Also, virtues are inspirational and aspirational ideals. Thus, virtue ethics are impractical for regulating our profession— can you imagine rescinding someone's registration as a psychologist because they were considered to be insufficiently humble? A psychologist with a reputation for being virtuous who does make a technical or ethical error, however, will tend to be dealt with in a more lenient manner and given the benefit of the doubt compared with someone who does not have such a reputation.

Relational ethics facilitate the incorporation of social and interpersonal factors that allow the placement of ethical considerations in the social context in which we are embedded (O'Neill & Hern, 1991). This directs us to consider our actions in context before deciding on their rightness or wrongness. A particular strength of this approach is its acknowledgement of the "messiness" of striving to be ethical and how established duties and good intentions may not always lead to good outcomes. In this aspect, relational ethics shares much with teleology. The major weakness with relational ethics is its experiential nature, which, as with virtue ethics, makes it impractical for regulating professionals. In the case of relational ethics, this impracticality arises out of the rightness or wrongness of ethical actions always being situation-specific. When asked to decide on the

ethical course of action, the relational answer will always be some variant of,
"It depends."

Clearly, each ethical system has its strengths and weaknesses. From a
practical point of view, Canadian society follows almost exclusively the deontological and teleological systems in its social and legal decisions. Essentially, all
Canadians are expected to act in accordance with deontological duties except
where doing so would obviously result in abhorrent consequences such as death
or extreme physical harm. Deontology and teleology are therefore appropriate
for understanding our ethical obligations and for regulating professionals. Virtue
ethics can provide an understanding of the personal qualities necessary to
enact our ethical responsibilities, while relational ethics are most helpful for guidance within each unique interpersonal circumstance in which ethical acts occur.
Virtue and relational ethics are therefore appropriate for cultivating our personal
ethical sensibility.

The Canadian Code of Ethics
for Psychologists

In the years following the Second World War, Canadian psychologists experienced increasing demands for their services (Dunbar, 1998). Just what constituted
a "psychologist," however, was open to considerable interpretation, and many
individuals had the job title of psychologist without a degree in psychology or
sometimes even any post-secondary education (Bois, 1948). In an attempt to
establish standards of certification, the Canadian Psychological Association
(CPA) arranged to have the American Psychological Association (APA) certify
CPA members. The APA agreed to do so provided the CPA adopt a code of ethics
(Wright, 1974). The CPA then spent the decade from 1949 to 1959 trying to develop
a Canadian code of ethics, which it failed to do, eventually adopting the APA's
code in 1963 (Dunbar, 1998).

By the late 1970s, Canadian psychologists were expressing dissatisfaction
with the APA code because it did not address concerns they felt were unique to
Canada. Many did not approve of its emphasis on commercial aspects of the
profession (Sinclair, Simon, & Pettifor, 1996), particularly around restrictions
on advertising to conform to US antitrust law, which were not relevant to the
Canadian context (Sinclair, 1993). Moreover, some argued that a made-in-Canada
code would appeal to a sense of national identity, address Canada's different
cultural context, and be more congruent with Canadian legal standards (Sinclair,
Poizner, Gilmour-Barrett, & Randall, 1987). In 1978, a decision was made to once
again undertake the development of a Canadian code of ethics.

DEVELOPMENT

The Canadian Code of Ethics for Psychologists can be said to be based on the "collective wisdom" of Canadian psychologists (Sinclair, 1998). Thirty-seven ethical vignettes were constructed to reflect conflicts between the ethical principles of the 1977 APA code of ethics in areas of applied psychology, teaching, and research. Fifty-nine members of CPA then responded to the following questions about each vignettes (Sinclair et al., 1987):

1. Indicate the individuals and/or groups that need to be considered in arriving at a solution to the psychologist's dilemma.
2. Take each of the individuals/groups in turn and explain in detail what considerations each is owed and why. (Think of the rights and responsibilities involved.)
3. What is your choice of action? Why?
4. What alternative choice(s) of action(s) did you consider? Why did you not choose them?
5. What is the minimal circumstance you can conceive in this situation that would lead you to a different choice of action? What would your action be? Why?
6. Do you have any further thoughts or comments about the above or similar situations? Please explain.

A content analysis of the responses was then conducted to look for reasons for particular courses of action (e.g., "Psychologists have a responsibility to inform clients of service limitations that might arise due to interference") or values expressed (e.g., "Clients have a right to choose their own therapist"). These were then grouped under four superordinate principles: Respect for the Dignity of Persons, Responsible Caring, Integrity in Relationships, and Responsibility to Society. A values statement describing each principle was then derived primarily from the psychologists' responses to the vignettes. Each principle was further elaborated through standards articulating the application of the principle to more specific situations. Ethics codes of other countries, ethical guidelines, and scholarly ethical writings were also reviewed, and additional standards were developed and incorporated into the appropriate principle. This is why standards exist for situations that were not dealt with in any of the vignettes, such as the treatment of animals in research.

The draft Code was then circulated to groups and individuals within and outside the discipline of psychology. Their feedback prompted a renaming of one of the principles and revisions to some of the values statements and standards.

The final four principles became Respect for the Dignity of Persons, Responsible Caring, Integrity in Relationships, and Responsibility to Society. Basing the Code in deontology had the particular benefit of rendering it consistent with Canadian laws and social norms. The Code even addresses the major criticism of deontology in that it presents a ranked ordering of the principles to assist decision making when ethical principles are in conflict. While certainly not a perfect solution, it does serve to make our ethical decisions more consistent within and across psychologists. The first edition of the Code was published in 1986, with minor revisions published in 1991 and 2000.

PRINCIPLE I: RESPECT FOR THE DIGNITY OF PERSONS

This principle was given the highest weight of the four principles. It is described in the Values Statement:

> Psychologists accept as fundamental the principle of respect for the dignity of persons; that is, the belief that each person should be treated primarily as a person or an end in him/herself, not as an object or a means to an end. In so doing, psychologists acknowledge that all persons have a right to have their innate worth as human beings appreciated and that this worth is not dependent upon their culture, nationality, ethnicity, colour, race, religion, sex, gender, marital status, sexual orientation, physical or mental abilities, age, socio-economic status, or any other preference or personal characteristic, condition, or status.

Respect for the Dignity of Persons corresponds to the foundational deonto-logical principles of autonomy and, to a lesser extent, justice. Autonomy literally means "self-rule" and deals with respect for the right of the individual to make choices about self-determination and to have freedom from the control of others. Respect for autonomy in the practice of psychology is most clearly expressed in allowing clients to decide for themselves whether or not to undertake psycho-logical services (see Chapter 5) and what private information is withheld from or disclosed to others (see Chapter 6). Justice is the deontological obligation to act fairly. In the context of professional ethics, it refers to avoiding bias or unfair discrimination in our professional actions (see Chapter 9), as well as fairness and equity in the allocation of and access to professional services (see Chapter 10).

PRINCIPLE II: RESPONSIBLE CARING

This principle was given the second highest weight. It is described in the Values Statement:

Responsible caring leads psychologists to take care to discern the potential harm and benefits involved, to predict the likelihood of their occurrence, to proceed only if the potential benefits outweigh the potential harms, to develop and use methods that will minimize harms and maximize benefits, and to take responsibility for correcting clearly harmful effects that have occurred as a direct result of their research, teaching, practice, or business activities.

Responsible caring embodies the deontological principles of beneficence and nonmaleficence. Beneficence involves actively contributing to the well-being of others. At a basic level it applies to all members of a society because we all have some responsibility to provide aid to those who are in need of assistance. For members of a profession, beneficence entails establishing and maintaining a minimum level of competence in order that professional services might be delivered in a manner that furthers the welfare of our clients (see Chapter 7). In addition to providing benefit, beneficence also obligates psychologists to balance the potentially beneficial consequences of an action against the potentially harmful ones, particularly the autonomy of our clients. Many a person refuses to accept a psychologist's good advice!

Nonmaleficence has a long history arising out of medical practice. It means not causing others harm. In more general terms for professionals, nonmaleficence means not inflicting intentional harm or engaging in actions that risk harming others, as well as being obligated to protect clients against harm (see Chapter 7). Most ethicists agree that, all other things being equal, our obligation to protect and not harm our clients is stronger than our obligation to contribute to their welfare (Beauchamp & Childress, 2012). In the medical arena, the concept of harm tends to be less controversially understood as physical bodily damage, pain, or death. Psychologists rarely deal in such matters, except in cases of suicide and homicide, and are more likely to be involved in instances of mental harms or thwarting significant personal interests such as reputation or privacy. There is much less agreement about our obligations with respect to these non-physical harms, especially when we consider such "harms" as annoyance or humiliation.

PRINCIPLE III: INTEGRITY IN RELATIONSHIPS

This principle was assigned the third highest weight and is described in the Values Statement:

The relationships formed by psychologists in the course of their work embody explicit and implicit mutual expectations of integrity that are vital to the advancement of scientific knowledge and to the maintenance of public confidence in the discipline of psychology. These expectations include: accuracy and honesty; straightforwardness and openness; the maximization of objectivity and minimization of bias; and, avoidance of conflicts of interest.

Integrity in relationships corresponds to the deontological principle of fidelity. Faithfulness, loyalty, honesty, and trustworthiness fall under the principle of fidelity and are at the core of the fiduciary relationship between professionals and the recipients of their services. Upholding the ethical principle of fidelity involves placing the interests of our clients ahead of our own, even when doing so is inconvenient or uncomfortable (see Chapter 8). Fidelity also extends to relationships with colleagues and other professionals. Integrity in relationships obligates psychologists to honour contracts with employers, for example, and to act in accordance with the rules of our profession.

PRINCIPLE IV: RESPONSIBILITY TO SOCIETY

This principle was given the lowest weight of the four principles and is described in the Values Statement:

> Psychologists, both in their work and as private citizens, have responsibilities to the societies in which they live and work, such as the neighbourhood or city, and to the welfare of all human beings in those societies.

Principle IV does not correspond directly to any deontological principles. It does address ethical duties associated with beneficence by expecting psychologists to increase knowledge and promote the welfare of human beings. Responsibility to society goes beyond beneficence as normally conceived, however, in broadening the ethical duty to society as a whole, thereby incorporating elements of justice (see Chapter 10).

Summary

Ethics represent the core values of a profession. By seeking to be accepted as professionals and thereby be granted the right to practice independently, psychologists are expected to abide by a code of ethics that strives to ensure that society benefits from our activities. Professional ethical behaviour, therefore, is predicated on considering the client's welfare as paramount. The major systems that guide ethical thinking are teleological, deontological, virtue, and relational. Teleology and deontology are best suited for regulating ethical behaviour, with virtue and relational ethics best for guiding individuals seeking to be ethical. The Canadian Code of Ethics for Psychologists is based primarily on the deontologic-al ethical system. It was developed by asking Canadian psychologists how they resolve ethical dilemmas and grouping their responses under four ethical prin-ciples: Respect for the Dignity of Individuals, Responsible Caring, Integrity in Relationships, and Responsibility to Society.

Discussion Questions

1. What do you like or dislike about each ethical system as applied to psychological practice? What do you like or dislike about each ethical system as applied to your own life?

2. Do you agree deontology should be the primary ethical system governing the practice of psychology? Why or why not?

3. Do you think that the Canadian Code of Ethics for Psychologists should have prescriptive statements? Alternatively, should it include only aspira-tional principles? Why?

4. Our Code of Ethics is almost completely silent with respect to virtue or relational ethics. Do you agree with this emphasis? Why or why not?

Your Reflective Journal

Think about an important ethical dilemma you faced in your personal life. Is there one that comes readily to mind? Or do you have to think long and hard to recall one? Does this tell you something about how prominent ethics is in your life? It may be that your ethical values and behaviours are highly congruent such that elaborate decision making is not required before acting. It may also be the case that you have not attended to your ethical beliefs as much as you should. Record your thoughts about this aspect of your ethical self.

Returning to your dilemma, think about the people that you considered in arriving at a solution. Did you think of the rights and responsibilities each was owed and why? Did you consider the consequences of alternative courses of action? Did your actions flow from your intuition, or was it more of a deliberate, logical process? Did you involve others in your dilemma or did you make a deci-sion on your own? What was your choice of action and what did you base it on? How comfortable were you with your action then? How comfortable are you with it now? What does your level of comfort tell you about your ethical self? Might you be inclined to act differently now? Why? Take some time to record any further thoughts.

Now go back and re-read the descriptions of the four foundational ethical systems in this chapter. To what extent does your ethical process reflect one of these systems? Record your thoughts about your personal system of ethics in relation to the foundational systems.

Case Study

Professor Under Pressure

You are a brand new professor in your first teaching position. During a departmental meeting, a review is undertaken regarding a student who is not going to be awarded a degree based, for the most part, on a failing grade assigned by you. You find yourself bombarded with questions about the validity of your marking and grading methods. Furthermore, a number of senior members of the professoriate speak glowingly of the student's personal qualities and how they are in favour of graduation. Going into the meeting you felt confident in the mark you assigned, but now you are questioning whether you should bow to the "wisdom" of your more experienced colleagues.

Case Study

Negative Outcomes

You are employed by a community mental health centre to evaluate their treatment services. You employ some established measures of outcome and some novel ones. In your analysis of the data you find some interesting results regarding the measures used that would be very helpful for other researchers. You prepare the study for presentation at a scientific conference and for publication in a peer-reviewed journal. After reading a draft of your paper, however, the director of the centre tells you that you are not to make the results public. You are told that your results put the centre in a bad light because their outcomes are not particularly good, and their funding could be terminated.

Case Study

Reluctant Parolee

You are providing services to a client who has been legally mandated to participate in psychological treatment by the court. She has a history of violence and will be having a parole hearing in three months. She participates reluctantly and discusses subjects in a superficial manner. She resists your efforts to focus on pertinent issues—in particular those relating to her violent behaviour—and is making very minimal progress, if any. She says that it was not her idea to receive treatment, that she thinks therapy is useless, and that the only reason she attends is that it would violate her parole if she refused, which would result in her being sent back to prison. You are asked by the court to submit a report of her progress and prognosis.

Recommended Reading

Beauchamp, T.L., & Childress, J.F. (2012). *Principles of biomedical ethics*. Oxford, UK: Oxford University Press.

Bergum, V., & Dossetor, J. (2005). *Relational ethics: The full meaning of respect*. Hagerstown, MD: University Publishing Group.

Meara, N.M., Schmidt, L.D., & Day, J.D. (1996). Principles and virtues: A foundation for ethical decisions, policies, and character. *The Counseling Psychologist, 24*, 4–77.

Sinclair, C. (2011). The evolution of the Canadian Code of Ethics over the years (1986–2011). *Canadian Psychology, 52*, 152–61.

2

Meeting Professional Standards

Case Study

A Psychologist by Any Other Name

Upon visiting a private practice psychology agency, you notice a flyer on a bulletin board announcing, "Joan Pending, PhD (Cand.), will be offering a counselling group for men who are divorced." You happen to know that Joan has a master's degree in career counselling with over twenty years of experience, has not earned a PhD, and is not a registered psychologist. When you ask her what "Cand." means, she explains that she is currently enrolled in the PhD program in applied psychology at your local university, that she has completed all of her required coursework and has passed her candidacy exam. She says it is an abbreviation of "Candidate," indicating that she is a PhD candidate, but has not yet completed her dissertation.

Questions for consideration

1. What ethical values are involved in this situation?

2. Would it make a difference if you were in a jurisdiction where the master's degree was the entry level to the profession? If the PhD was the entry level?

3. What do you think the typical member of the public would say about this situation?

4. If this situation were presented to you as a member of your provincial/territorial discipline committee, what would you want to ask of or say to Joan?

In order to be considered a profession, an occupation must be: 1) an intellectual activity based on a particular body of knowledge rather than a routine; 2) practical rather than theoretical; and 3) oriented toward service to society. Many occupations meet the first two criteria, while few meet the third. The most historically established professions—sometimes referred to as the *learned professions*—are the clergy, law, and medicine. Each requires years of education and training to acquire the necessary expertise that enables its practitioners to provide a unique and vital service. The clergy tend to the spiritual needs of the faithful, lawyers enact our legal system to maintain civil order, physicians treat the sick and injured. The degree to which a society considers each of these occupational groups to be professionals is dependent upon their honouring this social contract through contributing to the welfare of the public.

Members of the profession of psychology, or indeed any profession, are thereby expected to uphold this responsibility. That is why a term such as "professional athlete" is a misnomer. Here the word "professional" serves only to indicate that the individual is paid for their performance as a distinction from the "amateur," who is not, and does not denote membership in a profession or the need to meet ethical standards. That is, anyone who does not *act* professionally by fulfilling their ethical responsibility to society is not truly a professional. From a practical point of view, this responsibility is enacted in a profession's collective ability to ensure that its members behave in an ethical manner.

With the formation of Canada through the passing of the British North America Act (re-enacted and retitled the Constitution Act, 1867 by the Constitution Act, 1982), a framework for the regulation of professions was established that granted exclusive legislative authority to the provinces and territories to make laws governing professions. This framework continues to impact the profession of psychology in Canada and is quite different than that in the United States, where federal legislation has much greater authority. By placing the regulation of professions under regional auspices, no explicit constitutional recognition of any profession was granted. This also resulted in there being no national standards for the services that professionals provide.

The first Psychology Act defining the standards and procedures for such regulation was passed in Ontario in 1960. Today every province and territory in Canada, with the exception of the Yukon, has established a professional college to oversee the practice of some sixteen thousand psychologists. These colleges are accountable to society for setting standards admitting members into the profession, identifying members at risk to harm the public, and sanctioning those who have harmed a recipient of psychological services.

The Nature of Professional Standards

ENTRANCE STANDARDS

When the learned professions first emerged there were no established criteria for what constituted admission to the profession. Members were typically self-taught or apprenticed under someone considered to already be a member. One of the more obvious tasks of a professional regulatory college today is to set entrance standards deemed necessary to safely offer services to the public under the protected title of "psychologist." Note that professional registration does not deal with what professionals do, only what they call themselves. Thus, someone might talk to another with the intention of relieving their distress (i.e., offer counselling/psychotherapy) without ever making reference to being a psychologist. While they might be a regulated physician or social worker, they might also use the title "therapist" and thereby practice outside the authority of many professional regulatory bodies.

A particularly vexing consequence of delegating professional regulation to the provinces and territories has been that each has established idiosyncratic standards. In 1994, in part to address this issue, the federal, provincial, and territorial governments first signed the Agreement on Internal Trade (Government of Canada, 1994) with the goal of facilitating the mobility of Canada's people, investments, and services across the country. In 2001, the eleven regulatory bodies of psychologists in Canada signed a Mutual Recognition Agreement (amended in 2004), allowing psychologists who are registered to practice in one Canadian jurisdiction to have their qualifications recognized in any other jurisdiction. The intention was to enable properly qualified psychologists to have access to employment opportunities in all provinces and territories (Government of Canada, 2009). In order to reach this agreement, the signatory jurisdictions arrived at a consensus on five core competencies that undergird minimally acceptable psychological practice—that is, practice that will not harm the public. These competencies are: Interpersonal Relationships; Assessment and

Evaluation; Intervention and Consultation; Research; and Ethics and Standards. This was certainly a step in the right direction—there is no good reason for psychologists to meet different standards of education, training, and experience in one jurisdiction than another if the goal is protection of the public.

By signing the Mutual Recognition Agreement, all jurisdictions agreed to allow persons who have obtained the master's degree to practice psychology independently (i.e., without supervision) except Quebec, which will only admit applicants who have obtained the doctoral degree. British Columbia, Manitoba, and Ontario reserved the title of "Psychological Associate" for those who have a master's degree, while the rest allow all registered members to use the title of psychologist. Beyond degree status, each jurisdiction has varying requirements for completion of specific coursework, and all require at least one year of supervised practice subsequent to obtaining the master's degree. Some jurisdictions require an additional two or three years of supervised practice if the applicant does not have a doctoral degree, or one additional year subsequent to earning the doctoral degree. The exception is Quebec, where there is no practice requirement.

With the exception of the Northwest Territories and Quebec, all jurisdictions require the applicant to pass the Examination for Professional Practice in Psychology, a standardized multiple-choice examination developed, owned, and administered by the Association of State and Provincial Psychology Boards. All except Newfoundland, the Northwest Territories, and Quebec require the applicant to pass an oral examination. British Columbia and Ontario additionally require a written jurisprudence examination.

In 2009, the Agreement on Internal Trade was amended in an effort to ensure full mobility of workers because many professions (including psychology) were less than fully compliant. The 2009 amendment requires that provinces and territories agree to register professionals already registered in another jurisdiction without imposing further training, experience, examinations, or assessment. The reality is that persistent regional notions of what a psychologist ought to be makes movement to some jurisdictions from others rather difficult, and barriers clearly exist in practice if not in policy. This issue remains a challenge for the profession of psychology in Canada.

PRACTICE STANDARDS

In addition to guarding entrance to the profession, regulators must also ensure that psychologists provide benefit to their clients without harming them (see Chapter 7). While some jurisdictions employ a code of ethics for these regulatory functions, as discussed in Chapter 1 their aspirational and deontological nature makes them poorly suited for the task. Regulatory practice standards—variously called codes of conduct, standards of practice, or standards of professional con-duct, depending on the jurisdiction—do a much better job of protecting the public welfare by setting minimum prescriptive and proscriptive teleological standards of professional behaviour. Effective practice standards have several characteris-tics (Association of State and Provincial Psychology Boards, 2005):

1. They deal with the psychologist's professional behaviour and do not determine or dictate professional judgement.
2. They primarily protect the public interest and only secondarily protect professional interests through maintaining public confidence and trust in the profession.
3. They are as non-intrusive as possible, interfering with professional behaviour only when necessary to protect the public from harm.
4. They are as explicit as possible concerning what behaviour is acceptable and what is not.
5. They are sufficient unto themselves, without dependence for interpre-tation on additional explanatory materials.
6. They are compulsory, attainable, and crucial in that any violation is a basis for formal disciplinary action.

As with entry standards, each provincial and territorial regulatory body has the authority to establish or adopt practice standards. New Brunswick, the Northwest Territories, Nunavut, Saskatchewan, and the Yukon have not done so. Manitoba, Newfoundland, Nova Scotia, and Prince Edward Island have adopted the CPA's *Practice Guidelines for Providers of Psychological Services* (Canadian Psychological Association, 2001a); Ontario developed its own standards of professional conduct, which was also adopted by Nova Scotia; British Columbia has developed its own code of conduct; Prince Edward Island and Newfoundland have adopted the Association of State and Provincial Psychology Boards' (ASPPB) 2005 Code of Conduct; Alberta has adopted a modified version of the ASPPB's earlier 1990 Code of Conduct; and Quebec has developed its own unique code.

An important practical concern arising out of this situation is that psycholo-gists who access employment opportunities in more than one province or territory are responsible to act in accordance with the practice standards of the jurisdiction in which they are providing service. If the psychologist is physically present in one jurisdiction while the recipient of services is in another (such as when providing services via the Internet), the issue of which jurisdiction's standards are in force has not been entirely settled, although usually those of the client's jurisdiction will be applied.

PRACTICE GUIDELINES

Practice guidelines are intended to bridge the gap between the aspirational, more deontological expectations of the Code of Ethics and the minimal, more teleological expectations of practice standards. Some jurisdictions, such as Alberta, British Columbia, and Saskatchewan, periodically release statements regarding specific practice issues arising out of complaint investigations (see below) or legal decisions (see Chapter 3) called Practice Advisories that serve a similar function as guidelines.

Guidelines should be consistent with both the Code of Ethics and practice standards, while providing greater detail than either by integrating specialized knowledge into beneficent practice (Sinclair, 1993). Practice guidelines are typically developed to provide direction in general areas that are of concern to all psychologists, such as the Canadian Psychology Association's *Guidelines for Non-discriminatory Practice* (Canadian Psychological Association, 2001b) and *Guidelines for Ethical Psychological Practice with Women* (Canadian Psychological Association, 2007a), and in specialized areas that present unique challenges, such as the *Guidelines for Professional Practice for School Psychologists in Canada* (Canadian Psychological Association, 2007b) and *Ethical Decision Making in Supervision: Teaching, Research, Practice, and Administration* (Canadian Psychological Association, 2009). Guidelines therefore are usually a combination of prescriptive standards, proscriptive standards, and aspirational principles. Ideally, they ought not be definitive nor strictly enforceable because they would then usurp the authority of practice standards. In some cases, the language used and statements made are such that they are, for all intents and purposes, regulatory documents, and discipline committees and the courts will often refer to them to establish what the profession considers desirable practice. Whichever the case, psychologists who want to avoid sanctions and be as ethical as possible should be familiar with guidelines published by the Canadian Psychological Association, the regulatory body for the jurisdiction in which they are practicing, and any speciality organizations relevant to the psychological service they provide.

Professional Accountability

Various formal mechanisms have been established within the profession to protect the public from harm by psychologists. Ideally, professional standards for accountability should be sufficient to deal with the vast majority of situations. In those rare instances when our standards and mechanisms are not sufficient, external (i.e., legal) mechanisms can be invoked (see Chapter 3). In Canada, there are two means by which psychologists deal with professional misconduct: professional ethics committees and provincial/territorial disciplinary committees.

ETHICS COMMITTEES

Although membership in professional (i.e., non-regulatory) organizations is voluntary, membership typically provides benefits, such as reduced rates for malpractice insurance, to its members. To use the example of the Canadian Psychological Association (CPA), continued membership is dependent upon adherence to the Canadian Code of Ethics for Psychologists and other CPA guide- lines and is therefore something of an incentive for members to behave ethically. The CPA's ethics committee can negotiate informal resolutions of complaints with mutual consent of the concerned parties, conduct preliminary investigations of complaints made to CPA about the ethical behaviour of its members, and make formal ethics complaints to the board of directors when the preliminary investigation concludes that it is warranted (Canadian Psychological Association, 1990). The board of directors then has the authority to suspend or expel mem- bers. The CPA also encourages anyone who makes a complaint against a member to make a complaint with their regulatory college (Canadian Psychological Association, 1986).

In reality, the threat of dismissal is probably not much of a disincentive against behaving unethically, especially since many practicing psychologists are not members of any professional organization and are not required to be. Plus, such organizations rarely oust their members. Indeed, in its entire history, the CPA has only once invoked its authority to expel a member (although several psycholo- gists have chosen voluntarily to discontinue their membership when faced with a complaint) and the Committee on Ethics usually deals with only two or three complaints per year.

PROVINCIAL/TERRITORIAL DISCIPLINE COMMITTEES

All regulatory bodies of psychologists in Canada are required by law to have a mechanism for responding to complaints against their members. In most jurisdic- tions, the college, a member of the public, or a registered psychologist can initiate a complaint. The complaint can be made orally or in writing, although eventually a written complaint—whether in hard copy, electronic, or some other review- able form—must be made if matters proceed beyond preliminary considerations. Normally, the appointed representative of the college will discuss with the com- plainant the standards to which the psychologist will be held and the nature of the discipline process, and determine whether the complaint is obviously frivolous or in bad faith. Approximately two-thirds of all initial complaints are dismissed, withdrawn, or deemed to be outside the jurisdiction of the college at this point (Evans, 2011). If the jurisdictional legislation allows for it, the complainant can also elect for an informal resolution process. If the complaint is of a serious nature, however, the college may proceed with a formal investigation regardless of the wishes of the complainant.

If a formal complaint is initiated, the college representative will typically send a letter to the named psychologist inviting a response and, if needed, request further documentation from the complainant. The college may then appoint an investigator who reviews all materials, contacts any relevant parties, collects any necessary further documentation, and prepares a report summarizing the evidence. In some jurisdictions, trained investigators are employed. In others, a member of the college board or the discipline committee may be assigned. The method of investigation varies with respect to the nature of information necessary to clarify the complaint, and may include interviews or a review of clinical files and other correspondence. The college may also seek legal advice or an expert opinion as to whether any ethics codes or practice standards have been violated.

Once all necessary information has been gathered, most colleges typically have the option to dismiss the complaint, initiate a mediated or negotiated settlement, or proceed to a discipline hearing. If the complaint is dismissed, the complainant can appeal, usually to the college board or council. If a negotiated settlement is pursued, the psychologist undertakes whatever actions are agreed to be necessary to remedy the wrongdoing. This may involve a monetary refund if the complainant was overcharged, for example. In other cases, it may involve the psychologist undertaking ethics training or educational upgrading. If the psychologist breaches the terms of the settlement, the college typically will forward the matter to a discipline committee. If the terms are completed success-fully, the case can be closed.

If the case proceeds to a discipline hearing, the committee will hear evidence from the college and the psychologist. At this point in some jurisdictions, the client/complainant becomes a witness and the college becomes the complainant. In other jurisdictions, the client/complainant maintains "status" and has the right to legal representation, to question witnesses, and so forth. Typically, the college and psychologist will both have legal counsel. Any expert witnesses involved, either via the college or the defendant psychologist, may be called to testify and can be cross-examined by opposing legal counsel.

The penalties available to discipline committees are diverse, from a written reprimand to revocation of the psychologist's registration. Other possibilities include limits or conditions on the psychologist's practice, such as supervision, fines, or restitution to the aggrieved client, mandatory personal therapy for the psychologist, and successful completion of courses or exams.

Given that the discipline committee acts in a quasi-judicial manner and has the authority to impose rather severe penalties, there is a right of further appeal to the lower courts in each of the provinces and territories. The legislation governing this right of appeal varies between jurisdictions, with most allowing the courts to uphold, quash, or alter the committee's decision. In hearing an appeal, the courts will often defer to the expertise of the college and, by extension, the discipline committee to govern its own affairs. Thus, even where there has been an error in procedure, the result may be upheld.

COMPLAINTS AGAINST PSYCHOLOGISTS

It is almost impossible to form a precise idea of how many complaints are dealt with by provincial or territorial regulatory bodies due to the absence of a uniform system of classifying cases (Kirkland, Kirkland, & Reaves, 2004; Van Horne, 2004) and varying jurisdictional legislation around publication of matters of discipline. As many as forty cases per year are handled through negotiated or alternate dispute resolution procedures in some jurisdictions, with many more handled informally. The number of complaints that proceed to a formal discipline hearing are very low, however, from none to at most two or three per year in any given jurisdiction (Evans, 2011). In Newfoundland and Labrador, for example, only one case had gone to a hearing in twenty-five years (Garland, 2011). In that case, the psychologist's registration was suspended because of a serious criminal conviction, and then later reinstated when the conviction was overturned on appeal.

Based on a review of those colleges that publish any information regarding complaints (namely, Alberta, British Columbia, and Ontario), most complaints are in response to assessment and treatment, parental custody and access determinations, and professional boundaries (Evans, 2011).

Anatomy of a Complaint

Although all jurisdictions in Canada have slightly different rules for responding to complaints about their members, the following represents a composite of cases and processes that is fairly typical.

COMPLAINT

The Provincial College of Psychologists receives a telephone call from a woman who alleges that a psychologist verbally harassed her and threatened her physically. She states that she was in psychotherapy with the psychologist for eight months. She is requested to make her complaint in writing. She does so and it is received a few days later. An investigation is instigated.

INVESTIGATION

The psychologist is contacted and reports that the complainant was in psycho-therapy for relationship issues and that he had made a diagnosis of "borderline personality disorder." He admitted that he loaned the client two hundred dollars to cover a debt "out of compassion." After the client missed her next scheduled appointment, he contacted her by telephone and was surprised by her negative reaction to his call. The client did not return for therapy nor did she provide repay-ment of the loan. After some time, the psychologist again contacted the client to ask for repayment. The client became upset and hung up. The psychologist reported that he and the client met in person on one occasion subsequent to the two telephone contacts and that the client became upset and left. The psycholo-gist's case notes document the psychotherapy sessions and his diagnosis, but do not record the lending of any money or any contact to discuss it.

The complainant reported that she felt harassed and could no longer trust the psychologist. She stated that she felt the psychologist used knowledge of her weaknesses against her. She said the psychologist called her repeatedly over money he had "given" her. She reported that during their face-to-face meeting the psychologist became angry and she felt physically threatened.

An expert ethical opinion was sought. The expert opined that a) the psycholo-gist acted contrary to profession practice standards when he loaned the client money, b) that he should have foreseen the potential for difficulty in light of his diagnosis of borderline personality disorder, and c) he should have known that contact regarding money would upset the client.

Following a review of the materials produced by the investigation, a discipline hearing was convened.

DISCIPLINE HEARING

After hearing arguments from the complaints director and the psychologist, the discipline committee ruled that a dual relationship existed that violated profes-sional standards. The psychologist was found guilty of professional misconduct and ordered to successfully complete a course of study acceptable to the college regarding professional boundaries.

Regulating Ourselves

The essence of being a self-regulating profession is that each member is both regulated and a regulator. All of us, therefore, will find ourselves at some time faced with having to respond to unprofessional or unethical behaviour on the part of another psychologist. The CPA Code of Ethics encourages psychologists to:

IV.13   Uphold the discipline's responsibility to society by bringing incompetent or unethical behaviour, including misuses of psychological
knowledge and techniques, to the attention of appropriate authorities,
committees, or regulatory bodies, in a manner consistent with the
ethical principles of this Code, if informal resolution or correction
of the situation is not appropriate or possible.

Most psychologists find this a difficult and anxiety-arousing situation. In fact,
this is the most frequent type of ethical consultation with which psychologists
are presented. The following steps may be of some help when attempting to deal
with these situations in an ethically responsible manner.

CONFIRM THE ISSUE

Firstly, as best as you are able, try to assess the situation dispassionately. Are
you certain that you are competent to determine the appropriateness of your
colleague's actions? Are your motives personal, as opposed to protection of the
public? Do you have direct knowledge of your colleague's actions? You should be
particularly reluctant to act based upon rumours you have heard from others.
Similarly, if you are approached by someone who claims to have firsthand knowledge of the unprofessional behaviour of a colleague, you should be helpful and
encourage them to take appropriate action and be careful about how active a role
you take.

SAFEGUARD CONFIDENTIALITY

Except in situations that involve a threat of serious physical harm or a child in
need of protection (see Chapter 6), the client's right to confidentiality takes precedence over our professional obligation to correct or offset harm. If you become
aware of a colleague's behaviour in the context of a professional relationship
(such as in a psychotherapy session), therefore, the client's consent to reveal
information obtained in that relationship must first be obtained. If consent is not
granted, no further action on your part should be undertaken unless the situation
involves a mandatory reporting duty.

CONSULT WITH OTHERS

Discuss your concerns with trusted peers, making sure to protect the identity of
your colleague and any client(s). Do they agree that action should be taken? Are
there any practice standards or professional guidelines relevant to the issue?
Does the situation truly fall below acceptable professional standards?

ADDRESS THE ISSUE

When the action appears to be primarily a lack of sensitivity, knowledge, or experience, attempt to reach an agreement with your colleague on the issue and whatever appropriate action is to be taken. Your goal at this point should be to correct the problem, not to punish. Try to be calm, respectful, and constructive; imagine how you would like to be treated if you had made a professional mistake and were being confronted. Try to be open-minded and to understand your colleague's side of the story. A face-to-face meeting in professional surroundings is usually best.

INVOLVE OTHERS IN AN ACTION PLAN

If your colleague is unwilling to address the issue or if the action is of a seriously harmful nature, such as the sexual exploitation of a client, you should take your concerns to the provincial or territorial regulatory body best suited to investigating the situation and to stopping or offsetting the harm. You should be willing to make a written, signed complaint and to testify in a disciplinary hearing, if you proceed this far. You should record details of your actions and include specifics of any conversations if you reach this step.

Summary

The degree to which the public can trust the profession of psychology rests upon psychologists' ability to protect the public from harm caused by our members. Psychologists are therefore accountable to regulate ourselves by setting entrance standards into the profession to exclude those who would do harm, developing standards of professional conduct to establish expectations for practice that will not harm, publishing professional guidelines to facilitate competent practice, and sanctioning members who are at risk to harm or have harmed a recipient of psychological services. One of the more difficult situations we have to deal with is the possible unprofessional or harmful actions of a fellow psychologist. Psychologists who suspect a colleague has harmed or is at risk to harm a client should first ensure that they have adequate knowledge of the issue, consult with others if unsure, attempt to resolve the issue informally with the colleague, and involve others if necessary or if the issue is sufficiently serious.

Discussion Questions

1. What is the basis of standards of professional conduct, from what do they derive their binding power, and what do you see as their limits? Explain your answer.

2. How do you think regulatory colleges should deal with psychologists who violate the Code of Ethics because they hold personal values that are in conflict with the profession's values? Why?

3. What character traits, if any, do you think someone should possess in order to be considered a psychologist? Why?

4. Do you think the entrance standards for the profession of psychology are too low? Too high? Or just right? If you were given the responsibility and authority to set entrance requirements, what would they be? Explain your answer.

Your Reflective Journal

What is your experience with professionals? Is there a member of your family who is a professional? Perhaps even a psychologist? Have you had a negative experience with someone who was a professional but did not act like one? How has your familiarity—or lack of familiarity—influenced your conception of what a professional is? When you reflect on what it means to be a professional, what thoughts come to mind—money, social status, respect, something else? Do you have a negative reaction when you think of professionals, such as greedy "ambulance-chasing lawyers," self-serving physicians who practice "defensive medicine," or incompetent "baby-sitting" teachers? Perhaps you want to distance yourself from any considerations of a professional and focus exclusively on what psychologists do, like psychotherapy or assessment? Or have you had a positive experience or even many positive experiences such that you have very favourable associations with the concept of professional? Maybe even an idealized conception of being a professional? How have these experiences influenced your sense of yourself as a professional?

Take some time to reflect on the kind of professional psychologist you would like to be and how you might incorporate your preconceptions and what you have learned from this chapter into your developing professional self.

Case Study

One Too Many

You have recently joined an eight-member psychology group practice. One of the founding members of the practice has provided psychological services effectively for many years. She is well-known as an affable, gregarious person who rarely turns down a drink with her many friends. It is common knowledge that her twenty-year marriage recently ended in a bitter divorce that was financially and emotionally devastating to her. You notice that she is drinking a lot and often, and that she often contacts the office to cancel her morning appointments at the last minute. In fact, you have observed her prior to and after a number appointments to be obviously under the influence of alcohol.

1) Psychologist, patients, you
2) Integrity in relationships
   Responsible to Society ..

Case Study

Assessments Under the Table

You are providing supervision to paraprofessional support workers at a non-profit agency. The support workers' job is to determine the social and health needs of persons with low income and refer them to appropriate community services. Your job is to ensure that the support workers are competently fulfilling the requirements of their job. During a meeting with one of the workers you learn that she routinely provides psychological assessments for her clients. You also learn that she worked as a psychologist in another country and that her credentials have not been accepted by your provincial regulatory college. She says she cannot afford the coursework necessary to obtain registration in Canada because she is the sole breadwinner for her extended family. Upon further investigation you find that her assessments are appropriate to her clients' circumstances, are very competently done, and tend to facilitate more timely referrals.

Case Study

Meddling Misogynist

You are a psychologist providing psychotherapeutic services to a woman for treatment of her depression. She informs you that her husband is also in therapy and you obtain her consent to share information with the psychologist providing therapy to her husband so that services might be co-ordinated. Therapy is progressing well and your client reports feeling much less depressed and more optimistic about her life. After the fifth session with your client, her husband's psychologist contacts you to report that he is not doing well. It is clear that your client's increasingly assertive behaviour and pursuit of interests outside of the home are detrimental to her husband's satisfaction with their marriage. The other psychologist insists that your client's therapeutic goals be modified so that she resumes her former husband-centred role for the good of her husband and their marriage.

Recommended Reading

Cohen, K. (2009). Canada's Agreement on Internal Trade (AIT): Some things to think about for the practice and mobility of psychology and other health practitioners. *Canadian Psychology Association Psynopsis, 31,* 1–2.

Conway, J. (2011). National standards for the practice of psychology: A lesson from our history. *Canadian Psychology Association Psynopsis, 33,* 40–41.

Evans, D.R. (2011). *The law, standards, and ethics in the practice of psychology* (3rd ed.) Toronto: Emond Montgomery.

Shapiro, D., Walker, L., Manosevitz, M., Peterson, M., & Williams, M. (2008). *Surviving a licensing board complaint: What to do and what not to do.* Phoenix, AZ: Zeig, Tucker & Theisen.

3

Appreciating Legal Expectations

Case Study

Haines v. Bellissimo

Robert Haines was discharged from hospital following treatment of chronic schizophrenia under the care of a multidisciplinary team that included Dr. Bellissimo, a psychologist. A short time later, Mrs. Haines discovered a shotgun in their garage and telephoned Dr. Bellissimo, who then asked Mr. Haines to return to the hospital, which he did. Dr. Bellissimo assessed Mr. Haines's risk of suicide as not imminent and they arranged to accompany him home to take possession of the gun. When they arrived, however, it took more than three hours for Dr. Bellissimo to persuade Mr. Haines to surrender the gun. Later that night, Dr. Bellissimo telephoned Mr. Haines to check on his mental status and deemed him to be "all right." The next day, Mr. Haines purchased another gun and fatally shot himself. Mrs. Haines sued Dr. Bellissimo for malpractice.

Questions for consideration

1. *What ethical obligations do you think Dr. Bellissimo owed Mr. Haines's wife in relation to her husband's suicide?*

2. *Would you have gone to Mr. Haines's house? Why or why not? How does this affect your appraisal of Dr. Bellissimo's actions?*

3. *Do you think that Dr. Bellissimo should have done anything different to prevent Mr. Haines's suicide? Explain.*

4. *What do you think the average person would expect Dr. Bellissimo to do in this situation?*

Source: Taken from the case of *Haines v. Bellissimo*, [1977], 18 O.R. (2d) 177.

Is it necessary for psychologists to have the legal knowledge of a lawyer? Are we expected to keep up to date with court decisions of professional liability? The short answer to these questions is, "No." Psychologists are not trained in law nor expected to practice law, only to act in accordance with it. Law establishes expectations of behaviour that are acceptable to most people most of the time. In this way members of a society can know what is expected of them so that conflicts can be avoided or resolved without resorting to the courts. The same is true for psychologists. A basic understanding of the legal system and of how the profession of psychology is perceived by the Canadian courts can serve as a guide to how the courts are likely to judge us if our actions are brought before them. Armed with this knowledge, we can avoid behaving in ways that prompt others to seek legal remediation.

Characteristics of the Legal System
ADVERSARIAL
Our system of law pits one party against the other based on the premise that justice will emerge victorious when both sides in a dispute are given an equal opportunity to present their case and to challenge the other party's. This adversarial feature is often disquieting to those who are accustomed to non-competitive methods of resolving quarrels, but it is fundamental to the legal process. Fortunately, the situation is not usually as unpleasant as might be imagined (or presented on television) because only when a case reaches the courtroom is the adversarial process is fully enacted. Lawyers have a duty to first try to resolve their clients' disputes by agreement before resorting to court action. If they cannot, they are then expected to do their utmost to act as partisan advocates on behalf of their client within the limits of the law and their legal ethics.

VISIBLE
In order for the authority of the court to impact Canadian society at large and not only those directly involved in the proceedings, courtrooms are normally open to

all. This is what is meant by the saying, "Justice must be seen to be done." While a court may, in certain circumstances, ban the publication of information about a case or exclude the public entirely from the courtroom to protect the people involved—such as children who are victims of sexual abuse—an open court is generally considered to be essential to its function.

REMEDIAL

The obvious means by which the legal system maintains social order is by providing remedies to correct a wrong or settle a conflict. If the accused is found guilty in a criminal case (see below), for example, the court can impose a sentence. Sentencing may have a variety of objectives, including denouncing unlawful behaviour, deterring the offender, separating the offender from society, rehabili-tating the offender, providing reparations for harm done to the victims, and promoting a sense of responsibility in the offender. In a civil dispute (see below), the court will reach a decision regarding who is at fault and prescribe an appropriate remedy to rectify the injury. Such remedies include monetary compensation for damages, performance or discontinuance of specific activities, and payment of money to punish the wrongdoer.

Areas of Law

CRIMINAL

Criminal law deals with offences as set out in the Criminal Code of Canada (1985) and related federal statutes. A finding of criminal guilt can result in a monetary fine or loss of liberty. Since criminal acts are considered to be offences against society, the prosecution is conducted by the state, referred to as the Crown (a vestige of our history of having been a colony of the United Kingdom's monarchy). The role of the Crown is to prove beyond a reasonable doubt that the accused committed the offence with which they have been charged. The role of the court is to adjudicate between the Crown and the accused. Elaborate and detailed procedural rules exist to protect the rights of the accused given such an overwhelming discrepancy in power.

In Canada, the fundamental legal rights of individuals are enshrined in the Charter of Rights and Freedoms (1982) and include the right to life, liberty, and security of the person; to be safe from unreasonable search and seizure; not to be detained or imprisoned arbitrarily; to be informed of the reason for arrest; and to have legal counsel without delay. In addition to these Charter rights, case law and rules contained in various statutes promote due process and procedural fairness. Because the Charter and the Criminal Code establish that a person must be considered innocent until proven guilty, it is up to the Crown to prove beyond a reasonable doubt that the accused did what he or she has been accused of.

The Youth Criminal Justice Act (2002) applies in the case of crimes committed by persons between the ages of eleven and eighteen. Under this act, youths are treated differently from adults, and a wide variety of alternative measures other than custody are available. The Youth Justice Court can order a psychological assessment be done with or without the youth's consent and, if necessary, remand the youth for a period of up to thirty days in order to allow the assessment to be completed. The Youth Criminal Justice Act has extensive provisions dealing with confidentiality, including disclosures made by the youth during the course of a court-ordered psychological assessment.

CIVIL

Most of the laws that affect the practice of psychologists are civil laws. Civil law involves the regulation of relationships and the resolution of disputes between parties. It is based on common law, which has developed over the centuries in the United Kingdom, former Commonwealth countries, and the United States from incremental decisions made by the courts. In the common law system pivotal cases—known as "leading" cases—that settled contentious issues establish principles that assist in deciding future similar disputes. Unlike the rest of Canada, the laws of Quebec are based on the European system, in which a single authoritative set of codes are established through a political process, rather than common law.

Civil law can compensate the wronged party by awarding damages, establish standards for the limits of behaviour, educate the public, and provide a means for parties to address their differences in a controlled setting. In civil law the complaining party is referred to as the *plaintiff*, while the party responding to the complaint is referred to as the *defendant*. It is the plaintiff's burden to demonstrate a valid basis for their complaint when it is filed. If they cannot, the court will refuse to hear the case. Many complaints fail at this point, and almost all of the claims involving psychologists that pass this test are settled by the parties without ever going to court.

The courts recognize that wrongs perpetrated by one person against another can be intentional or unintentional. Intentional wrongs involve deliberate interference with another person through battery, trespass, invasion of privacy, assault, false imprisonment, or infliction of mental suffering. In the case of battery, assault, and false imprisonment, it is not necessary for the plaintiff to prove that any loss or injury occurred in order to recover damages—only that the conduct was intentional. In the case of mental suffering, however, the plaintiff must establish that it is a result of the defendant's intentional conduct. This obviously has important implications for psychologists, given that we primarily deal with mental suffering.

Canadian case law regarding psychologists is actually quite limited. The reasoning upon which complaints brought against psychologists are decided is well-established in related fields such as medicine, nursing, and social work, however. The few cases involving psychologists and the many involving other similar professions tell us that the vast majority of harms that we are likely to be accused of are those resulting from negligence.

Negligence

Negligence, as the term is used in law, refers to professional actions that fail to meet the standard required of society. A valid basis for negligence must generally establish five elements. First, there must be a *duty of care* owed by the defendant to the plaintiff. Second, there must be a failure to provide *reasonable care*. Third, and perhaps most difficult to understand, there must be a degree of *causation* between the defendant's conduct and the injury. Obviously, there must be some damage or *injury* to the plaintiff, and, finally, the *plaintiff's conduct* cannot have been such that it would preclude recovery.

DUTY OF CARE

In most cases, the duty of care owed to a client by a psychologist arises out of a professional relationship that may or may not involve a contractual arrangement between the parties. When a legal duty of care exists, the professional is expected to behave in a particular manner in relation to a client. Such duties may be created by the legislature, by the courts, or by the general understandings of everyday existence. In the absence of such a duty, there is no obligation to act in a non-negligent manner.

REASONABLE CARE

The question of what constitutes "reasonable care" is ultimately decided by the courts, stated in *Crits v. Sylvester* (1956) as:

> Every medical practitioner must bring to his [*sic*] task a reasonable degree
> of skill and knowledge and must exercise a reasonable degree of care. He
> is bound to exercise that degree of care and skill which could reasonably
> be expected of a normal, prudent practitioner of the same experience and

standing, and if he holds himself out as a specialist, a higher degree of skill is required of him than of one who does not profess to be so qualified by special training and ability.

Note that the relative inexperience of a psychologist is not a defence; once you are registered as a psychologist, you are deemed to meet the same standard of reasonable care whether you have been practicing for two months or two decades. Thus, while experience or specialization may result in a higher standard of care being required, there is a minimum expected of all practitioners within the profession.

The standard, however, is not one of perfection. The law recognizes that mishaps can and will occur without necessarily being negligent. Similarly, while a psychologist is expected to remain knowledgeable of developments in the field, liability will not be imposed for something as trivial as failing to read a recent professional article on the topic, for example. Finally, the circumstances in which the service is being provided will be taken into account by the courts. A psychologist providing a service in an emergency situation will likely have to meet a lesser standard of care than another doing so under more favourable conditions, for instance.

CAUSATION

The question of causation is one of the most difficult issues to be resolved in professional malpractice cases and is often the basis for plaintiffs being unsuccessful. Legal causation has two aspects: factual and proximate. The classic description of factual causation is that if not for the defendant's negligence, the plaintiff would be uninjured. However, in the real world there are often multiple causes for events, or the causes may be suspected but not certain. The Supreme Court of Canada has therefore reiterated that the civil law standard is a balance of probabilities and emphasized that causation need not be proven with scientific precision (*Snell v. Farrell*, 1990).

Proximate causation recognizes the general societal expectation that a defendant should not be responsible for damages that have practically nothing to do with his or her conduct. In addition to factual causation, therefore, the plaintiff must also establish a sufficient degree of proximity between the cause and the damage. You would not be liable for having provided career counselling to someone who then made a career choice that resulted in their being disentitled when a long-lost relative's will is enacted, for example. The test here is whether the damage is foreseeable by a reasonable person in the defendant's situation.

In instances where there are multiple causes for an injury, defendants are responsible only for that portion of the harm attributable to their conduct. Similarly, where there are multiple defendants, each will be adjudged at fault to the extent of their own contribution to the plaintiff's suffering.

PLAINTIFF'S CONDUCT

Even when plaintiffs can establish that they sustained foreseeable damages as a result of negligence on the part of a defendant psychologist, their own conduct may disentitle them from remediation in some circumstances. A defendant psychologist might successfully argue, for example, that the provision of a service that caused harm was based on false information provided by a client. Usually, however, the court will address this issue by apportioning some degree of causation to the plaintiff's conduct, rather than dismissing the claim entirely.

Relationships and Consequences Relevant to Legal Expectations

SUICIDE

The most obvious duty psychologists have is the protection of our clients' lives. The court's perception of psychologists' responsibility in such instances are highlighted in the 1977 Ontario decision of *Haines v. Bellissimo* (the case study preceding this chapter). The court found that Dr. Bellissimo was not negligent, and the reasoning is worth quoting at length:

> Having undertaken to treat Robert Haines, the defendants owed to him a duty to exercise that degree of reasonable skill, care, and knowledge possessed by the average of like professionals. If the patient's mental conditions and actions were such that a reasonably prudent psychiatrist or psychologist would under the circumstances have anticipated a suicide attempt, then the concept of "reasonable care" in treatment requires the therapist to take all reasonable steps including hospitalization of the patient, if necessary, to prevent or reduce the risk of self-destruction. To this should be added the fundamental principle of law that governs all professionals that the psychiatrist or psychologist who makes a diagnostic mistake or error in judgement does not incur liability what ever the harm, provided he exercised reasonable care and skill and took into consideration all relevant factors in arriving at his diagnosis or judgement. Psychology and psychiatry are inexact sciences and the practice thereof should not be fettered with rules so strict as to exact an infallibility on the part of the practitioners which they could not humanly possess.

Another case where a suicide attempt led to an action for professional negligence is the 1992 British Columbia Supreme Court case of *Stewart v. Noone*. Mr. Stewart sought emergency care for irregular sleep patterns and manic feelings. After being discharged he went home and unsuccessfully attempted suicide through an overdose of prescription drugs. He called an ambulance and was taken to another hospital and admitted. The following day he denied any suicidal thoughts, requested that he be discharged, and promised to keep an appointment at a community clinic. The psychiatrists believed that his suicide risk was sufficiently low and discharged him. Later that day he drove to a parking garage and jumped from the fourth floor. He survived and sued the hospital and the psychiatrists for discharging him prematurely. The court agreed with the defendants that Mr. Stewart's discharge was appropriate, reaffirming the legal standard of reasonable care rather than perfection.

Note that there is no legal requirement to intervene if someone who is mentally competent (see Chapter 5) decides to take his or her own life. In fact, in the eyes of the law interfering with someone who is attempting suicide can be an assault. Of course, the mental competence of someone who wants to commit suicide is always an open question, making it difficult to defend oneself by claiming that the plaintiff was competent. On the other hand, plaintiffs who sue or bring charges against you for saving their life are not likely to be viewed too sympathetically by the courts.

It is also worth noting that the act of suicide is not—as is often thought—illegal. Legal sanctions did exist at one time to supplement religious prohibitions against suicide, but in 1972 attempted suicide was decriminalized. Section 241 of the Criminal Code of Canada (1985) does, however, make it a criminal offence to counsel or assist someone to commit suicide.

PSYCHOTHERAPY

Claims can be made against psychologists for damages resulting from psychotherapy. In the Ontario case of *S.T. v. Gaskell* (1997) a client argued that revisiting her past sexual abuse as a child without being first provided the proper support systems caused her to resort to drinking and violence. Her claim included legal fees incurred in defence of criminal proceedings, damage to her motor vehicle caused by driving while impaired, and loss of potential employment as a police constable because of her criminal conviction and lifetime ban from owning a firearm. The court did not accept the client's claim that her criminal behaviour was caused by the therapy given that she had a stable home environment at the outset of the therapy, she freely related her past, and there was no indication during therapy that the client was experiencing undue turmoil.

There have been a number of Canadian cases where sexual relationships between a psychologist and client have been found to be negligent (as well as unethical and unprofessional; see Chapter 8). In the case of *N.V. v. Blank* (1988) the psychologist was found to have manipulated his client into having sex with him. The court, following a number of earlier decisions, noted that even if a client consents to such acts, they still constitute a breach of duty in that they are contrary to the best interests of the client. Other cases have gone further and held that even where the professional relationship has ended, an enduring influence over the client by the psychologist precludes the client giving true consent to sexual contact (Seto, 1995).

ASSESSMENT

The duty of psychologists includes accurate assessment of their clients' condition. An interesting line of legal argument has developed in England and Australia— likely to be followed by Canadian courts because of our mutual common law system—where mental health professionals hired by school boards have been sued for failing to properly assess a need for special education. In one English case (*P.H.P. v. Hillingdon London Borough*, 1998) parents sued the school board for the failure of an educational psychologist to diagnose their daughter's dyslexic condition when she was a child. The parents unsuccessfully argued that, if their daughter had been properly diagnosed, a special teaching program would have prevented her subsequent difficulties in employment and life skills. The court ruled that damages could be awarded only if an injury is exacerbated by delayed treatment, and, given that dyslexia is not an injury, the psychologist was not negligent. However, the court did note that if the psychologist had been hired privately by the parents, rather than employed by the school board, liability might be found for failure to fulfill a contract.

Underlying this decision is a strong legal view that claims such as these, brought against psychologists many years later, would be counter to the societal interest in providing free education. While there are no reported cases in Canada where this issue has been addressed, under Canadian law there may be instances where liability would be found against a privately employed psychologist. The courts would likely consider whether the psychologist met the standards of the profession for detecting a psychological condition.

THIRD PARTIES

Few practicing psychologists are unaware of the *Tarasoff v. Regents of the University of California* (1976) decision and the impact it has had on the profession. In that case, Mr. Poddar, under the care of a psychologist and psychiatrist, confided that he intended to murder Tatiana Tarasoff. The psychologist notified the campus police who decided that there was insufficient basis for having him involuntarily committed. A few weeks later Mr. Poddar murdered Ms. Tarasoff, and her parents sued the psychologist and the psychiatrist. The court ruled that there was a valid basis for the claim to proceed, stating:

> Where a therapist determines, or pursuant to the standards of his profession should determine, that his patient presents a serious danger of violence to another, he incurs an obligation to use reasonable care to protect the intended victim against such danger. The discharge of this duty may require the therapist to take one or more of various steps, depending upon the nature of the case. Thus, it may call for him to warn the intended victim or others likely to apprise the victim of danger, to notify the police or to take whatever steps are necessary under the circumstances.

The case was settled out of court, and it is generally believed that the psychologist would not have been found negligent (Truscott, 1993).

The leading Canadian case is *Wenden v. Trikha* (1991), in which Mr. Trikha was placed under close supervision in a psychiatric ward under the care of a psychiatrist. Shortly after his admission, he escaped from the hospital and was involved in a car accident in which Ms. Wenden was seriously injured. Ms. Wenden commenced a civil action against the hospital and the psychiatrist. The court held that when a psychiatrist becomes aware that a patient presents a serious danger to the well-being of a third party there arises a duty of care to take reasonable steps to protect that person if the requisite proximity of causation exists (Truscott & Crook, 1993). In *Wenden* the court ruled that the psychiatrist had met the standard of reasonable care and thereby no negligence was found.

If a client under our care harms another individual and that harm is related to our failure to provide reasonable care to our client, we may be found partially responsible. Note that the extent of our responsibility is typically very limited. The duty to protect is triggered when your client is a foreseeable threat to the life or physical integrity of a reasonably identifiable victim or victims and you have an opportunity to prevent the harm from occurring (Truscott & Crook, 1993). It is the standard of foreseeability that presents the most serious challenge for psychologists because it is well-established that even experts employing the best methods available do a poor job of predicting violence (McGuire, 2004; Norko & Baranoski, 2005; Rice, Harris, & Quinsey, 2002). The legal expectation is "reasonableness," not "certainty," however. In other words, we are held to the standard of whether a reasonable psychologist would have foreseen violence on the part of our client (*Smith v. Jones*, 1999).

What tends to be particularly troubling for psychologists about the duty to protect third parties is that whether our client harms someone seems quite obviously to be the result of the client's choice or forces outside of our control (Truscott & Evans, 2009). Society, however, expects psychologists to have unique skills beyond the average person for predicting and influencing how others will act. A failure to properly exercise these skills that results in serious harm to a third party by one of our clients can therefore be a basis for negligence.

A variant of the *Tarasoff/Wenden* duty occurs when it is the therapeutic process itself that causes harm to a third party. The most common instance where this arises is a client undergoing psychotherapy to deal with the effects of past sexual abuse and the alleged perpetrator brings a civil action against the therapist. In the British Columbia case of *Carnahan v. Coates* (1990), a father sued a psychologist who gave evidence based on interviewing the children that resulted in the father's access to them being substantially reduced.

Counsel for the psychologist applied to have the claim dismissed on the basis that the psychologists did not owe a duty of care to the plaintiff father. The court rejected this argument noting, "the state of law regarding the nature and extent of a professional person's duty towards those who come within the range of foreseeable harm arising from professional misconduct is unsettled," and thereby a suit might proceed on the grounds that the father was owed a duty of care. On the basis that a witness must be free to testify in court without fear of reprisal by civil suit, the court held that the psychologist, absent malicious intent toward the father, was immune from suit.

These legal reasons preventing liability when a child is at risk of harm do not arise in cases involving adult clients, however. The leading case in Canada is the British Columbia decision of *I.G. v. Rusch* (1999) where a number of family members accused of sexual abuse sued their accuser's therapist for breaching the duty of care owed to them as persons wrongfully accused. The court observed that being falsely accused of child abuse is a devastating tragedy and thus there may be good reasons for extending a duty of care from a therapist to a falsely accused third party. The court ultimately concluded that the detection and reporting of abuse are more important societal goals and noted that the duty of care could be extended to include third parties had the therapist suggested to his client that she confront her family, or if he had reported the matters to the police or encouraged his client to do so.

Summary

A basic understanding of the legal system and of the expectations of the profession of psychology by the Canadian courts can serve as a guide to how the courts would likely judge us if our actions were to be brought before them. The Canadian legal system is adversarial, visible, and remedial in nature and deals with disputes either through the criminal or civil courts. If psychologists are involved with the legal system, they tend to be defendants in civil suits, which deal with professional negligence. Negligence involves a duty of care, a failure to provide reasonable care, an injury, the failure having caused the injury, and an absence of actions on the part of the injured party that would preclude recovery. Relationships and legal consequences of note for psychologists are suicide, psychotherapy, assessment, and third parties.

Discussion Questions

1. How do legal standards differ from ethical and professional standards for professionals?

2. Could a psychologist ever ethically break the law? If so, under what circumstances or by what justification? What system of ethics does your answer represent?

3. What are the limits of legal decisions as a guide for professional behaviour? Explain.

4. Given the fundamental differences in how the legal system and psychologists arrive at the "truth," what is psychology's rightful place in courtroom proceedings?

Your Reflective Journal

What has been your experience with the law? Have you been issued a lot of speeding or parking tickets, for example? Perhaps you or someone close to you has had a more serious involvement with the law. Have you broken the law and never been caught? Or are you an especially law-abiding person? Do you think that Canadian society is generally too lenient in enforcing its laws? Or too severe? When John Mortimer's fictional defence lawyer, Horace Rumpole of *Rumpole of the Bailey*, was asked about how we might have fewer criminals he responded, "By having fewer laws." What do you think of this position—are there too many laws, or too few? Take some time to think about your personal relationship to the laws of our society, law enforcement, and any other questions you may wish to consider.

To get a flavour for the law's adversarial approach to finding truth, re-read what you have written. Do you notice any themes or biases? Once you have identified one or more, take some time to consider an opposing position. Try your best to construct a valid counterposition to your initial one. Once you have done so, journal your reactions.

Case Study

R.G. v. Christison (1996)

A mother who has joint custody of her two children, aged four and six, brings them to you for counselling. She says that they are upset as a consequence of having to live with her ex-husband and his wife. After three sessions the children describe experiencing physical abuse at the hands of their father and you believe them. Their mother asks you to write a report to the court stating same and you do so. The court does not alter the parental arrangements, citing medical evidence and an investigation by Child Protection Services disputing any abuse. The mother then makes a complaint to the police, who investigate and find no compelling evidence of abuse. The case has now gained some notoriety—in part because the father is well-known in the community—and you are contacted by the local newspaper and television station. The mother implores you to give the interviews "for the sake of the children."

Source: Taken from the case of *R.G. v. Christison* (1996), S.J. No. 702.

Case Study

Said Too Much

You are employed as a school psychologist at a detention facility for adolescents who have been convicted of criminal offences. You find that establishing trust is the major obstacle to the provision of effective services, and you have been struggling to develop a rapport with one particular resident. During a conversation with her about her intense dislike of one of the other staff, she mentions rather offhandedly that some of the residents have stolen and hidden tools to use as weapons. You gradually come to understand that they are planning to escape, and you are reasonably confident that their intention is to harm the disliked staff member in the process. Your body language betrays your growing concern and the resident realizes she has said too much. With obvious fear and poignant sincerity she begs you not to tell anyone, saying that she will be assaulted by the other residents if they find out she talked to you.

Case Study

Wrong Man

You are a psychologist providing psychotherapeutic services to a client with emotional difficulties resulting from having been sexually assaulted. Much of the content of your sessions has been devoted to how she has been dealing with the lengthy legal process. Her case was recently heard in court where her accused was found guilty and sentenced to prison. During a session shortly after the trial, your client says that she is feeling conflicted. She tells you that the man convicted of assaulting her was not actually the man who did it. She states in a cold and angry voice, "I know that he's done lots of things that he was never convicted of, so I hope he rots in jail." She refuses to reveal this to anyone else and insists that you not tell anyone either.

Source: Taken from the case of R. v. R. (K.A.) (1993), 121 N.S.R. (2d) 242.

Recommended Reading

Boyd, N. (2007). *Canadian law* (4th ed.). Toronto: Thomson Nelson.

Gall, G.L. (2004). *The Canadian legal system* (5th ed.). Toronto: Carswell.

Ogloff, J.R.P., & Olley, M.C. (1998). The interaction between ethics and the law: The ongoing refinement of ethical standards for psychologists in Canada. *Canadian Psychology, 39,* 221–30.

4

Making Ethical Decisions

Case Study

Child Abuse

You are providing therapy to Mrs. and Mr. Jones and their two children, aged eleven and thirteen. They sought help because they "argue too much," and have made good progress so far. In the third session, the oldest child reports that their father has hit them in anger on numerous occasions over the past ten years. Approximately one year ago, his arm was broken when his father threw him against a wall. Mr. Jones expresses considerable remorse and asks for your help to curb his violent behaviour. He says that he was removed from his family as a boy because his father beat him and that he could not bear to have his children taken away. There is a real risk that he will seriously harm himself if the children are apprehended. Mrs. Jones and the children state that they want to remain together as a family and work things out.

Questions for consideration

1. *What individuals or groups ought to be considered in this situation? Why?*

2. *What feelings are aroused in you? How might they influence your decision making?*

3. *What ethical duties are relevant? Which do you most value? Which are most valued by the profession?*

4. *What outcomes are likely? Which are most important to society? Which are most important to the family?*

Source: Adapted from the *Companion Manual to the Canadian Code of Ethics for Psychologists*, 3rd ed. (Sinclair & Pettifor, 2001).

Even sincere and earnest psychologists will fairly often find themselves in situations that are difficult to resolve in a manner that satisfies our professional ethical standards. Nonetheless, we are expected to make conscientious decisions whenever we are faced with situations in which ethical values are at stake. This can be very difficult, however, when situational pressures or interpersonal complexities cloud the issue, strong feelings or personal biases impair our judgement, ethical duties conflict with one another, or harms are likely to result no matter what we do.

Deciding what to do when faced with a situation that calls for ethical reasoning usually occurs very rapidly. This is particularly true when the circumstances are familiar to us, our motives are uncomplicated, our professional duties are clear, and our past actions in similar situations resulted in satisfactory outcomes. As professionals, however, even these snap decisions must be able to withstand ethical scrutiny. If the situation is unfamiliar to us, for example, we can still decide what to do in a relatively straightforward manner if there are applicable guidelines or standards and when there is no conflict between the ethical duties articulated within them. Situations that are complex, emotionally arousing, or for which there are no clear directives, however, are not easily resolved and require careful deliberation if we are to meet our professional ethical responsibilities.

Ethical reasoning is actually the product of two levels of processing—*experiential* and *analytical*—operating on two kinds of information—*social* and *personal*—and not, as is often thought, simply the outcome of logical analysis (Craigie, 2011). Only by deliberately incorporating all four of these aspects into our ethical reasoning can we make reliable and responsible decisions. This is where the four foundational ethical systems introduced in Chapter 1 are put to use, because each of them deals with one of these facets of ethical reasoning. The relationship between the two levels of processing, two kinds of information to be processed, and the four foundational ethical systems is diagrammed in Figure 4.1.

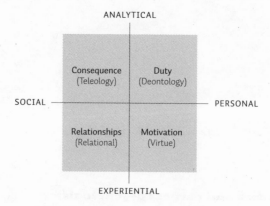

Figure 4.1 A model of ethical reasoning

Experiential ethical reasoning tends to be automatic, holistic, and emotional with little, if any, conscious awareness of even having made a decision (Haidt, 2001; Rogerson, Gottlieb, Handelsman, Knapp, & Youngren, 2011). It is based upon our appraisal of the situation—the most important aspect being the interpersonal context—which is then filtered through our emotional reaction to that understanding (Ochsner & Lieberman, 2001). These emotions are the product of our personal moral system and motivate us to value some actions over others. Early in our careers, professional ethical standards typically play a rather feeble role in our personal moral system. When we encounter novel or ambiguous situations, or have strong emotional reactions, our experiential reasoning can lead us astray of professional expectations (Cacioppo, 2002; Kahneman & Klein, 2009; Reynolds, 2006). Conversely, for those who have dealt with a variety of ethical challenges by diligently applying the values of our profession, experiential reasoning tends to lead to sound ethical decisions. Note that it is the assimilation of professional values into our personal moral system that is the crucial factor in becoming more ethical, because experience alone is actually inversely related to willingness to choose the most ethical course of action (Haas, Malouf, & Mayerson, 1988).

Analytic ethical reasoning involves a deliberate, logical, rational process of problem solving (Craigie, 2011; Reynolds, 2006) based on professional ethical duties, standards, and expectations. As professionals, our actions are expected to be justifiable according to such critical-evaluative reasoning, and thus we are required to incorporate analytic reasoning into our ethical decisions (Kitchener, 1984).

When we are strongly motivated toward a particular course of action we can experience conflict between what we want to do and what we know we should do. Given that there are many potential ways by which we might logically reason our way through to an ethical decision, in these instances we are prone to *rationalizing* our behaviour after the fact rather than *reasoning* our way to an ethical course of action (Bandura, 2002; Haidt, 2001; Reynolds, 2006; Smith, McGuire, Abbott, & Blau, 1991). To make decisions genuinely guided by professional ethical values that you would truly act upon, therefore, you should incorporate experiential *and* analytical reasoning into your decision making.

When confronted with ethical dilemmas that are new or particularly challenging to us, psychologists are expected to proceed through a deliberate decision-making process so that we might *discover* what course of action is best, rather than *justify* what we want to do or what we have done. As we encounter new situations and this reflective process is reiterated, our implicit moral values become more congruent with the explicit ethical values of our profession through greater awareness of ethical circumstances, enhanced ability to incorporate our personal motives into our ethical reasoning, repeated exposure to our professional ethical duties, and experience with the consequences of our actions (Rest, 1984). In this manner, we can develop a more "informed intuition," and ethical decisions that are congruent with professional ethical expectations become more reflexive. It also helps us to become more internally motivated, which results in higher engagement in ethical tasks, better decision making, more persistence, and assumption of greater responsibility for the outcomes (Ryan & Deci, 2000).

Making Ethical Decisions Via the CPA Process

Most readers will recognize that the situation presented in the case study at the beginning of the chapter requires us to make an ethical decision, and that doing so will not be easy. The Canadian Code of Ethics for Psychologists presents a decision-making process in the preamble to the Code proper. While the utility and authority of the Code of Ethics is not dependent upon using this process, it is very thorough and comprehensive (Cottone & Claus, 2000) and thus represents an excellent choice. The CPA process comprises ten steps, of which steps 2 and 3 have been re-ordered here to correspond with the model presented in Figure 4.1:

1. identification of individuals and groups involved or likely to be affected by the decision;
2. consideration of how personal bias, stress, or self-interest might influence the development of or choice between courses of action;
3. identification of relevant ethical principles, standards, and guidelines;
4. development of alternative courses of action;

5. analysis of likely risks and benefits of each course of action for the individuals and groups involved or likely to be affected;

6. choice of course of action after conscientious application of steps 1 through 5;

7. action;

8. evaluation of the results of the course of action;

9. assumption of responsibility for consequences of action, including correction of negative consequences, if any, or re-engaging in the decision-making process if the ethical issue is not resolved; and

10. appropriate action, as warranted and feasible, to prevent future occurrences of the dilemma.

1. IDENTIFICATION OF INDIVIDUALS AND GROUPS LIKELY TO BE AFFECTED BY THE DECISION

In the simplest circumstance, the only parties legitimately concerned with the outcome of an ethical decision would be the psychologist and the client. In practice, however, others are almost always involved. In some circumstances, a third party, such as an insurance company or a school, is paying for the professional service. In other situations, a parent or the courts may have directed that psychological services be provided. In all cases, an important first step is to consider who ought to be taken into account when ethical decisions are being made, what their preferences and interests are, and how the nuances and the interpersonal context impact our appraisal of the situation.

Relational ethics points us toward paying close attention to these interpersonal issues. This particularly involves listening carefully to what the affected parties have to say about their experience of the situation and incorporating this into our appraisal. Doing so will often involve a consideration of the larger cultural and social context as well (see Chapters 9 and 10).

To return to the example from the beginning of the chapter, the individuals and groups involved or likely to be affected by our decision are the children, father, mother, family as a unit, you the psychologist, and society in general. The circumstances are complex given that a number of individuals with conflicting preferences are involved and that these individuals are members of a family. We are in a position to help the children and their parents resolve their family difficulties in the manner of their choosing.

2. CONSIDERATION OF PERSONAL BIAS, STRESS, OR SELF-INTEREST

Doing the right thing professionally demands that we consider our personal motives and commitment to being of service to others. This does not mean that all psychologists must be saints, only that we should regularly consider how our own interests and biases influence our ethical reasoning. In response to financial stresses, for example, we may make ethical compromises in hopes that no harm will result and we will profit. Sometimes a situation will arouse feelings in us that cloud our ability to understand and reason through the problem (Betan & Stanton, 1999), such as a psychologist who has recently gone through a trying parental custody dispute and finds it difficult to provide an impartial opinion in a custody assessment.

Often, we may be able to resolve our personal issue that is interfering with a conscientious deliberation of our professional obligations before we attempt to take ethical action. In other situations, it may be possible to recognize that our personal biases are influencing our reasoning and acknowledge them as something to remain aware of as we proceed through the decision-making process. Seeking consultation from a trusted colleague would be well-advised in either situation.

Virtue ethics points us toward paying close attention to these motivational issues. When considering our motives, Hass and Malouf (1995) suggest the "clean, well-lit room" standard, which asks, "How would you feel presenting your preferred action to a group of your colleagues in a professional setting?" If you imagine yourself feeling uncomfortable, you can be pretty confident that you would not be behaving virtuously.

When we become aware of self-interests unduly influencing our reasoning, we should, quite simply, refrain from acting on them. It is not that our rights and preferences should be disregarded—they are certainly legitimate considerations in our ethical decision—but rather that we should not benefit at the expense of our clients. We can also use our reaction to inform us about possible situational influences that are "pulling" us toward certain actions or "pushing" us away from others.

In our example, you may have strong feelings about the importance of family integrity, self-determination, and responsibility with respect to suicide and the protection of vulnerable children. Additionally, you may be very concerned about your potential legal risk to the extent that a relatively higher value might be placed on avoiding liability than on helping the family.

3. IDENTIFICATION OF RELEVANT ETHICAL PRINCIPLES, STANDARDS, AND GUIDELINES

After taking into account the interpersonal circumstance and our personal motives, we next turn our attention to deontologic considerations by asking, "Does a relevant professional ethical duty, standard of conduct, or guideline exist?" This question obligates a review of relevant professional documents, starting with the practice standards of your jurisdiction, the CPA Code of Ethics, professional guidelines, and perhaps even the scholarly ethics literature. Indeed, as one student suggested to us, a test of ethical prudence might be to measure the distance between a psychologist's office chair and their copy of the Code of Ethics. Nowadays, I suppose we might look to see if it is bookmarked in their Internet browser or downloaded onto an electronic reader.

In some situations, especially for students and beginning practitioners, our decision-making efforts may stop at this point when a relevant standard or guide-line is found. Even highly experienced practitioners often find that a review of the Code of Ethics or their jurisdiction's practice standards turns up information that they had missed before or forgotten. The codes are, after all, quite detailed, such that you may have difficulty recalling specifics when they are hypothetical, and it is hard to imagine exactly how they might apply to circumstances you had not previously encountered.

If there is no single professional standard that applies, psychologists are expected to identify the ethical principles that are relevant and whether they are in conflict. Once you have done so, you will sometimes be able to identify an over-riding or primary ethical principle. With the four ethical principles of CPA Code of Ethics being ordered by their relative importance, prioritizing conflicting principles is made somewhat easier (Seitz & O'Neill, 1996). Thus, Principle I: Respect for the Dignity of Persons should generally be given the highest weight, except in circumstances when doing so would threaten the life of another person. Principle II: Responsible Caring should be given the second highest weight. Principle III: Integrity in Relationships generally should be given the third highest weight. And lastly, Principle IV: Responsibility to Society should generally be given the lowest weight of the four principles when it conflicts with any of them.

Next, we can compare and contrast our experiential preference with our duties as professionals. If there is an incongruence, we are expected to think long and hard before acting and to be prepared to justify our decision if we choose to act in a manner inconsistent with our ethical duties. Ideally, we can consider our moti-vation in a new light and perhaps even experience a shift in our personal morality such that we feel differently about what we prefer to do.

In our example, the CPA Code of Ethics encourages psychologists to:

I.45   Share confidential information only with informed consent, except as required by law, or in circumstances of actual or possible physical harm or death.

II.39   Do everything reasonably possible to stop or offset the consequences of actions by others when these actions are likely to cause
serious physical harm or death. This may include reporting to
appropriate authorities (e.g., the police) or an intended victim,
and would be done even when a confidential relationship is involved.

Thus we can see that there is a conflict between wanting to respect the
family's expressed wish that the children not be apprehended (Principle I) and
wanting to ensure that the children are safe from harm (Principle II). Additional
considerations are: not wanting to precipitate circumstances that could prompt
the father to harm himself (Principle II); honouring a commitment to help the
family (Principle III); and respecting society's value of protecting children from
harm (Principle IV) as well as maintaining the public's trust in the confidentiality
of psychological services (Principle IV).

4. DEVELOPMENT OF ALTERNATIVE COURSES OF ACTION

In situations when no single ethical principle outweighs the others, a number of
actions may be ethically appropriate. Time spent "brainstorming" and generat-
ing possible solutions that address the conflicting principles without being too
concerned with the feasibility of the alternatives is often of benefit at this point.
When at all possible, the client and concerned parties should be involved in the
development of possible solutions. If steps 1 through 3 have been applied diligently, the number of possible courses of action will typically have been reduced
considerably.

In our example, there are only two viable alternate courses of action:

1. report to the appropriate authorities;
2. do not report and continue to provide therapy to the family.

Although you might well be able to think of other alternatives, if you examine
them closely you will find that they are either variations of one of these two or
fail to address the essential ethical issue. This may seem obvious, but practitioners often focus on practice issues—such as what would "address the client's
maladaptive thinking" or "resolve the client's transference"—rather than on
the ethical issue, such as, in this situation, the conflict between the principles of
autonomy and beneficence.

Also, you want to be sure that the course of action you are considering could
actually be implemented. For example, psychologists often would like to change

social policies or laws, when in fact such changes cannot be implemented in a particular situation or in time to resolve the dilemma (see Chapter 10 for a further discussion of this issue). Moreover, you should consider how practical a particular alternative is for you personally. The time and effort that a course of action may require can sometimes be out of proportion to the ethical conflict it is intended to resolve.

5. ANALYSIS OF LIKELY SHORT-TERM, ONGOING, AND LONG-TERM RISKS AND BENEFITS OF ALTERNATIVES

When evaluating the alternative courses of action generated in step 4, psychologists are expected to consider the extent to which each alternative:

Satisfies the preferences of the affected parties. Given that the Code of Ethics obligates psychologists to promote human welfare by respecting the dignity of persons first and foremost, in particular situations this translates into promoting the preferences of the affected parties. Thus, if no ethical duty or professional standard exists that resolves the dilemma, a course of action that satisfies—or at least takes into account—the preferences of affected parties should be developed. ·

Presents no new ethical problems. The nature of ethical dilemmas is such that attempts to resolve them can create new problems. In particular, one may feel tempted to do something "a little unethical" such as telling a partial truth in order to avoid addressing larger ethical issues. Such alternatives are really based on expediency rather than ethical responsibility, however, and usually cause more problems than they solve.

Advances one principle over the other(s) in conflict. Often what makes an ethical dilemma a challenge is that each alternative advances one ethical principle while compromising another. The idea of considering risks and benefits is not to have you simply adopt a teleological approach to ethical reasoning. Rather, the best (or sometimes least undesirable) alternative may be the one that compromises fewer deontological principles or compromises conflicting principles to a lesser degree than the other alternatives.

Once we have considered these aspects of our potential alternative actions and eliminated those that do not pass muster, we can then turn to teleological thinking and take into account their foreseeable consequences. If the likely consequences are too undesirable, we should either reconsider or be prepared to defend our actions as the product of a thorough process of ethical reasoning.

To return again to our example, if the children's possible need for protection is reported to the authorities, you would not be satisfying the preferences of any of the affected parties except society in general. Doing so would also result in a high likelihood that the father will harm himself and that the family will terminate therapy, thereby resulting in undesirable consequences. You would, however, be advancing the ethical principle of offsetting or preventing harm by responding to the children's need to be physically safe from their father's violence.

If you do not report, you would be satisfying the preferences of the family, and they will likely continue in therapy where you may well be able to help the father reduce his violent behaviour. A new ethical problem may be created, however, if continued therapy does not result in reducing the father's violence and the children suffer further harm.

6. CHOICE OF COURSE OF ACTION

After conscientious application of steps 1 through 5, you are ultimately expected to make a choice. Ideally, the choice will be experientially justifiable to you and analytically justifiable to others. It may help to remember that no one can be held to a standard of perfection; you must simply try your best to do the right thing. In our example, both courses of action address the ethical principles in conflict and have the potential to create new ethical dilemmas, while having advantages and disadvantages with respect to satisfying the interests of the affected parties and advancing one ethical principle over another. Given that neither alternative is clearly superior, the circumstance of dealing with the physical safety of children who are not in a position to champion their own interests, tips the balance toward the best course of action being to inform the authorities of their need for protection.

7. ACTION

Making a decision is not the end of the process of ethical reasoning; you must act in order to truly be ethical. Remember that even not doing anything is an action. Sometimes taking action can be a relief from the tension of anticipation. Being ethical can also result in increased work, pressure, and anxiety, however. It can also sometimes necessitate defying or confronting others who have power over us, such as supervisors or employers. Implementing our choice of course of action therefore may involve additional skills such as assertiveness, fortitude, and tenacity.

This is not to say that acting ethically is always unpleasant. Doing the right thing can provide a sense of professional pride and mastery and instill confidence in your ability to master future ethical challenges. It can also evoke respect in colleagues and facilitate a more ethical interpersonal environment.

In our example, we would inform the family of our decision and the reasons for it, give them every opportunity to participate, contact the authorities, and do our best to maintain a positive—or at least respectful—relationship with the family.

8. EVALUATION OF THE RESULTS OF THE COURSE OF ACTION

Evaluation of the consequences of your actions ought to go hand in hand with implementation and brings us back to relational ethics. Ideally, you will be able to follow up with all parties affected by your actions, although this is not always possible. Certainly, the most ethical course of action will not always please everyone, and some people will not want to have further contact with you. Whenever possible, however, you should include the direct recipients of your services in the ongoing process of evaluating whether your actions have resolved the ethical dilemma. Finally, you should take stock of the new circumstances— especially interpersonal relationships—in light of the effects of your actions and continue the ethical reasoning process until an ethically satisfactory resolution is achieved.

In our case example, you would be expected to follow up with the family and the authorities to ensure that appropriate steps have been taken.

9. ASSUMPTION OF RESPONSIBILITY FOR CONSEQUENCES OF ACTION TAKEN

Although we are expected to consult with others and be guided by professional codes and standards, the responsibility for our actions remains with us as individual psychologists in accordance with virtue ethics. Often, our actions bring to light additional dimensions of the situation that may lead to a redefinition of the problem or change the circumstances in significant ways, necessitating consideration of further alternatives that have impactful consequences and so on. This is why the model in Figure 4.1 is presented in a circular, iterative form.

Hopefully, the family in our example will maintain their trust in your intentions to act in the best interests of everyone involved and you can continue to provide therapy. If so, you would be expected to be particularly mindful of the father's suicide risk and respond as appropriate. If the family does not stay in therapy, you should offer referrals and seek the family's consent to co-ordinate the transfer of services.

10. APPROPRIATE ACTION TO PREVENT FUTURE OCCURRENCES
OF THE DILEMMA

Every experience changes the people involved. Ethical dilemmas tend to change us rather profoundly. Often, the emotional toll prompts a psychologist to conclude, "I'm never going to provide that type of service (or provide services to that type of client, etc.) again!" Such a reaction, although understandable, is counterproductive to being an ethical psychologist. In fact, what tends to happen when psychologists adopt such an attitude is that they become more rigid in their interactions with others and actually increase the likelihood of establishing distrustful and adversarial relationships. This, in turn, can result in more ethical challenging situations, which can provoke a more guarded approach to clients, and so on in a non-virtuous, non-relational downward spiral.

An approach that is more likely to promote your ethical development and decrease future dilemmas is to take time to reflect on what you have learned from the situation in accordance with deontological and teleological ethics. Ask yourself the following questions and any others that occur to you:

- Are there things that I would do differently next time?
- Am I as familiar as I ought to be with ethical codes, standards, and literature?
- Do I have a professional network with whom I can effectively consult?
- Are there changes that I could or should make in my professional practices that may prevent future occurrences of similar dilemmas?
- Are there changes that could or should be made in the policies and procedures of the institution that may prevent future occurrences of similar dilemmas?

In our example, you would probably want to consult with colleagues to review your ethical reasoning and to debrief emotionally, and you may want to review the professional and ethical literature dealing with treating family violence and maintaining confidentiality in circumstances involving vulnerable children.

Summary

Ethical actions should be the result of careful reasoning. A ten-step process for making ethical decisions begins with (step 1) identification of the individuals and groups potentially affected by the decision and moves to (step 2) consideration of the influence of any personal biases, stresses, or self-interest. In step 3, psychologists identify relevant ethical principles, standards, and guidelines, and then (step 4) develop alternative courses of action. Step 5 involves analysis of likely consequences of each course of action. At step 6, psychologists choose a course of action, then (step 7) act, (step 8) evaluate the results of the course of action, and (step 9) assume responsibility for the consequences of action. Finally, in step 10, the psychologist takes appropriate action, as warranted and feasible, to prevent future occurrences of the dilemma. Although the process appears time consuming at first, through greater familiarity with ethics codes and standards, consultation with colleagues, and reflecting on your personal moral system, ethical decisions that are justifiable and congruent with professional values will become more intuitive.

Discussion Questions

1. What do you think are some of the reasons that psychologists don't always behave as ethically as they ought to? What source of knowledge did you draw on to answer this question?

2. How would you go about choosing which colleague(s) to consult with about an ethically challenging situation you encounter? What qualities should such a person possess? Why?

3. Under what circumstances would you feel tempted to disregard ethical standards in favour of your intuitive judgement? Under what circumstances would you feel justified in doing so?

4. Do you agree with how the ethical dilemma was resolved in this chapter? Why or why not? If not, how would you resolve it?

Your Reflective Journal

You have been exposed to quite a number of ethical case studies now. Take some time to consider your reactions to them. You may want to go back and re-read them and any impressions you recorded at the time you first read them. What trends or commonalities do you notice in your reactions and responses? What does this tell you about your intuitive ethical self? Do you notice any incongruence or contradictions between your intuition and what you publically avow? Or between your intuition and the rules and obligations of the profession? What does this tell you about your analytical ethical self? How might you facilitate a greater reconciliation of your experiential and analytical reasoning?

Case Study

Offender Treating Offenders

You are a psychologist employed by Correctional Service Canada and are chairing a selection committee to hire a psychologist for a sexual offender treatment program. Inmates are admitted to the program by court order to receive individual and group therapy. Correctional Service has had a very difficult time filling the position due to a lack of applicants. In fact, the position has remained unfilled for over two years and the inmates in the program have been receiving very limited treatment. There is only one psychologist under consideration. He has credentials and experience that make him a good candidate. In addition, however, he was recently found guilty by his provincial regulatory college of sexually exploiting two female clients. His practice is restricted to providing services only to men and only under the supervision of a psychologist acceptable to the college. Your manager is urging you to hire—and supervise—him.

Case Study

Deinstitutionalized

You are a psychologist working in a large regional psychiatric hospital. You have been given the responsibility of overseeing a project designed to transfer long-term care patients into community settings. The project is predicated on establishing community-based boarding homes, hiring and training staff, and providing ongoing support for the patients and staff. The time frame for the project is eighteen months. Five months into the project you receive notice from a senior administrator that all of the patients must be moved within one month and that no funding will be available for ongoing support. You respond by explaining that it would be impossible to arrange for even rudimentary placements for all of the patients in that time and that without support the well-being of the majority of patients would be seriously jeopardized. You are told that the directive comes from "the highest levels of government," is not open to debate, that you are expected to do your best, and someone else will be given the task to complete if you do not.

Source: Adapted from the *Companion Manual to the Canadian Code of Ethics for Psychologists*, 3rd ed. (Sinclair & Pettifor, 2001).

Case Study

Need to Know?

You are a psychologist providing psychotherapeutic service to a twenty-two-year-old man who suffered a brain injury a few years ago. Much of his sense of self-worth is based on his high intelligence. He was a varsity athlete with a promising future in law prior to his injury. He now vacillates between concern that he has lost his mental capabilities such that he will never be a lawyer and frantic bursts of unfocused enthusiasm for regaining his former glory. When his pessimism is dominant, he becomes very depressed and at times even suicidal. A copy of a recent neuropsychological assessment is on his file. The test results are consistent with his having experienced a marked decline in his intellect. In fact, there is not even a remote possibility that he could handle the cognitive challenges of a legal career. He asks you for a copy of his file.

Recommended Reading

Craigie, J. (2011). Thinking and feeling: Moral deliberation in a dual-process framework. *Philosophical Psychology, 24,* 53–71.

McCarron, M.C.E., & Stewart, D.W. (2011). A Canadian perspective on using vignettes to teach ethics in psychology. *Canadian Psychology, 52,* 185–91.

Pettifor, J.L. (1998). The Canadian Code of Ethics for Psychologists: A moral context for ethical decision-making in emerging areas of practice. *Canadian Psychology, 39,* 231–38.

Sinclair, C., & Pettifor, J.L. (2001). Use of the code in ethical decision making. In C. Sinclair & J.L. Pettifor (Eds.). *Companion manual to the Canadian code of ethics for psychologists, 3rd ed.* (pp. 105–43). Ottawa: Canadian Psychological Association.

5

Obtaining Consent

Case Study

Parental Refusal

You have undertaken a psychological assessment of an eight-year-old child referred by the school to address the possibility of being held back a grade. The parents have given consent to have their child assessed and to release the report to the school, which is your normal practice. Upon completion of the assessment and prior to providing the report to the school, you discuss the results with the parents. You tell them that their child has a learning disability for which the school will provide additional in-class tutoring under their policy for children with special needs. The parents then tell you that they do not want the assessment report shared with the school because they do not want their child to be labeled as "retarded." Despite your best efforts at explanation and persuasion, they will not relent.

Questions for consideration

1. *What individuals and groups are affected in this situation? Why?*

2. *Would it make a difference if the assessment was paid for by the school? If it was paid for by the parents?*

3. *How do you feel about the parents' reaction and decision? How might your feelings influence your ethical reasoning?*

4. *What are the ethical values in conflict in this situation? Explain.*

All other things being equal, the right to make decisions about whether or not to receive psychological services, and the nature of those services, belongs to the client. This conclusion finds support in psychologists' ethical values—particularly those arising out of the social contract between a profession and society (see Chapter 1)—and also in our professional standards (see Chapter 2) and law (see Chapter 3). Indeed, consent is the most represented value in the Canadian Code of Ethics for Psychologists. It is rather curious to note, therefore, given its central importance today, that the topic of consent did not even appear in the ethical literature until the late 1950s, and only received detailed consideration beginning in the early 1970s (Beauchamp & Childress, 2012). Prior to the Nuremberg trials of World War II and at least as far back as Hippocrates (400 BCE), patients were given almost no input into treatment decisions because it was thought that too much explanation would either confuse them or arouse so much anxiety that their care and treatment would be compromised. Largely as a result of the consumer movement in health care, this attitude has changed (Kapp, 2006). In fact, over the last few decades the focus has shifted from the professional's legal obligation to disclose information in order to minimize harm—primarily that arising out of exploitation—to respect for autonomous choice (Fontigny, 1996).

When a client gives consent for a service we are, in effect, entering into a contractual professional relationship with them. The client agrees to receive a psychological service that will be provided by us. We, in turn, agree to provide the specified service within the limitations and under the conditions set down by both parties. Unlike most other types of contracts, however, the consent agreement is based on a special relationship often called a fiduciary relationship. This refers to the circumstance in which, because of our superior knowledge and training relative to our clients, they place their trust in us and we are expected to act in such a way that benefits them.

Duties and Virtues Underlying Consent

AUTONOMY AND RESPECT

The ethical foundation for consent is derived from the principle of autonomy whereby each person's right to be free from controlling influence by others is respected. As a society, we regularly allow one another to make decisions that are of questionable benefit to our well-being—such as smoking—so long as it does not impinge on the autonomy of others—as in the case of second-hand smoke. Equally important is that we normally allow members of our society to make these decisions relatively unfettered by controlling constraints. In the circumstance of consent for professional services, this includes freedom from limitations imposed by inadequate understanding or undue pressure that would prevent meaningful and voluntary choice. Virtually all professional codes of ethics now hold that free and informed consent must be obtained prior to undertaking any professional service. Indeed, our Canadian Code of Ethics for Psychologists includes the following standard:

> I.16   Seek as full and active participation as possible from others in decisions that affect them, respecting and integrating as much as possible their opinions and wishes.

Relationships and Consequences Relevant to Consent

STANDARDS OF DISCLOSURE

It is essential that clients have the necessary and sufficient information about a service if they are to decide to enter into a professional relationship. It also follows that clients cannot act as autonomous persons if they are unaware of alternatives from which they may choose or the implications of choosing or rejecting these alternatives. Psychologists have an obligation to ensure that our clients have this information because the very nature of a profession is that we have specialized knowledge not available to the average person (see Chapter 2). The need for information is heightened by the fact that most people's presuppositions about psychology often are mistaken (Farberman, 1997; Murstein & Fontaine, 1993). Many people, for example, believe that psychologists can "read their minds" or dispense medications (Orchowski, Spickard, & McNamara, 2006). We are expected, therefore, to do whatever is reasonably possible under the circumstances to provide clients or potential clients with information adequate and sufficient to allow them to exercise their right to choose. But how much information is adequate and sufficient? There are three possible standards of disclosure to consider: full, professional, and objective reasonable person.

The standard of full disclosure would require that *all* information relevant to a given situation be provided. Such a standard would require that collectively and individually psychologists would be able to foresee all the possible outcomes of receiving or not receiving all possible psychological services and their alternatives, both psychological and non-psychological. Given the impossibility of anyone being omniscient, such a standard is neither practical nor professionally or legally enforceable.

For a brief historical period in the 1970s, psychologists were expected to disclose as much information as a similar colleague would under similar circumstances (*Kelly v. Hazlett*, 1976). The problem with this "professional standard" was that it ignored the status of the client as an autonomous agent and placed the decision in the hands of the professional. Not surprisingly, the courts revised this standard quite soon after the *Kelly* decision and replaced it with the *objective reasonable person* standard (*Reibl v. Hughes*, 1980).

The objective reasonable person standard holds that professionals have an obligation to ensure that our clients have whatever information a reasonable person would want to know in their situation in order to make the decision under consideration. This means that as psychologists are expected to pay due regard to our clients' particular circumstances from the perspective of their personal, cultural, and other needs and characteristics. It is quite reasonable that a person with a particular cultural background would want to know (or not know) what a person with a different background would not (or would), for example. In a multicultural society such as Canada, this is a very important consideration (see Chapter 9). This legal standard is completely consistent with our profession's ethical standards:

I.23   Provide, in obtaining informed consent, as much information as reasonable or prudent persons would want to know before making a decision or consenting to the activity. The psychologist would relay this information in language that the persons understand (including providing translation into another language, if necessary) and would take whatever reasonable steps are needed to ensure that the information was, in fact, understood.

I.24   Ensure, in the process of obtaining informed consent, that at least the following points are understood: purpose and nature of the activity; mutual responsibilities; confidentiality protections and limitations; likely benefits and risks; alternatives; the likely consequences of non-action; the option to refuse or withdraw at any time, without prejudice; over what period of time the consent applies; and, how to rescind consent if desired.

I.25 Provide new information in a timely manner, whenever such information becomes available and is significant enough that it reasonably could be seen as relevant to the original or ongoing informed consent.

III.14 Be clear and straightforward about all information needed to establish informed consent or any other valid written or unwritten agreement (for example: fees; concerns; mutual responsibilities; ethical responsibilities of psychologists; purpose and nature of the relationship; alternatives; likely experiences; possible conflicts; possible outcomes; and, expectations for processing, using, and sharing any information generated).

From an ethical (and legal) point of view, however, it is not sufficient to simply impart information; it must be understood if it is to be used to make a decision. The importance of truly informed consent is probably underestimated by many psychologists, and some even tend to view it somewhat cynically as a onetime hurdle to overcome before getting down to business. This attitude is manifested in an overemphasis on content issues—what do I need to include to make this a valid consent?—and comparatively little attention paid to the process of obtaining consent (Johnson-Greene, 2007).

FREEDOM OF CONSENT

Obviously, consent that is not obtained voluntarily does not represent true consent at all. Given that the value underlying consent is respect for the dignity of the individual and the right to autonomy, clients must freely give their consent. Threats of harm or undue incentives—whether physical, emotional, monetary, or social standing—therefore negate consent. Similarly, manipulation by presenting information in a biased fashion, withholding certain facts, or outright deception, does not represent ethically—or legally—valid consent. The Code of Ethics advises psychologists to:

I.27 Take all reasonable steps to ensure that consent is not given under conditions of coercion, undue pressure, or undue reward.

I.29 Take all reasonable steps to confirm or re-establish freedom of consent, if consent for service is given under conditions of duress or conditions of extreme need.

I.36   Be particularly cautious in establishing the freedom of consent of any person who is in a dependent relationship to the psychologist (e.g., student, employee). This may include, but is not limited to, offering that person an alternative activity to fulfill their educational or employment goals, or offering a range of research studies or experience opportunities from which the person can select, none of which is so onerous as to be coercive.

III.32 Not offer rewards sufficient to motivate an individual or group to participate in an activity that has possible or known risks to themselves or others.

PROCESS OF CONSENT

It is sometimes mistakenly thought that informed consent is dealt with during our first contact with the client and then can be forgotten. Indeed, if a client expresses surprise or dissatisfaction with some aspect of service, psychologists with this mind-set might be tempted to remind them that they had previously given consent! Such a stance does not reflect true consent. Likewise, signing a consent form does very little good from the point of view of protecting the client's autonomy. A signed consent form may serve the interests of the psychologist or some other third party by providing documentation that something took place, but the issue of what the client actually understood they were agreeing to or whether the client felt pressured to consent remains open to argument. Even the Code of Ethics is equivocal on this issue:

I.17   Recognize that informed consent is the result of a process of reaching an agreement to work collaboratively, rather than of simply having a consent form signed.

I.21   Establish and use signed consent forms that specify the dimensions of informed consent or that acknowledge that such dimensions have been explained and are understood, if such forms are required by law or if such forms are desired by the psychologist, the person(s) giving consent, or the organization for whom the psychologist works.

I.22   Accept and document oral consent, in situations in which signed consent forms are not acceptable culturally or in which there are other good reasons for not using them.

Certainly, reading a form does not ensure that the content is understood. Studies of patients who sign consent forms find that comprehension and memory of the purpose, nature, and risks of the treatment is poor (Brezis et al., 2008; Cassileth, Zupkis, Sutton-Smith, & March, 1980; Shurnas & Coughlin, 2003). Even when a consent form satisfies administrative and legal requirements, signed written consent does not function primarily in our clients' interests or as a way of making their interests known. The greatest ethical concern with using a consent form is that it can tempt us to treat consent as a discrete task that is accomplished once the client has signed the form. Providing information relevant to consent in writing that the client can keep and review whenever and as often as they wish, on the other hand, can obviously serve to further their autonomy, regardless of whether they sign a copy.

True consent requires the client to do more than simply express agreement or comply with a proposal that we might make. The client must intentionally authorize us to do something to or with them. Thus, consent for a psychological service involves initiating and maintaining a collaborative relationship with our clients. This is not to say that obtaining consent is merely a process of shared decision making. A client may have already made an informed and voluntary choice prior to meeting us by having researched the service to be provided or spoken with a knowledgeable individual, for example. In most circumstances, we have far more information and experience with similar situations than the client, however, and so have a greater responsibility to contribute to the decision to be made. Ideally, consent is never "obtained"—at any point in time the client should feel free to ask questions about the service being undertaken and consent to its continuation, alteration, or discontinuation. Ultimately, the responsibility for ensuring that consent is truly informed and freely given—whether through the use of a consent form or documented oral consent—is ours.

It may be most helpful to think of consent as a process of working collaboratively with your client. That is, the goal of consent is never completely met. As circumstances change—which is often the very goal of psychological services—so too does the information needed by the client to decide whether to continue, alter, or discontinue the service. While most psychologists will recognize that a collaborative process of negotiating consent can clear up clients' misconceptions, it can also be an opportunity for clearing up our misconceptions. An open dialogue can make us aware of features of the client's circumstances that depart from our preconceptions and previous experience, and thus serve as a corrective to any personal or professional biases (O'Neill, 1998), thereby enabling us to provide better service.

From a practical point of view, therefore, you should explain the purpose and nature of the service to be undertaken, the reasonably foreseeable benefits and risks, and any alternative services. You should then make sure that your client understands these elements. This initial discussion should be documented either in case notes or using a consent form. Once services are initiated, you should remain alert to indicators of client collaboration and agreement and discuss them openly with your client, particularly if reluctance or disagreement is sensed, or if significant alterations to the service are indicated by changing circumstances and—yet again—document these discussions. This process is not necessarily the most expeditious one in the short term. We must be prepared to go slowly and listen carefully—experientially and analytically—if we are to truly hear our client's preferences. Sometimes it is a barely perceptible hesitation, or a too-quick agreement. Ultimately, however, taking as much time as is necessary will allow us to respect the interpersonal context, our motivation, and our client's autonomy and achieve more desirous outcomes for everyone involved.

MINOR CLIENTS

Uniquely difficult practical problems arise when obtaining consent for psychological services from minors, who may not yet have developed the capacity to give it. The Code of Ethics advises psychologists to

I.33   Seek to use methods that maximize the understanding and ability to consent of persons of diminished capacity to give informed consent, and that reduce the need for a substitute decision maker.

I.34   Carry out informed consent processes with those persons who are legally responsible or appointed to give informed consent on behalf of persons not competent to consent on their own behalf, seeking to ensure respect for any previously expressed preferences of persons not competent to consent.

I.35   Seek willing and adequately informed participation from any person of diminished capacity to give informed consent, and proceed without this assent only if the service or research activity is considered to be of direct benefit to that person.

Every jurisdiction in Canada has set a legal age of majority. Above this age, competence to consent is assumed. Below it, competence is not assumed. In most jurisdictions that age is eighteen, although in some it is nineteen (Rozovsky, 2003). As a society, therefore, parents (or guardian substitutes) are charged with the legal obligation to provide care and support for their minor children, and this translates into the legal right to direct and supervise them. Proxy consent from parents or guardians is thus sought for many activities involving persons under the age of majority. This age criteria is based as much on convenience as ethical and legal considerations, however. Ethically, the duty of respect for autonomy obligates us to allow anyone capable of consenting the opportunity to give or withhold it. This would cause the day-to-day functioning of many social institutions to grind to a halt if we had to determine the capacity to consent of every individual for every decision they have to make, and so it is seldom enacted.

Further complicating matters, different ages have been set for different purposes by federal and provincial law. Provincial legislation establishes ages for voting, drinking alcoholic beverages, and driving, for example. Legislation does not establish an age for consent for psychological services, however. The fact that a person is under the age of majority does not bar that person from consenting to psychological services—the courts presume that each individual is capable of giving consent in the absence of proof to the contrary (Rozovsky, 2003). Unfortunately, many psychologists are reluctant to accept the consent of clients under the age of majority for fear of incurring the wrath of angry parents and running the risk of having to defend against a professional or legal complaint.

The most typical situation psychologists face is that where a parent (or guardian) brings their minor child to receive services and gives consent on behalf of the child. In this case, the psychologist's task is fairly straightforward: to deliver the service and inform the parent/guardian of anything arising during the provision of that service that they would reasonably want to know in order to maintain consent. While parental consent is in effect we are expected to provide minor children with as much information as they are capable of understanding and obtain their agreement to begin or continue services. This agreement should be commensurate with the minor's capacity. With very young children, for example, agreement is more the form of a mutually friendly, trusting relationship. The greater the capacity of the minor child to understand—usually but not necessarily a function of age—the greater the amount and depth of the information provided and agreement expected.

A minor who does not want to participate in psychological services to which their parents have consented on their behalf should be provided as much choice as possible around aspects of the service that are negotiable. You should attempt to build a trusting relationship with the child and thereby secure their agreement. Ultimately, if the minor steadfastly refuses to agree to participate in the

psychological service—particularly intervention—it will be of little if any benefit
and the parents should be so informed: No psychologist should continue to provide a service that does not help the client (see Chapter 7).

If a minor seeks a psychologist's services and does not want to involve their
parents, the matter becomes more difficult. Common law recognizes the principle
of a *mature minor*. Minors are considered "mature," and thereby capable of providing their own consent, if they have sufficient understanding and intelligence
to enable them to fully appreciate the service being proposed (*A.C. v. Manitoba
[Director of Child and Family Services]*, 2009; *J.S.C. and C.H.C. v. Wren*, 1986). Although
chronological age is only one of several factors to be considered (Fischer, Stein, &
Heikkinen, 2009; Steinberg, Cauffman, Woolard, Graham, & Banich, 2009), legal
precedent suggests a benchmark: a minor would rarely be considered mature
before the age of fourteen. Minors aged fourteen years and older of average intelligence are typically competent to consent to psychological services (Adelman,
Lusk, Alvarez, & Acosta, 1985; Kaser-Boyd, Adelman, & Taylor, 1985; Lewis, 1981;
Schachter, Kleinman, & Harvey, 2005; Weithorn & Campbell, 1982). Indeed, on
some characteristics they cannot be distinguished from young adults of the age
of majority. It would be an exceptional child below the age of fourteen who is
able to understand the complexities and consequences of psychological services
(Weithorn & Cambell, 1982), and considerable caution should be exercised under
such circumstances.

If the minor's understanding and appreciation of the service is sufficient to
warrant being treated as a mature minor, his or her consent is therefore sufficient
(Rozovsky, 2003). This determination should be tempered by the degree of risk
inherent in the situation, however. Situations involving greater or longer-term
risks, such as life-threatening sexually transmitted diseases, require a greater
capacity than might be the case where risk is more trivial, such as the dissolution
of a friendship. Also, care should be taken with children under the age of fifteen
with respect to freedom of consent in light of their tendency to acquiesce to
authority (Grisso & Vierling, 1978; Mann, Harmoni, & Power, 1989). Keep in mind,
however, that the case of *A.C. v. Manitoba (Director of Child and Family Services)*
(2009) involved a fourteen-year-old girl who was deemed competent to reject
a life-saving blood transfusion over the objection of her physicians. Rarely—if
ever—will psychological services entail risks as serious as these. Thus, concerns
about the risks associated with a minor's decision should not be weighed too
heavily as a justification for denying a minor's wishes.

Psychologists who work in schools should be aware of the legislation in their
jurisdiction relevant to obtaining consent from minors. In Alberta, for example, a
student under the age of eighteen may be considered "independent" as defined in

the School Act and thereby competent to give consent to psychological services. These statutes are merely codifications of principles that we as psychologists and Canadian citizens value, however, and should be used for guidance where they exist, without allowing them to override our best judgement of the capacity and preferences of our clients.

DEPENDENT ADULTS

Persons of the age of majority are assumed to be competent to make decisions for themselves unless there is convincing and overwhelming evidence to the contrary. As a society, we regularly respect an individual's right to make decisions that are of questionable benefit to their well-being. Equally important is that we allow members of our society to make these decisions regardless of any personal characteristics, conditions, or status. At the individual level, therefore, allowing others to decide for themselves without interference is normally given precedence over promoting their well-being. When a service is for the benefit of the individual, free and informed consent—including the choice of refusing the service—should be respected regardless of our opinion of what would promote their welfare.

As already stated with regard to minors, the only ethically justifiable circumstance in which psychologists would decide for others whether they should be subjected to any form of psychological service is when they are not competent to decide for themselves. The relative weighting of respect for the dignity of persons (Principle I) over responsible caring (Principle II) is now adjusted based on individuals' inability to make decisions in their own best interest. Considerations of self-determination are now subsumed under considerations of well-being. Respect for the dignity of the individual is not abandoned, however. When individuals are incompetent to make a decision for themselves, therefore, the proxy decision maker should attempt to replicate as much as possible the decision that the client would make under the circumstances if they were competent. The dependent adult's opinions and wishes should also be respected and integrated into any decision as much as possible.

In most cases, the dependent adult will have a legally appointed guardian. In cases where the individual does not, the psychologist should either petition the court to appoint a guardian to make decisions on the individual's behalf, or seek a family member's consent. The latter is permissible in some jurisdictions but is less preferable because judicial involvement affords the individual substantially greater protection from exploitation.

ASSESSING COMPETENCE

Competence (or incompetence) does not describe a trait or even state of an individual—it describes an individual's ability (or inability) to perform a particular task, such as making a decision. Thus, competence in the context of consent is decision-relative, not a global appraisal. A person may be competent to make a particular decision under certain circumstances, such as which account to debit at an automated teller machine without time constraints or social pressure, and not competent to make a different decision, or even the same decision under different circumstances, such as when there is a queue of people waiting to use the ATM. Assessing competence, therefore, should involve a determination of an individual's ability to make a particular decision at a particular time under particular circumstances. Thus, in the course of normal practice, assessment of competence will be an ongoing process.

Whenever in doubt about competence to consent, the assessment to be made is whether or not the individual is capable of consenting to the psychological service in question. The psychologist should determine if the client understands the following:

- the nature and purpose of the psychological service;
- the risk and benefits of the psychological service; and
- the nature, purpose, risks, and benefits of alternatives to the psychological service.

If the client does not understand all three of the above issues, a legally recognized decision maker (e.g., parent or guardian) should make the decision.

Summary

Obtaining consent is a process of collaboration whereby the client understands whatever information is necessary to make a decision about undertaking, altering, or continuing psychological services and willingly agrees to them. Consent is required by our Code of Ethics and is based on the ethical principle of respect for the dignity of persons. Psychologists are expected to disclose whatever information a reasonable person would want to know in their particular circumstance in order to give informed consent and ensure that the information is understood. Freedom of consent is addressed by taking all reasonable steps to ensure that consent is not given under conditions of coercion, undue pressure, or undue reward, and respecting the right of persons to discontinue the service at any time.

In situations where the individual is not competent to give consent, psychologists should obtain the consent of a parent or guardian, as appropriate, while incorporating the wishes and preferences of the non-competent person as much as possible.

Discussion Questions

1. Do you think a client should have the right to be ignorant of risks associated with a psychological service if they don't want to know? Explain.

2. Can there be truly informed consent in court-mandated situations? If so, explain how. If not, how can you ethically justify providing services under such situations?

3. Under what circumstances would you allow an adolescent to consent to psychological services without parental knowledge or consent? Explain your position.

4. By law, people with severe mental disorders have the right to refuse treatment. How do we reconcile their right to—and our ethical value of—autonomy with the ethical value of beneficence?

Your Reflective Journal

In our personal lives we are faced with many situations where complete candour may not be in our best interest. Think about times when you were not fully disclosing to others. Or when you convinced someone to do something that you knew they didn't really want to do. What was significant about those situations? How do you feel about yourself in light of what you did? Were your actions justified? Or do you feel guilty? Why? Is there something unique about professional circumstances with respect to disclosure and consent? If so, what is it? Take as much time as you need to consider these and other questions that may occur to you around this issue.

Case Study

Eternal Soul

A sixteen-year-old young man seeks your services for treatment of depression. It is clear that he understands the nature, benefits, and risks of therapy, and willingly gives permission to contact his parents, who consent on his behalf with the understanding that you will involve them if their son is at risk of harm to himself or others. In the third session of therapy, he confides that he is romantically attracted to other young men and that he is conflicted about how to tell others—especially his parents—that he is gay. He says that this is why he is depressed and that he really wants to talk to someone about it. Later that week his father calls you and accuses you of "filling [his] son's head with homosexual filth" and thereby "harming to his eternal soul." He demands that you stop talking to his son about "sexual deviance" or he and his wife will withdraw their consent.

Case Study

Mind Reader

You undertake an assessment of a woman charged with killing her two infant children. You explain to her that your role is to assess her mental state and prepare a report for court. You inform her that anything she tells you will not be kept confidential and can be used in your report. You answer her few questions, she appears to understand the nature and purpose of the assessment, and she signs a consent form. She then asks, "You're a shrink, right?" You respond by telling her that you are a·psychologist, re-state your role as an assessor on behalf of the court, and re-emphasize that whatever she tells you is not confidential. She does not seem to be actively listening and then asks, "You can read minds though, right?" You tell her that neither you nor anyone else can read minds. She appears crestfallen and dejectedly says, "But I thought you would be able to tell me why I killed them."

Case Study

On His Own Terms

You have a contract to provide psychological services to employees covered under an employee assistance program. The contract will reimburse ten sessions of psychotherapy if the client is abusing alcohol, six sessions if depressed, and three sessions if having interpersonal problems. An individual covered under the plan presents to you saying that he is experiencing conflict with a co-worker. After your initial assessment, it is clear that he is depressed and alcoholic. You explain that the best approach is to treat his drinking and depression, and that it will likely take all of the sixteen sessions that his insurance will cover. He denies that he has any personal problems and insists he wants to deal only with the interpersonal difficulty. You explain that therapy is unlikely to be effective, in part because you will only have three sessions in which to work together. He replies by stating that if you won't provide the treatment he wants, he will find another therapist who will.

Recommended Reading

Crowhurst, B., & Dobson, K.S. (1993). Informed consent: Legal issues and applications to clinical practice. *Canadian Psychology, 34,* 329–46.

O'Neill, P. (1998). *Negotiating consent in psychotherapy.* New York: New York University Press.

Schachter, D., Kleinman, I., & Harvey, W. (2005). Informed consent and adolescents. *Canadian Journal of Psychiatry, 50,* 534–40.

Tymchuk, A.J. (1997). Informing for consent: Concepts and methods. *Canadian Psychology, 38,* 55–75.

6

Protecting Confidentiality

Case Study

Marital Secrets

Many months after having provided marital therapy to a couple, you receive a telephone call from a lawyer representing the husband. The lawyer tells you that the couple is now separated and is disputing the custody of their child. The lawyer requests on behalf of the husband that you testify at a custody hearing. You will be asked to verify the wife's admission during therapy that she had numerous extramarital affairs. The lawyer intends to argue that these affairs make her an unfit mother. You contact the wife to obtain her consent to present this information in court and she refuses.

Questions for consideration

1. What ethical values are in conflict in this situation?

2. What implications does your choice of action have for the profession as a whole?

3. Would it make a difference if you had never discussed confidentiality with your clients before or during therapy? Why or why not?

4. How might your feelings about marriage and interpersonal commitment affect your ethical reasoning?

Source: Adapted from the *Companion Manual to the Canadian Code of Ethics for Psychologists*, 3rd ed. (Sinclair & Pettifor, 2001).

The confidential relationship between psychologist and client has long been regarded as one of the cornerstones of the professional relationship. The trust embodied in promising and maintaining confidentiality is so critical that most psychological services may well be worthless without it. Most clients expect that almost everything they say to a psychologist will be held in strict confidence (Miller & Thelen, 1986; VandeCreek, Miars, & Herzog, 1987). Certainly, without assurance of confidentiality, many potential clients might never seek psychological services. People generally worry about being judged negatively for private thoughts and feelings about which they themselves feel uncomfortable or ashamed. Once services are undertaken, fear of confidentiality being breached can prompt clients to be less than fully disclosing, potentially resulting in ineffectual or compromised services. For these and other reasons, confidentiality is the most common source of ethical concern for psychologists (Pettifor & Sawchuk, 2006). These concerns are often aroused by misunderstandings about the terms *privacy, privilege,* and *confidentiality.* While conceptually related, they have quite distinct meanings and important differences.

Privacy is the right of individuals to choose the time, circumstances, and extent of their personal presence, property, thoughts, feelings, or information being shared with or withheld from others. It is a basic human right guaranteed in the Charter of Rights and Freedoms (1982) and is considered essential to human dignity and freedom of self-determination. The concepts of privilege and confidentiality both grew out of the much broader concept of an individual's right to privacy.

Privilege is a legal concept that addresses the right of an individual to withhold information from court or other legal proceedings (see Chapter 3). Normally, anything germane to the issue at hand in a legal proceeding can and should be admitted as evidence. Communications in a psychologist–client relationship are *not* guaranteed privileged except in some circumstances when the psychologist is the agent of a lawyer or during negotiations to mediate a divorce settlement. This means that anything disclosed by a client to a psychologist could potentially be required to be revealed in court. In fact, the Supreme Court of Canada has held that privilege should be determined on a case-by-case basis. Perhaps equally important, privilege as a right belongs to the client, not to the professional or anyone else. If your client waives privilege regarding communications between the two of you in a professional relationship, you can be compelled to testify in court regardless of your opinion of what is best for you or your client.

Confidentiality is a professional expectation that information about a client not be disclosed to anyone except under conditions agreed to by the client. It is an implicit promise or sometimes an explicit contract on the part of a psychologist to keep private any information disclosed in the psychologist–client relationship. A promise to keep information confidential does not mean that the information is privileged. With few exceptions (see below), however, all communications between psychologists and clients are considered confidential. As with privilege, confidentiality belongs to your clients. It is up to them to decide what will or will not be revealed and to whom. Even disclosure of insignificant material—such as hobbies or food preferences, which may not seem particularly personal to you—without your client's consent is a violation of confidentiality.

Duties and Virtues Underlying Confidentiality

AUTONOMY AND RESPECT

The importance of confidentiality is derived first from the ethical principle of autonomy through acknowledging that all persons have the right to decide who has access to their private information. Respecting the right to privacy is essential to maintaining individuality and selfhood. In many ways, the loss of the power to make such decisions is the loss of one's sense of self. It is no coincidence that most forms of torture and imprisonment have loss of privacy as an essential cruelty. Legal arguments in support of confidentiality have been made on both teleological and deontological grounds. The utilitarian argument is that to force disclosure of private information made in a professional relationship would degrade those socially valuable relationships. This is particularly pertinent to psychologists because it is generally held that even the possibility of confidentiality being broken will be gravely detrimental to the professional relationship. Similarly, in most legal cases, the reasoning for granting privilege is that the damages that would result from disclosure outweigh the damage done to the judicial process by not having access to the information (see Chapter 3). More recently, however, claims of privilege have been justified in courts on broader deontological claims that the privacy of some relationships is fundamental to human dignity and should be free from state interference, particularly those recognized in the

Charter of Rights and Freedoms. This deontological stance is reassuringly consistent with our Code of Ethics, which advises psychologists to:

> I.43   Be careful not to relay information about colleagues, colleagues'
> clients, research participants, employees, supervisees, students,
> trainees, and members of organizations, gained in the process of their
> activities as psychologists, that the psychologist has reason to believe
> is considered confidential by those persons, except as required or
> justified by law.

Relationships and Consequences Relevant to Confidentiality

MANDATORY REPORTING OF A CHILD IN NEED OF PROTECTION

All jurisdictions in Canada, with the exception of the Yukon, have legislation that make it mandatory to report a child in need of protection (Walters, 1995). All of this legislation, with the exception of Saskatchewan's, make the individual who fails to report subject to criminal prosecution. The Code of Ethics supports this law in requiring that psychologists:

> I.45   Share confidential information with others only with the informed
> consent of those involved, or in a manner that the persons involved
> cannot be identified, except as required or justified by law, or in
> circumstances of actual or possible serious physical harm or death.

More fundamentally, these laws codify a societal recognition that the rights of one individual must sometimes give way to the rights of another, more vulnerable individual. This recognition is also articulated in the Values Statement of Principle I of the Code of Ethics:

> Although psychologists have a responsibility to respect the dignity of all
> persons with whom they come in contact in their role as psychologists, the
> nature of their contract with society demands that their greatest responsi-
> bility be to those persons in the most vulnerable position.

As a society, we recognize that children are our future, and, therefore, acknowledge a collective interest in their safety. Normally, parents' determination of what is in the best interest of children in their care is considered synonymous with the child's best interest (see Chapter 5). Sometimes—as psychologists well know—parents do not adequately protect their children or may actually harm them. To counter the strong social norms against interfering in private family matters, we have decided collectively to make reporting of a child in need of protection a legal requirement for *all* Canadians, including psychologists.

Note that there is no legal or ethical requirement to report "childhood sexual abuse," as is often mistakenly thought. The standard is "a child in need of protection" (or similar language), and legislation typically includes neglect of a child's basic needs as well as physical harm, such as physical or sexual abuse. The requirement to report is invoked when anyone has reasonable grounds to suspect that a child is in need of protection. That is, it is not necessary that you be *certain* that a child is being neglected or harmed. The reporting authorities (such as Children's Aid or Child Welfare) are responsible for assessing the need for intervention. When a psychologist makes a report, the authorities will obviously often put greater weight on our opinion than a member of the general public, but it remains their determination to make.

DUTY TO PROTECT THIRD PARTIES

The duty to protect third parties from our clients' violent behaviour is established in law (see Chapter 3) and our code of professional ethics (Truscott & Crook, 1993). Psychologists often mistakenly believe that we are legally obligated to *warn* the potential victims of our clients' violent behaviour (probably because of the first *Tarasoff* decision; see Truscott, 1993). This is not true. The courts in Canada have stated that we are expected to do whatever is reasonable under the circumstances to protect third parties from our clients' violence, which *may* include warning the foreseeable victim *if* this is the best available course of action (Truscott & Evans, 2001). The intention of the courts is to *permit* psychologists to break confidentiality if necessary, not to *require* us to do so. We are expected under normal circumstances to maintain our clients' confidentiality and indeed can be found liable for damages resulting from harm to our client caused by violating confidences, even if we are trying to prevent them from seriously harming someone (*Young v. Bella*, 2006). The Code of Ethics thus states that psychologists are expected to:

II.39   Do everything reasonably possible to stop or offset the consequences of actions by others when these actions are likely to cause serious physical harm or death. This may include reporting to appropriate authorities (e.g., the police), an intended victim, or a family member or other support person who can intervene, and would be done even when a confidential relationship is involved.

Also, breaking confidentiality is only legally permissible under circumstances of possible serious physical harm or death. In the Nova Scotia case of *R. v. R. (K.A.)* (1993) a physician informed the courts that he had reason to believe a patient was lying in a criminal case. The physician was suspended for three months by the College of Physicians and Surgeons for violating confidentiality. A comparable fate would befall a psychologist who acted similarly.

Note also that the permissibility of breaking confidentiality in order to protect a third party does not apply to suicide. There is a legal expectation that parents of minors be notified when their children are suicidal (*Eisel v. Board of Education,* 1991), and there certainly are also circumstances where other individuals should be involved in order to properly implement a treatment plan. Psychologists are in no way obligated to break confidentiality when a client is suicidal, however, and doing so without the client's consent is a violation of confidentiality.

THIRD-PARTY ACCESS TO INFORMATION

Psychologists are expected to make all reasonable efforts to ensure that no information collected or recorded about a client is revealed to anyone without the client's consent. There are, however, certain statutes that may compel the release of information with or without the client's consent, such as in worker's compensation cases. Similarly, when clients submit a claim for benefits to an insurance company, they may also be agreeing to allow the insurance company to obtain information from their psychologist, such as diagnosis or type of service offered. The ethical concerns here are protecting clients' confidentiality and the potential for harm once information is no longer under the clients' or our control.

In addition to federal and provincial statutes that set out when disclosure of a client's records to a third party may take place, there have been a number of Canadian cases where release of information has resulted in claims of negligence or libel and slander. In instances where a psychologist provides evidence in a court proceeding, the disclosure is protected from liability (*Boychyn v. Abbey,* 2001). However, a psychologist who makes the same comments outside of court such as, for example, to the press, could be providing legitimate grounds for being sued (*R.G. v. Christison,* 1996).

When undertaking to provide services that are being paid for by a third party, psychologists are expected to inform the client of the reasonably anticipated use that will be made of information collected and the limits on confidentiality before obtaining consent. In response to third-party requests, we are expected to make every reasonable effort to inform our clients of the request and to obtain their valid consent to release the information (see Chapter 5). In circumstances where the party requesting the information asserts a legal right to access without client consent, we are expected to make every reasonable effort to resolve the request in a manner that protects the client's confidentiality, and would do well to obtain legal advice.

Note also that our responsibility to protect our clients' confidentiality continues even in the event of their death. Family members and other interested parties (such as the police) may request records after a client suicide, for example, and we are expected to proceed cautiously. In some instances, the right to privacy will be transferred to the executor of the client's estate.

CLIENT ACCESS TO RECORDS

There has been some professional controversy on the subject of clients having access to a psychologist's records about them. The Supreme Court of Canada decision of *McInerney v. MacDonald* (1992), however, has clearly established that society expects psychologists to allow clients access to any and all information in their files that the psychologist has drawn upon to inform the provision of services. Yet, the court notes that there is not an absolute right of access. A client may be refused access to their records if it can be established that doing so would result in harm either to the client or to a third party. Similar restrictions can be found in some legislation, including the Youth Criminal Justice Act. Psychologists should also be aware of any specific provincial or territorial legislation dealing with client access to institutional records.

While only a few Canadian jurisdictions have updated their standards of professional conduct for psychologists to reflect the *McInerney* decision, none expressly prohibit such action on the part of a psychologist. Given that our ethical obligation to protect confidentiality stems from respect for the client's autonomy, it would be a rare circumstance where we could justify refusing to release our records to a client. Harm to the client or a third party would be obvious—and very uncommon—examples. A good rule of thumb is to assume that any client may someday ask to see his or her records and that all who persist will ultimately be able to do so (Hamberger, 2000). It can also be helpful to remember that the purpose of maintaining records is to ensure continuity of care—either supplementing our memory or assisting someone else who assumes responsibility for the provision of services—so that the client will benefit, and keep records accordingly.

One area that remains problematic, however, is client access to original test protocols. The profession—to say nothing of the publishers of psychological tests—has an interest in keeping the content of most tests from the general public in order to maintain their utility. If people were able to obtain a copy of an intelligence test and study the correct answers, for example, it would invalidate their score. Yet, an individual requesting access to his or her records could not make any sense out of a test answer sheet without the test questions. Often a thorough explanation of the issue to the client requesting his or her file will suffice to settle the matter. In other situations such as legal cases, however, great effort may have to be expended in trying to maintain test integrity. Arranging to have the test materials given to another psychologist hired by the other parties to the legal issue is a common approach. Another strategy can be to refer the person making the request directly to the test publishers.

COURT ORDERS AND LEGAL PROCEEDINGS

In instances where a party to a lawsuit seeks disclosure of your records, protecting your client's confidentiality can be an onerous task. First, an attempt should be made to determine whether your client opposes disclosure of the records. If not and there are no other impediments to disclosure—such as requirements of the institution in which you are employed—then compliance is straightfor-. ward. If your client will not consent, the party seeking the records should be instructed to make an application to court. At a hearing the seeker of the records will be required to establish that the records are likely relevant to an issue in the proceedings. Assuming that the records are those of a party to a lawsuit, your involvement at the hearing may be minimal, usually being asked to swear an affidavit by your client as to the confidential nature of the records. Typically, you will not attend nor be expected to have counsel of your own, although that is an option you can choose. If an order is made, it may specify that the records be provided either to a party or to the court. In the latter instance, a judge will review them to determine what should be disclosed.

If you are called to give evidence in a civil trial (see Chapter 3), it will usually be by means of a subpoena, which requires attendance with records. Again, the question of confidentiality arises if your client does not consent, and in such circumstances engaging the services of a lawyer is recommended.

In criminal proceedings (see Chapter 3), there are no mechanisms for pre-trial disclosure of documents from third parties, so you would usually be called to trial by way of subpoena. Where confidences are revealed in a forensic setting, however, such as assessing competency to stand trial or pre-sentence examinations, before proceeding clients should be informed that confidentiality is not guaranteed because the evaluation is for the benefit of third parties, and that they should consult their lawyer if they have questions.

Clients who initiate a civil lawsuit claiming malpractice (see Chapter 3) or a professional disciplinary complaint against you (see Chapter 2) should be informed that by doing so they waive their right to confidentiality. While psychologists might justifiably have concerns as a profession that the possibility of revealing embarrassing confidential information may deter clients from exercising their right to legal remediation, the law recognizes that we also have the right to defend ourselves. Procedurally, such concerns are dealt with by conducting hearings in private by excluding the public from courtrooms and sealing records involving sensitive testimony.

GROUP AND FAMILY THERAPY

Despite the difficulties of protecting clients' confidentiality, our ethical responsibility to do so does not change in group and family therapy. We are still expected to not disclose to those who have no right to the identity of or information revealed by clients. The fact that the other group or family members are now privy to this information, however, does complicate matters considerably. It simply becomes impossible for you to guarantee that what is disclosed will not be revealed by others. The need to protect confidentiality on the part of everyone in attendance should be stressed, while acknowledging that you have no real power to enforce this request short of threatening to terminate someone from the group.

Legally, the question of whether information revealed in group or family therapy can even be regarded as confidential remains open. When an individual has revealed personal information in the presence of a third party, the courts have not tended to regard such information as confidential. This does not excuse us from our professional obligations, however. Probably the best that can be done, therefore, is to discuss the issue openly and ensure that everyone understands the limitations so that they can make an informed decision about what to reveal or not to reveal in group or family therapy. The Code advises psychologists to:

I.44   Clarify what measures will be taken to protect confidentiality, and what responsibilities family, group, and community members have for the protection of each other's confidentiality, when engaged in services to or research with individuals, families, groups, or communities.

MINOR AND DEPENDENT CLIENTS

Psychologists providing services to minors are required to protect confidentiality in most of the same ways as with adults. You should not gossip about a minor client nor share client information with people other than the minor's parents or legal guardians without proper consent (see Chapter 5). The rationale for this position is the same as for adults—respect for the client's autonomy and welfare. Children as young as six years of age are sensitive to issues of privacy and gradually become more sensitive to control over their personal information as they mature (Wolfe, 1978).

The issue is more complicated than with adults, however, because minors are not fully autonomous individuals in the eyes of society or their parents. Society has an interest in fostering the development of responsible citizens and in maintaining public safety. Likewise, parents have an interest in raising their children according to their own standards, which may be at odds with those of society. Even if the interests of the state and the parents are congruent, however, parents may not wish to allow others to access certain information about the child because to do so would compromise the family's privacy.

In addition to this general interest in socializing their children, parents also have a duty to protect their children from harm. This duty sometimes cannot be fulfilled without access to information that their children would prefer to keep from them. Given the nature of psychological services, psychologists often are privy to just such information. If the minor's parents have given consent for their child to receive psychological services, what will and will not be disclosed should be clarified with them and the child, and an ongoing dialogue should be maintained. Legally, the parent or guardian who consents to services on the minor's behalf has the right to know the content of the child's service. Thus, a minor should not be promised that information will be kept from a parent who has legal custody.

If a child requests certain confidences, the degree to which confidentiality can be honoured is directly related to whether or not the child is determined to be a *mature minor* (see Chapter 5). If the minor's capacity is sufficient to warrant being treated as a mature minor, the parent or guardian no longer has the right of access to the child's confidential information. If not, you must still deal with the matter of limits to confidentiality. That is, minor children should be informed in language that they can understand that their parents or guardians have the right of access to all information that is revealed during the provision of services. Regardless of whether the minor client agrees to have information disclosed to a parent, the child should be informed—beforehand whenever possible—about what information will be shared.

TECHNOLOGICAL THREATS

With the ever-expanding use of computers, the Internet, "smart phones," and other technologies to generate, store, retrieve, and transmit information, new threats to privacy are continually arising. Most psychologists, for example, keep their client records on computer. If this computer is connected to the Internet, files can be accessed by and distributed to others through a variety of means such as "worms" and "viruses" (programs that access a computer without the user's knowledge), often via email attachments. In one instance, a confidential disciplinary investigation report written by a psychologist about another psychologist was emailed to hundreds of people by a computer virus specifically programmed to look for the words *private* or *confidential* in documents stored on the user's computer. To protect against just such an occurrence, many psychologists keep a computer specifically for their client files that is not connected to the Internet. Indeed, encryption of files and other such safety measures are now expected of all professions.

Problems associated with technology can also arise in keeping communications between client and psychologist confidential. Clients or psychologists may have shared Internet access accounts that inadvertently allow other users to read their email. Email can also be forwarded to unintended recipients through accidentally clicking the "reply all" button of one's email application. These and other potential risks to confidentiality call for vigilance on the part of psychologists.

To protect our clients from technological threats to their confidentiality, psychologists would do well to be aware of two important issues with regard to technology. First, do not take anything for granted with new technologies. A good rule of thumb is: *If you do not know how secure the technology is, do not use it.* Before using new technologies, therefore, consult an appropriate expert. Second, the same ethical, professional, and legal expectations apply to technologies as to non-technological situations. In fact, psychologists may be held to a higher standard with new technologies than with old. It is the "psychological privacy" that is important, not the actual privacy. That is, although in reality it is quite simple to open a paper envelope marked "confidential," there is a shared understanding of the risk and protections of doing so that gives us a sense of security and thereby constitutes acceptable professional practice. With new technologies, however, there may be no shared understanding. In fact, many people probably have an exaggerated fear of privacy violations through Internet use and email. Thus, even if email, in reality, provides greater privacy protection than mailing a letter, if confidentiality is breached through using a new technology, clients are very likely to feel that they have been betrayed as a consequence lack of due diligence. Therefore, clients' understanding, familiarity, and comfort with any proposed technology used in the delivery of psychological services should be discussed with them, and that technology should be used (or not) in accordance with the client's wishes.

Summary

Confidentiality is central to the professional psychological relationship. It is founded on the ethical principles of respect for the dignity of the individual in that it acknowledges that each person has the right to decide who has access to their private information. It also has implications for responsible caring because breaches of confidentiality can "undo" the benefits of psychological services by betraying a client's trust. Psychologists are expected to be aware of important limits to confidentiality: mandatory reporting of a child in need of protection; duty to protect third parties; client and third-party access to records, group, and family therapy; court orders; and malpractice and discipline. In situations with minor children or dependent adults, psychologists should discuss with the parent (or guardian) and the client what information will be kept within the professional relationship and what will be disclosed. Psychologists are responsible for addressing the threats to confidentiality that are being posed by new technologies for the storage and transmission of information.

Discussion Questions

1. Are you in agreement with the Wenden court's conclusion that our duty to protect others overrides our duty to maintain confidentiality? Why or why not?

2. Does the fact that most child protection service agencies are overworked and far from perfect affect your decision to report suspected child abuse? Explain.

3. Do you think that children should have the right to keep material confidential from their parents? Why or·why not?

4. Even though there is no legal requirement to do so, do you think that confidentiality should be broken in the case of suicide? Why or why not? What ethical system does your position represent?

Your Reflective Journal

Most of us love gossip, if only as a "guilty pleasure." Think about when you have participated in gossiping and why. Some theorists have proposed that gossiping serves to facilitate social cohesion. Others have observed that it often takes the form of passive-aggressive hostility, even bullying. Do either of these motives resonate for you? Think about times when you have disclosed information to others in an indiscreet manner that was first shared with you in confidence. How did you feel during or afterward? Or perhaps you have been the subject of gossip. Did it result in any harm coming to you or others? Or were there benefits? How is your experience relevant to your professional ethics regarding confidentiality?

Case Study

Cooking the Books

You are employed as a psychologist at a community mental health clinic known for serving disadvantaged individuals of Aboriginal heritage. You decide to undertake a research study using data from Aboriginal assessments done at the clinic because there is so little research with this population and you see an opportunity to make a contribution. When you gather basic data on the number of assessments provided, however, you find it impossible to reconcile your data with that published by the clinic director in her annual reports to the board of directors. After having your efforts to discuss the matter with the director repeatedly rebuffed, she finally tells you that her numbers are intentionally "overstated" because the majority of the clinic's funding is for Aboriginal assessments, while the majority of requests for service are from non-Aboriginal clients. If the clinic's funding was based on actual numbers, it would have to close and no one would receive services.

Case Study

Troubled Student

You are a psychologist and a professor on faculty in a professional psychology graduate program. A student that you are supervising tells you in confidence that a dear friend has recently died. She says she is depressed and finding it very difficult to concentrate on her studies. She has been attending psychotherapy, which she says is helping. She tells you that she wants to continue in the program and "just get through the year" until she can fully recover over the summer while she continues her therapy. She asks that you not tell anyone because she fears being judged unfit to practice psychology. In a staff meeting the student's poor performance is discussed. The consensus of the staff is that she is not suitable for the profession due to her apathy and should be asked to leave the program. As her supervisor, you are given the task of so informing her.

Case Study

Whose Records?

You are a psychologist who has been contracted to provide psychological services to persons referred by an employee assistance program (EAP). In accordance with your jurisdiction's standards of professional conduct, you keep detailed records, including the presenting problem, the nature of each session, progress toward the goals of each service, and copies of testing and consultative reports. After almost a year of providing services, a case manager from the EAP contacts you to obtain copies of all of your records pertaining to clients funded by them. The case manager reminds you of the contract agreement you and the client signed allowing the EAP "access to information necessary to administer the account" and tells you that they have a legal opinion stating that this means they have the right to access your entire professional file. You explain that much of what is in your files is of a very sensitive personal nature and irrelevant to their business. The case manager is unrelenting.

Recommended Reading

Bemister, T.B., & Dobson, K.S. (2011). An updated account of the ethical and legal considerations of record keeping. *Canadian Psychology, 52,* 296–309.

Cram, S.J., & Dobson, K.S. (1993). Confidentiality: Ethical and legal aspects for Canadian psychologists. *Canadian Psychology, 34,* 347–63.

Fisher, M.A. (2008). Protecting confidentiality rights: The need for an ethical practice model. *American Psychologist, 63,* 1–13.

Werth, J., Welfel, E.R., & Benjamin, A. (2009). *The duty to protect: Ethical, legal, and professional considerations in risk assessment and intervention.* Washington, DC: American Psychological Association.

7

Helping Without Harming

Case Study

To Treat or Not to Treat?

You are a psychologist providing psychological assessments for an urban hospital. A young woman is self-referred complaining of anxiety. Through the process of the assessment you learn that she is concerned about being "fat," often induces vomiting after meals, uses laxatives frequently, restricts her caloric intake, and exercises daily. She says that she feels you understand her and would like you to provide treatment. You tell her that you do not consider yourself competent to provide treatment for her eating disorder. You do have training and experience in the assessment of eating disorders, and a well-informed opinion on how best to treat them. Your therapeutic preparation, however, consists only of having read several of the major works on the topic and attending a two-day workshop on treatment. She says that she has never told anyone about her problem and that if you do not treat her she will not seek therapy from anyone else.

Questions for consideration

1. *What ethical considerations are owed to this client? Explain.*

2. *Do you think you would be more likely to help or harm the client in this situation if you were to provide treatment? Why?*

3. *How do you think your decision would be influenced if you had a personal history of having recovered from an eating disorder?*

4. *If this client were to complain to your regulatory college because you refused to treat her, how would you defend your inaction?*

Helping without harming is the cornerstone of what the public expects from professionals. People seek services from a psychologist because they expect us to be better able to help them than a non-professional can. Harmful actions on the part of psychologists are unethical, unprofessional, and, under certain circumstances, grounds for malpractice (see Chapter 3). A psychologist who is not able to provide services that will help his or her clients, in other words, should not practice. This is why the ethical principle of Responsible Caring in our Code of Ethics includes competence. Being competent is knowing what to do to be helpful and how to do it without harming the recipients of psychological services.

The matter of whether or not academic degrees, professional registration, and credentials are indicators of competence is a controversial one. Such designations typically only recognize the acquisition of knowledge, and often don't even do that very well. Academic degrees are awarded upon the successful completion of various course requirements that may have a practical component, yet they rarely assess whether the individual is able to provide psychological services competently. Whereas competence is of course assumed to result from understanding course content believed to be relevant to competent practice, very few training programs actually require trainees to demonstrate their ability to be helpful. Professional registration recognizes the completion a minimum level of academic training and the passing of various additional exams, with the additional requirements being almost exclusively knowledge-based. Registration typically does little to guarantee that the holder is competent to do all that their registration permits them to do and relies on complaints to monitor whether psychologists are practicing within their competence (See Chapter 3). Credentials bestowed by professional or special interest groups usually rely on evidence that the individual has obtained a particular type of academic degree and is registered to practice, and therefore rarely add any new information as to the holder's competence (Koocher, 1979). It thereby falls on individual psychologists to attend to their ability to be helpful and not harmful.

The professional regulation of competence is similarly fraught with difficulty (Kaslow et al., 2009; Leigh et al., 2007). This is because, at a very basic level, to be competent is to be able do something (Jensen, 1979). Ideally, the regulation of psychology would therefore be based upon what psychologists actually do to benefit our clients. Yet, it is next to impossible for regulators to oversee what psychologists do, especially taking into account that we are engaged in a multitude of activities. Just imagine what it would take to evaluate the professional activities of the more than sixteen thousand psychologists in Canada. Some jurisdictions would have to conduct at least two evaluations each day, every day of the year if they wanted to review every psychologist once every five years! In light of the near impossibility of this task, regulators rely on entrance requirements and the discipline process (see Chapter 2) as indirect measures of whether we can and are helping and not harming our clients.

Many jurisdictions also have continuing competence requirements that mandate psychologists to engage in activities designed to promote our ability to be professionally helpful and not harmful. Unfortunately, most focus almost exclusively on continuing education. Although time spent in educational activities is easily quantifiable, it has almost no relationship with competence (Daniels & Walter, 2002; Davis, O'Brien, Freemantle, Wolf, Mazmanian, & Taylor-Vaisey, 1999; Neimeyer, Taylor, & Wear, 2009). This is because professional competence comprises at least three components: *knowledge*, *skills*, and *judgement* (Lichtenberg et al., 2007; Overholser & Fine, 1990).

Knowledge involves having absorbed and understood a body of information sufficient to understand the range of professional situations that psychologists can reasonably be expected to encounter. Knowledge is a necessary but not sufficient precondition for competence. Knowledge covers a continuum from basic information that all psychologists should know—such as ethics—to specific knowledge necessary for specialized areas of practice—such as neuropsychology. In Canada, basic knowledge is initially demonstrated by completing a graduate-degree program in psychology, which must involve the completion of certain required courses, and by passing the Examination for Professional Practice in Psychology (see Chapter 2). Obviously, however, the knowledge base for a discipline is not static and continued study is considered necessary to stay current with developments in knowledge relevant to your practice. The CPA Code of Ethics encourages psychologists to:

> II.9   Keep themselves up to date with a broad range of relevant knowledge, research methods, and techniques, and their impact on persons and society, through the reading of relevant literature, peer consultation,

and continuing education activities, in order that their service or
research activities and conclusions will benefit and not harm others.

Skill is the ability to apply knowledge effectively in actual practice. As with
knowledge, skills cover a continuum from basic—such as interviewing—to technical proficiency for specific psychotherapeutic, assessment, or other professional
procedures. Much more difficult to assess and even more difficult to instill, yet
considered necessary, are personal skills such as self-awareness, tolerance for
ambiguity, interpersonal sensitivity, and openness to exploring personal biases.
It is generally accepted that supervised practica and internships are necessary to
acquire the fundamental skills for the practice of psychology.

Judgement involves knowing when to apply what knowledge and which skills
under particular circumstances in order to be helpful without harming. Good
judgement incorporates the intent of increasing the probability that activities
will benefit and not harm the individuals, families, groups, and communities with
whom you have a professional relationship (Keith-Spiegel, 1977). It also involves
self-reflection on how our values, attitudes, experiences, and social context
influence our choices, recommendations, and actions. Judgement is much harder
to assess than knowledge and skills because it is more of a global tendency than
a specific quality. It is usually indirectly addressed by its absence during supervised experience—if a psychologist under supervision for a sufficiently long
time does not make any serious errors in judgement, they are assumed to have
good judgement.

Duties and Virtues Underlying Helping Without Harming

BENEFICENCE AND BENEVOLENCE

Beneficence refers to an action done to help others. In the Canadian Code of
Ethics for Psychologists beneficence is subsumed within the principle of Responsible Caring. The duty of beneficence establishes a professional obligation to help
our clients further their interests via psychological services. Rules of beneficence
state positive requirements of action need not always be followed impartially
and rarely, if ever, provide grounds for sanctions when psychologists fail to abide
by them (see Chapter 2). The extent to which we are obligated to help others
is dependent upon what we are capable of providing. At the very least we are
expected to provide services commensurate with that of an average fellow
psychologist in good standing. If we have specialized training that sets us apart
from the average practitioner, however, our duty to be helpful is correspondingly
higher. The Code therefore expects psychologists to:

II.6 Offer or carry out (without supervision) only those activities for which they have established their competence to carry them out to the benefit of others.

II.8 Take immediate steps to obtain consultation or to refer a client to a colleague or other appropriate professional, whichever is more likely to result in providing the client with competent service, if it becomes apparent that a client's problems are beyond their competence.

Benevolence is a character trait of concern for bettering the welfare of others that is manifested in a habit or tendency to be helpful. Benevolence is associated with feeling pleasure when someone else succeeds. It is not the same as altruism, which dictates that you sacrifice yourself for the benefit for others such that their need is a claim on your actions. Benevolence can be understood as optimism applied to other people. Like all virtues, it does not consist of any particular set of actions. Rather, benevolence is a general goodwill toward others based on the premise that successful relationships are to be expected, and we should act as if they will be successful.

NONMALEFICENCE AND NONMALEVOLENCE

The duty of nonmaleficence asserts an obligation that we not inflict harm on others. Obligations arising out of nonmaleficence are typically less demanding than those of beneficence. Rules of nonmaleficence are negative prohibitions that provide ethical justification for professional and legal restrictions of certain forms of conduct. Generally speaking, obligations of nonmaleficence are more specific than those of beneficence, and, in most situations where nonmaleficence and beneficence are in conflict, nonmaleficence is given priority. If we had an opportunity to deceive someone (i.e., cause harm) so that they might thereby be happier (i.e., bring about benefit), for example, the duty of nonmaleficence would obligate us to refrain from doing so. Similarly, sexual involvement with clients (see Chapter 8) is considered to be so harmful that no justification is sufficient to condone it under any circumstances (for an example of a failed attempt to justify it, see Shepard, 1971).

Nonmalevolence is the absence of cruel intent or motive. Rather than being a tendency to be helpful to others, therefore, it is a character trait of caring and compassion. It is associated with feeling sorrow at another's misfortune. Obviously, sometime we may cause harm without intending to. This would be case of maleficence without malevolence. When doing good cannot be done without causing harm (as in some situations of being "brutally honest") the non-malevolent individual will do so only if his or her benevolent motives outweigh his or her nonmalevolent ones and strives to inflict the least harm possible.

DILIGENCE

Diligence is the habit of consistently attending to our knowledge, skills, and judgement as they are applied in our professional activities so that our clients might benefit and not be harmed. Diligence involves a willingness to work hard to provide the best service possible for each and every client, honestly evaluating our professional performance, and seeking additional training when appropriate. Diligent psychologists seek out professional standards and guidelines essential to their practice. Being diligent also incorporates self-awareness of any personal or situational circumstances that might diminish one's competence. The CPA Code of Ethics encourages psychologists to:

II.10   Evaluate how their own experiences, attitudes, culture, beliefs, values, social context, individual differences, specific training, and stresses influence their interactions with others, and integrate this awareness into all efforts to benefit and not harm others.

II.11   Seek appropriate help and/or discontinue scientific or professional activity for an appropriate period of time, if a physical or psychological condition reduces their ability to benefit and not harm others.

II.12   Engage in self-care activities that help to avoid conditions (e.g., burnout, addictions) that could result in impaired judgement and interfere with their ability to benefit and not harm others.

Relationships and Consequences Relevant to Helping Without Harming

MAINTAINING COMPETENCE

The knowledge, skills, and judgement considered essential to being even minimally competent in the basic tasks of the profession are not static. In constantly striving to deliver helpful services to our clients, the average competence of the profession continues to rise over time. Psychologists are expected, therefore, to continually keep abreast of new developments in the field in order to maintain professional competence. New developments are typically knowledge in the form of new scientific and practice findings and skills in the form of new intervention

techniques and assessment procedures. There are even developments in professional judgement from time to time when what was once considered marginal but
acceptable behaviour is no longer acceptable at all, such as some dual relationships (see Chapter 8). Professional organizations also periodically produce revised
practice guidelines (see Chapter 2).

Equally important is that we as persons are not static. The profession is generally understood to be personally stressful (Figley, 2002). Psychotherapy is particularly so with its intense interpersonal, yet non-reciprocal, circumstance (Farber &
Heifetz, 1982; Raquepaw & Miller, 1989). We also age, experience joy and suffering,
form new relationships and end others, and generally change as people. Thus, our
judgement also changes—often for the better (Craig & Sprang, 2010), and sometimes for the worse (Thoreson, Miller, & Krauskopf, 1989). Psychologists are also
expected, therefore, stay abreast of our own personal changes and continually
evaluate how these changes impact our competence, if we want to remain helpful
and not harm our clients.

What should be obvious is that there is no single way to maintain competence
(Jensen, 1979). It is incumbent upon psychologists to continually monitor our
practice relative to the state of the profession. When developments occur that
"raise the bar," we are expected to assess the extent of the gap between our
knowledge, skills, and judgement, and then take appropriate steps to upgrade.
It is also necessary to monitor yourself as a person and professional, assess how
any changes affect your skill and judgement, and take whatever steps are necessary to maintain your competence. Among the activities to consider, in order from
least to most extensive, are:

- continuing education;
- peer consultation/supervision;
- formal consultation;
- formal supervision;
- additional training; and
- retraining.

EXPANDING SERVICES

For various reasons psychologists may wish to enhance or change their areas
of practice or the psychological services that they offer. You may wish to offer
additional services in assessment, intervention with individuals or groups,
consultation, program development, or some other area. In order to fulfill our
professional obligation of helping and not harming our clients, it is necessary
to obtain whatever additional knowledge and skills are essential for practicing

competently in the new area, as well as refining our judgement. You should become familiar with the standards of knowledge, skills, and judgement considered necessary for competent practice in the area into which you are considering expanding, compare them with your own, and develop a plan to acquire what you lack. The means for doing so are identical to those used to maintain competence, although of course you will typically have to undergo more extensive training. For example, if you are competent to provide psychotherapeutic services with adults and want to provide psychotherapeutic services to children, retraining in basic and applied knowledge regarding normal and abnormal development of children, as well as training in psychotherapeutic skills with children, would probably be necessary. This would likely necessitate coursework and supervised practice, which may involve additional training under the auspices of a postgraduate institution that offers these specialties. It is expected that you select an institution that will provide the psychological education and training generally recognized as meeting professional standards of quality and appropriateness.

INTRODUCING EMERGING SERVICES

Another consideration when seeking to enhance your ability to be helpful is whether doing so involves the introduction of services that are new not just to you but also to the profession. Psychologists are expected to provide services that are based on reasonable psychological theory and evidence and any relevant practice guidelines or documents (See Chapter 2). It is incumbent on us, therefore, to critically evaluate the relevance and soundness of new services. This can be accomplished through several routes, such as examining the scientific literature pertaining to the topic, consulting other professionals with expertise and experience in the area, and the exercise of critical judgement. Often all of these routes are required for a thorough evaluation of emerging services to be offered.

This standard is usually relatively straightforward when applied to emerging assessment services because proof of their validity can be established and some are found to be unhelpful or ineffective. In the case of treatment services, however, no bona fide treatment offered to willing recipients has ever been found to be unhelpful (Wampold, Imel, & Miller, 2009). There is evidence that the misapplication of treatment services—both established or emerging—can cause harm, however (Lilienfeld, 2007). Harm is more likely to result when the service is delivered ineptly, the client does not agree with the goal or procedures of the service, and the service is not adapted to the client's needs or characteristics (Castonguay, Boswell, Constantino, Goldfried, & Hill, 2010). Therefore, introducing an emerging service should only be considered when:

- established services have been tried and the client has not benefitted;
- the emerging service is based on a reasonable psychological rationale and does not contradict the rationale underlying established services;
- good evidence exists that the emerging service is helpful or at least none exists that it is harmful;
- there is no reasonable expectation of harm in the client's particular circumstance;
- the emerging service is compatible with the client's needs and characteristics; and
- you have adequate preparation such that you are able to deliver the emerging service competently and have access to appropriate supervision.

AVOIDING IMPAIRMENT

Beyond becoming out of date relative to the state of the profession, psychologists are expected to be vigilant with respect to becoming impaired in our ability to provide services for which we have already established our competence. Because competence is based on performance, not ability, circumstances may arise whereby your application of already acquired knowledge, skills, and judgement becomes impaired (Laliotis & Grayson, 1985). Reasons for this can be emotional— such as burnout or distress—or cognitive—such as substance abuse or dementia (Ackerley, Burnell, Holder, & Kurdek, 1988; Bram, 1995; Guy, Poelstra, & Stark, 1989; Guy & Souder, 1986). Whatever the reason, you are expected to do what you can to avoid becoming impaired, be vigilant with respect to impairment, and take appropriate steps to limit harm to others if you should become impaired (Mahoney, 1997).

The following suggestions may be helpful for avoiding becoming impaired:

- Limit the scope and amount of your professional practice to what you can competently handle.
- Develop referral sources to whom you can send clients with problems you are not competent to handle.
- Develop and nurture a strong interpersonal support system.
- Develop co-operative relationships with fellow professionals.
- Take time to nurture your personal well-being.
- Stay involved in professional development activities.

If you should find yourself impaired for whatever reason, the following steps are recommended:

- Remove yourself from professional activities that could lead to harming others, especially your clients.
- Arrange (or have someone else arrange) for your professional obligations to be met by terminating services or transferring responsibility to another psychologist.
- Seek appropriate professional help, including psychotherapy if indicated.
- Return to professional activity gradually as appropriate to the rate of your recovery.
- Review and revise your self-care practices.

AVOIDING ACCUSATION OF HARM

A review of Canadian case law suggests that malpractice claims against psychologists continue to be a rarity, although they are more common than in the past. Despite this happy news, however, no one is immune from being named in a lawsuit or discipline complaint. It is pretty safe to assume that you will have at least one complaint made against you during the course of your career. And a professional liability claim, no matter how ill-founded, is a source of considerable stress. The costs in time and personal turmoil cannot be overstated. Once a claim is brought, you will sustain a loss regardless of the ultimate outcome. Your approach, therefore, should be first to minimize the potential for accusations (which may or may not be warranted). Beyond reasons of self-interest, psychologists do not practice in isolation of society and have an obligation to act in accordance with the standards of our society as reflected in the law (see Chapter 3). And, if you conduct your practice in such a way as to avoid accusations of harm by striving to maintain the highest standards of the profession, you are thereby providing the highest standard of care to *all* of your clients.

Most professionals are surprised to learn that making a mistake has essentially no bearing on whether or not you will be accused of harming a client (Fielding, 1999). People who bring a complaint against a health professional typically do so because they feel uncared for either by the professional (Beckman, Markakis, Suchman, & Frankel, 1994) or the system. Physicians who have been sued twice or more, when compared with those who have never been sued, for example, spend less time with their patients, do not solicit their patients' opinions, are more interpersonally dominant, and express less concern (Ambady et al., 2002; Beckman et al., 1994; Hickson et al., 1994; Levinson et al., 1997). Complaints against psychologists are most likely to occur for boundary violations (see Chapter 8) and in child custody cases (Evans, 2011) where strong emotions are involved and clients feel they have been treated unfairly. The common thread is that people who seek legal remedy against a professional usually do so because they feel hurt and angry.

Keeping lines of communication open not only with the client, but also with the client's family as appropriate, may do as much to avoid claims as any other precaution. A significant number of claims are made not by the actual recipient of your services—although his or her name may appear on the complaint—but by the person who is responsible for their day-to-day support (Beckman et al., 1994).

Professionals are more likely to have a claim brought against them by clients for whom they have just begun providing services. It is imperative, then, that during the initial visit as much time as is necessary be spent obtaining information about the client, including their relevant history. Psychologists are expected to consult with previous caregivers or, at the very least, review the client's records within a reasonable period of time after—and ideally before—commencing services. A client's satisfaction, or lack thereof, with previous services is a strong indicator of the expectations they bring to their encounter with you. Time taken to discuss these expectations is well-spent.

The following are suggestions for consideration to help avoid accusations of harm:

- Present yourself honestly to your clients.
- Take time to discuss the service to be undertaken and your client's circumstances—and don't rush to conclusions.
- Be especially cautious and careful in third-party situations.
- Keep relationships with clients on a strictly professional level.

RESPONDING TO ACCUSATION OF HARM

If you have knowledge of a potential complaint against you, notify your malpractice insurer and co-operate with the investigation. Failing to do so can in itself be grounds for discipline. The lawyer appointed to represent you will likely request a copy of your records. You should provide as much material as possible and allow your lawyer to determine what is, and what is not, relevant to your case. The material you provide should not be altered or edited in any way.

Prior to any lawsuit or disciplinary investigation, your case records should be as thorough as possible. Given that an action may be delayed considerably, by the time a claim is brought it is unlikely that you will be able to recall many details of the service provided. In British Columbia, for example, the ultimate limitation period is thirty years, although most actions must be brought within six years. The value of case records is dependent upon their trustworthiness. Notes taken contemporaneously or shortly thereafter will be given more weight than notes entered a week later, for example. Significant statements by the client should be recorded verbatim, if possible, and indicated as such by quotation marks. Once a claim is made against you, it is too late to make any changes to your records as this will be taken as an admission of guilt. So make an effort to ensure your records are always up to date.

If you should find yourself the defendant in a malpractice suit or discipline complaint, the following steps may also be helpful:

- Stop being a service provider to the client suing you and respond cautiously without hostility.
- Do not initiate any further contact with your client and contact a lawyer immediately.
- If you do consult with anyone about the complaint—especially anyone connected with your practice—do so judiciously and discreetly, if at all.
- Assemble all relevant records and continue to document all client contact, and show them only to your lawyer.
- Be patient.

If the unthinkable occurs and judgement is rendered against you, it may help to ease your pain by keeping the finding in perspective. The court is not commenting on your general abilities as a practitioner, nor on your competence in the future. A judgement for malpractice or unprofessional conduct means nothing more than, based on the evidence before them, the trier of fact found that, for the particular act or acts alleged, your actions did not meet the relevant standard. After a period of "licking your wounds" you can use the experience as a learning opportunity to become a better psychologist.

Summary

Psychologists are expected to be fully trained and keep up to date personally and within the scope of their practice so as to be able to be helpful and not harmful. Otherwise they should not be providing professional services. Psychologists should know their limits and refer cases they are not competent to handle. Competence comprises three major components: *knowledge, skills,* and *judgement.* The science and profession of psychology is always changing, and it is important to be aware of new developments. Many avenues are open to psychologists for professional development to keep up with these changes. It is also our professional and ethical responsibility to evaluate the merits of new procedures and services for the best interests of our clients. Psychologists should take steps to avoid becoming impaired and to limit harm to others should they become so.

While complaints against psychologists are uncommon, the risk can be reduced by taking sufficient time for your clients to feel understood, presenting yourself honestly, being especially cautious and careful in third-party situations, documenting carefully, consulting with colleagues on a regular basis, and reducing or suspending your practice when in personal distress.

Discussion Questions

1. Some say that the standards for practicing within the limits of one's competence are unreasonable for rural practitioners who must try to provide a wide range of services to a wide range of people. What do you think of this position?

2. Quite a few people enter the profession desiring to help others in response to their own histories of dealing with personal problems. Do you think such a history is an advantage or disadvantage with respect to helping without harming? Why?

3. To what extent do you think that burnout is inevitable in the profession of psychology? Explain.

4. What continuing competence activities do you consider necessary for the well-functioning of all professional psychologists? Explain your position.

Your Reflective Journal

What is your experience with becoming and maintaining professional competence? Are you currently in the process of becoming a professional psychologist? Or are you already registered to practice? How is your professional developmental level related to your needs around competence? What sort of plans do you have for staying healthy and vital? Are they informed by past experience you may have had? If so, in what way? If not, why not? This may be a good time for you to sketch out a personal continuing competence plan.

Case Study

Recovering Alcoholic

You are a psychologist in private practice specializing in the assessment and treatment of clients with substance abuse problems. You have been very successful both as a practitioner and in your business. You are also a recovering alcoholic and have not had a drink for over ten years. It has not been easy for you to abstain, and you have used your ongoing struggle for both professional motivation and therapeutic self-disclosure, which is standard practice in the field. A few weeks ago you were diagnosed with cancer. More diagnostic tests are scheduled, and it is possible that the type of cancer you have will hasten your death considerably. You are worried, though not overly upset. You decide that, given your current circumstances, you will allow yourself to drink one alcoholic beverage a day. You vow to cease providing psychological services if your intake exceeds your self-imposed limit. It is not possible for you to pay all of your medical expenses unless you continue to practice.

① Use guideline.

Case Study

Revitalized Professor

You are a professor who has been teaching for many years. You have a reputation in your field based on impressive early career success, and in your prime your courses were in great demand. You have not made any significant contributions for quite some time, however, and your classes—which are required in your department's prestigious professional psychology program—are sparsely attended and lacklustre. In a fit of enthusiasm, you decide to attempt to regain some of your past glory and are going to revise your course. You are thinking of using your lectures as an opportunity to develop some radical new ideas that you have long been considering. Students would learn the material necessary for competent practice by reading the required textbook, which is excellent. Half of their grade would be based on mastery of content from the textbook, a quarter on attendance, and a quarter on material you present in your lectures.

Case Study

An Epiphany

You are a psychologist trained in assessment of children's academic needs. Your mother, with whom you were very close, died unexpectedly a few months ago. You found the loss very distressing and took two months away from practice to deal with it. It has become clear to you that your relationship with your parents was pivotal in your academic success and career choice. You realize that no one can be certain they will have another chance to restore their relationships with important people in their lives. Upon your return you find that you have a new passion for your work and a renewed sense of purpose. You resolve to refocus your assessments to help families, teachers, and school personnel appreciate how positive expressions of connection and love are vital to academic achievement.

Recommended Reading

Kaslow, N.J., Grus, C.L., Campbell, L.F., Fouad, N.A., Hatcher, R.L., & Rodolfa, E.R. (2009). Competency assessment toolkit for professional psychology. *Training and Education in Professional Psychology, 3,* S27–45.

Shen-Miller, D.S., Grus, C.L., Van Sickle, K.S., Schwartz-Mette, R., Cage, E.A., Elman, N.S., Jacobs, S.C., Kaslow, N.J. (2011). Trainees' experiences with peers having competence problems: A national survey. *Training and Education in Professional Psychology, 5,* 112–21.

Skovholt, T.M., & Trotter-Mathison, M. (2011). *The resilient practitioner: Burnout prevention and self-care strategies for counselors, therapists, teachers, and health professionals* (2nd ed.). Boston: Allyn & Bacon.

Spengler, P.M., White, M.J., Ægisdóttir, S., Maugherman, A.S., Anderson, L.A., Cook, R.S., Nichols, C.N., Lampropoulos, G.K., Walker, B.S., Cohen, G.R., Rush, C.N. (2009). The meta-analysis of clinical judgment project: Effects of experience on judgment accuracy. *The Counseling Psychologist, 37,* 350–99.

8

Maintaining Professional Boundaries

Case Study

The Dating Game

You are providing career counselling to a client who you find quite attractive. You notice that this client makes subtle overtures of being romantically interested in you. You attribute this to a positive therapeutic relationship and deal with it by behaving in a professional, friendly manner. After four sessions, the client decided on a new career. In the final few minutes of your last scheduled session, the client obliquely indicates a desire to spend time with you socially. In order to keep the busy agenda of termination as first priority, you decide not to address the issue directly, and services end satisfactorily. One year later, you happen to meet your now former client at a community event. The two of you easily enter into a most amicable conversation. The client tells you that the career change has been very fulfilling. The fact that neither of you is in a committed relationship is established. The (ex-) client then asks about the possibility of the two of you having lunch together.

Questions for consideration

1. *Is there any additional information you would want before deciding on a course of action in this situation? If so, what? How would it affect your decision?*

2. *Would the ethical duties owed be different if the service provided was more involved—such as weekly psychotherapy for two years—or of the client's problem was more severe—such as suicide? Explain.*

3. *Do you think that the attraction between the two of you should have been discussed while you were still in the professional relationship? If so, how? If not, why not?*

4. *If you learned that the client has a history of romantic relationships that ended badly, how would it affect your decision about meeting for lunch? Why?*

① No data

② Date

Professional boundaries are the role expectations for the psychologist–client relationship that makes it safe and beneficial for the client (Smith & Fitzpatrick, 1995) and is the interpersonal territory where ethics are enacted (Austin, Bergum, Nuttgens, & Peternelj-Taylor, 2006). Indeed, boundary violations are the grounds on which psychologists are most frequently disciplined (Evans, 2011; Kirkland, Kirkland, & Reaves, 2004). The construct of boundaries originated in structural family therapy (Minuchin, Montalvo, Guerney, Rosman, & Schumer, 1967) to describe how the interpersonal rules governing family relationships affect individual functioning. If family role boundaries are too rigid—with family members being underinvolved with one another—then each individual's development is impeded through denial of their attachment needs. Conversely, if boundaries are too diffuse—with family members being overinvolved in the personal domain of one another—each individual's autonomous functioning is impeded through denial of their self-determination needs. In a healthy interpersonal relationship, role boundaries are neither too diffuse nor too rigid, but rather sufficiently flexible to meet individual needs without stifling individuality (Minuchin, 1974).

The concept of role boundaries was introduced into professional ethics by feminist scholars who decried the (mostly sexual) exploitation of (mostly female) clients by (mostly male) professionals. It was found to be so useful that we are now expected by regulation to establish interpersonal role boundaries in our professional relationships that protect our clients from harm. Their origin in the recognition of overly diffuse, harmful boundaries, however, has resulted in a tendency to prescribe professional roles that are more toward the rigid end of the continuum. If we are to be helpful to our clients—rather than only not harmful (see Chapter 7)—we must establish an appropriate position between protecting personal autonomy and facilitating interpersonal engagement. That is, we are expected to find that professional stance between under-involvement and over-involvement, as depicted in Figure 8.1.

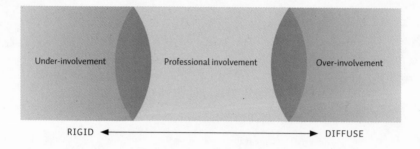

Figure 8.1 Relationship between boundaries and professional involvement

Boundaries are so important to professional ethics because there is an inherent power imbalance in our relationships with clients. Our power relative to that of our clients is derived from our (typically) higher social status as professionals, our ability to offer assistance, and the client's trust that we have the expertise to help them with sensitive personal issues. This makes it difficult for clients to negotiate boundary expectations or defend themselves against boundary violations. Most clients are also unaware of the need for professional boundaries and may at times even initiate behaviour or make requests that could result in their being harmed. In view of how psychologists are portrayed in the popular media (Orchowski, Spickard, & McNamara, 2006; Vogel, Gentile, & Kaplan, 2008), many clients might well expect us to establish overinvolved boundaries. Given the potential harms arising from this power differential, all jurisdictions in Canada that have adopted practice standards explicitly prohibit harmful dual relationships (see Chapter 2), and we are thus accountable should harms result from boundary violations.

Dual relationships involve role boundaries in which we have a professional relationship and another significant role in relation to the same person. The other role can be professional, authoritative, or emotional and examples include course instructor, work place supervisor, romantic partner, and friend. The concept of dual relationships is generally considered to be outdated because avoiding having more than one relationship with a client is almost impossible, particularly in settings such as rural communities. It has now been superseded by the idea of *harmful* dual relationships. That is, we are not expected to avoid all dual relationships, only those that are harmful to our clients. Harm arising out of a dual relationship results when the rules governing the two relationships interfere, conflict, or are incompatible with each other, leading to a situation in which the client is exploited, betrayed, or receives compromised services.

Duties and Virtues Underlying Boundaries

NONMALEFICENCE AND NONMALEVOLENCE

The primary concern in establishing and managing boundaries with each client must be not harming them. As the professional in the relationship, you have the responsibility to ensure that you gain only the fee paid for the service (or salary), and perhaps a sense of professional satisfaction for a "job well done." Thus, it must be only the client's agenda that is intentionally furthered in the professional relationship. This means that you should not meddle in the affairs of your clients that are outside of the professional agenda, nor share unsolicited personal opinions, for example.

The CPA Code of Ethics advises psychologists to:

III.31 Not exploit any relationship established as a psychologist to further personal, political, or business interests at the expense of the best interests of their clients, research participants, students, employers, or others. This includes, but is not limited to: soliciting clients of one's employing agency for private practice; taking advantage of trust or dependency to encourage or engage in sexual intimacies (e.g., with clients not included in Standard II.27, with clients' partners or relatives, with students or trainees not included in Standard II.28, or with research participants); taking advantage of trust or dependency to frighten clients into receiving services; misappropriating students' ideas, research or work; using the resources of one's employing institution for purposes not agreed to; giving or receiving kickbacks or bonuses for referrals; seeking or accepting loans or investments from clients; and, prejudicing others against a colleague for reasons of personal gain.

III.33 Avoid dual or multiple relationships (e.g., with clients, research participants, employees, supervisees, students, or trainees) and other situations that might present a conflict of interest or that might reduce their ability to be objective and unbiased in their determinations of what might be in the best interests of others.

INTEGRITY

More so than any other ethically challenging circumstance, the maintenance of professional boundaries requires of us the virtue of integrity. Integrity, in the ethical sense, is the character trait of having a congruent relationship between our ethical intentions, duties, actions (including our words), and role expectations.

Integrity is primarily a formal relation one has to oneself, or between parts or aspects of one's self, therefore, and to acting in accordance with well-ingrained ethical values (Cox, La Caze, & Levine, 2003). The absence of integrity is manifested in hypocrisy or insincerity at best, and betrayal or exploitation at worst. While it is easy to appreciate how vain, lustful, greedy, or angry motives can be damaging, harmful dual relationships can also result from virtuous motives such as compassion and justice.

To appreciate the role of integrity, remember that both experiential and analytic reasoning takes place when we are confronted with ethical choices (see Chapter 4). If we have well-ingrained preferences and lack integrity, it is far too easy to rationalize behaving in a manner that is congruent with our predilections and incongruent with our ethical, professional, and legal obligations (Truscott, 2011).

Relationships and Consequences Relevant to Boundaries

BARTERING AND BUSINESS RELATIONSHIPS

The practice of bartering or entering into a business arrangement with a client is problematic because additional interests beyond fee for professional services are now germane to the expectations of the original relationship. When bartering for services, you assume the added role of recipient of the client's service or product. Expectations can easily become conflicted when a client views you as an employer. The power to complain about working conditions or address problems in the service arrangement, for example, is thus compromised. A client expressing discontent with the bartering arrangement might well worry that you will terminate professional services. Such conflicts can easily lead to feelings of betrayal. Your professional stance can also be compromised by being invested in the service or product the client is providing. If a client is bartering carpentry services for psychotherapy, for example, and completes therapy before the work is completed, you may be motivated to prolong therapy. Conversely, you may want to foreshorten services if the work is done before the client completes therapy. Also, if you are not satisfied with the quality of the client's work, it can be very difficult to address your concerns without altering the professional relationship for the worse.

GIVING AND RECEIVING GIFTS

Giving or receiving gifts of more than token value is problematic because of the risk of changing the role expectations of the professional relationship to the client's detriment. A client who receives a gift from a psychologist, for example, can feel pressured to reciprocate in order to avoid receiving inferior care (Hahn, 1998). Conversely, accepting a significant gift from a client can leave you feeling pressured to reciprocate by offering "special" care. One must also be sensitive to cultural and individual differences when gifts are offered so that the client is not dishonoured. A frank yet sensitive discussion of the client's motives, preferences, and intentions can usually provide the necessary information to make an ethical decision (Knox, Dubois, Smith, Hess, & Hill, 2009). The decision should not be based upon your desire for the gift or to avoid discussing the client's motives. It should be made based on a collaborative consideration of whether the client's autonomy would be furthered or compromised and whether the client would be more harmed than helped by your refusal or acceptance.

RURAL PRACTICE

Psychologists in large urban centres have a much easier time avoiding multiple relationships because of the large population of potential clients from which to draw, their workplace life is much more likely to be separate from their home life, and they can more readily refer clients to other professionals. Urban psychologists also have the benefit of the relative anonymity of the large city so that dual relationships—whether harmful or not—are less likely to occur.

Psychologists in rural settings, by contrast, have more challenging circumstances to deal with as a result of different cultural norms and professional–personal contexts (Malone & Dyck, 2011; Werth, Hastings, & Riding-Malon, 2010). The pool of potential clients is much smaller such that turning away referrals can represent a very real financial hardship, and referral sources are limited and distant so that clients can be severely disadvantaged. And unless one is willing to live as a hermit, multiple relationships are a fact of life (Helbok, Marinelli, & Walls, 2006).

In a rural setting, the potential for harm by turning away a client with whom we have another significant relationship must be weighed more heavily against the potential for harm arising out of the dual relationship. Jennings (1992) recommends that rural psychologists develop a generous capacity for tolerating ambiguity in their relationships, make use of more extensive consent procedures (see Chapter 5), and consider providing briefer and less intense professional services to clients in proportion to the length and intensity of the other relationship.

FORENSIC SERVICES

Some of the most troublesome professional role relationship conflicts, for both client and psychologist, occur in the forensic setting. Clients who are involved in legal proceedings typically have much at stake, from custody of their children to personal liberty. Psychologists participating in such proceedings run a great risk of having their client feel betrayed. Even if you do not choose to practice in forensic settings, you can find yourself involved in legal disputes, most commonly as a therapist required to provide an opinion to the courts. Whereas a therapist is expected to be supportive, accepting, and empathic (i.e., engagement-promoting), when psychologists enter the legal arena in the role of an opinion-provider, they have the legal system as a client and are expected to provide an opinion that is neutral, objective, and detached (i.e., autonomy-protecting). Psychologists must take extra care, therefore, to clarify the nature of role expectations with clients when entering into a legal role. Potential role conflicts should be discussed thoroughly ahead of time and often thereafter as events proceed and circumstances change.

TEACHING AND SUPERVISION

Post-secondary faculty roles implicitly involve multiple relationships with students. Professors can serve as instructor, evaluator, advisor, research supervisor, mentor, and collaborator with the same student. Many programs also encourage informal, friendly interactions between professors and students. Although these more involved roles can foster student development, they can also become quite difficult for both parties as the risk of exploitation increases (Rupert & Holmes, 1997). Friendly relationships can present problems for both professors and students in that the role expectations in a friendship are for a higher level of personal involvement than are teaching relationships. Information disclosed in a friendly relationship and the expectation for greater reciprocity may then present complications leading to feelings of betrayal when decisions are made in the teaching relationship (Owen & Zwahr-Castro, 2007).

Given the power imbalance between professor and student, and the relatively diffuse boundaries inherent in the roles, it is no surprise that approximately 10 to 30 per cent of female graduate students in psychology report having received sexual overtures from a professor, with between 2 and 15 per cent reporting having engaged in sexual activity with a professor (Glaser & Thorpe, 1986; Pope, Levinson, & Schover, 1979; Zakrzewski, 2006), although rates appear to be decreasing (Zakrzewski, 2006).

Psychologists serving in the role of supervisor are expected to avoid relationships that may harm or exploit supervisees, impair the supervisor's judgement, or otherwise degrade the professional services provided to the supervisee. Given that supervision inherently involves multiple role boundaries—supervisor–supervisee, supervisee–client, supervisor–client—particular diligence is required to identify and avoid potentially harmful boundary crossings (Thomas, 2010; Truscott, 2006). A common problem area occurs when psychologists' supportive and facilitative roles conflict with their evaluative role (Rosenberg & Heimberg,

2009). Trainee's progress requires that struggles, concerns, and difficulties be shared with their supervisor in order that they can be addressed (Stark, 2011). If that same person also has the role of evaluator—as most supervisors do—a conflict arises between helping the trainee master their difficulties and thereby improve, while also worrying about their ultimate competence (Gottlieb, Robinson, & Younggren, 2007). Perhaps even more problematic, supervisees are faced with the dilemma of having to decide whether or not to expose their struggles and risk being evaluated negatively, or to keep them hidden and risk impeding their development.

SELF-DISCLOSURE

While psychologist self-disclosure is appropriate in some professional circum-stances (Henretty & Levitt, 2010), care needs to be taken that the focus of service does not shift from the needs of the client to the needs of the psychologist, or change the relationship toward one that is more personal than professional. Such diffusion of role expectations can degrade the quality of the professional services. The primary question to be asked is always, "Is my self-disclosure for the client's benefit?" Self-disclosure as instructive or illustrative can be a powerful interven-tion when used judiciously, and it may be necessary at times to inform the client of any personal circumstances that will interrupt services. Self-disclosure should not involve details such as personal problems, sexual fantasies, social activities, or financial circumstances that serve no professional function, however (Fisher, 2004; Smith & Fitzpatrick, 1995). Particular care must be taken on social network-ing sites such as Facebook regarding what information you post about yourself, what privacy settings are used, and who you allow to access your page (Gabbard, Kassaw, & Perez-Garcia, 2011).

PHYSICAL CONTACT

There are a variety of ways of using touch to communicate nurturing, understand-ing, and support, such as a hug, a pat on the shoulder, or a handshake. Touch can also be perceived by clients as intrusive, sexual, or both, however, necessitat-ing sound professional judgement and interpersonal sensitivity (Bonitz, 2008). Psychologists are expected to be cautious when any physical contact is initi-ated, recognizing the diversity of individual norms with respect to touching, and cognizant that such behaviour can easily be misinterpreted. In Montreal, where the dominant culture is French-Canadian, for example, kissing on both cheeks is a widely practiced greeting among friends, casual acquaintances, and, on occasion, between a psychologist and client (Smith & Fitzpatrick, 1995). Such a greeting would likely arouse shock or confusion in settings outside of Quebec, however.

Assessment and therapeutic work with children requires special consideration (McNeil-Haber, 2004). Some agencies, for example, advise their staff to avoid any touching of children. In other settings, touching is permitted in such a manner that would be open to public scrutiny. Most children expect and seek out physical contact, and it is disturbing to them if we are too distant. Much of the anxiety of agencies and professionals is the result of fear of being accused of sexualized touching of children. This is where awareness of our intentions is paramount to ethical practice. In working with children and considering the question of touching, one might ask, "Would I do this in the presence of my colleagues or this child's parents?" Even more importantly, "Am I touching this child out of my desire (sexual or otherwise) or the child's need?" Again, considered professional judgement should prevail for the protection of you and your client.

SOCIAL RELATIONSHIPS

Generally, psychologists should avoid socializing with clients. In the course of providing professional services, psychologists may, on occasion, engage in activities that resemble friendship, such as going on an outing with a child or adolescent, or attending a client's wedding or another special event. Such activities can be an important component of your services, particularly when working from a feminist perspective to minimize role expectations that entrench the power differential with your clients (Brabeck, 2000). In all cases, however, it remains your responsibility to ensure that the relationship remains professional and in the best interest of your clients. This includes social media Internet activities such as "friending" someone on Facebook (Gabbard et al., 2011).

Although there are no explicit guidelines that prohibit friendships from developing once professional services have terminated, we are expected to use our best judgement in assessing the appropriateness for the individual client (Anderson & Kitchener, 1998). The power imbalance may continue to exist and influence your client's expectations of you well past termination of the professional relationship.

SEXUAL EXPLOITATION

There are *no* circumstances in which sexual activity between a psychologist and client is ethically acceptable or legally permissible. Sexual relations between a psychologist and a client are prohibited in all jurisdictions in Canada that have adopted practice standards (see Chapter 2). Under Canadian law, sexual contact between a psychologist and client is considered assault whether the client gives consent or not (see Chapter 3). This is because the unequal balance of power and influence inherent in a professional relationship makes it impossible for a client to give valid consent to any sexual involvement (see Chapter 5). Client agreement or willingness to participate in a sexual relationship, therefore, does not relieve psychologists of our responsibility to refrain from doing so.

While it is obviously difficult to get an exact figure for the incidence of psychologist–client sexual exploitation, a reasonable estimate appears to be 10 per cent for male psychologists and 2 per cent for female psychologists, although rates appear to be on the decline (Holroyd & Brodsky, 1977; Pope, 1990a). The vast majority of clients who have been sexually involved with their psychologist report that the experience was exploitative and resulted in significant ill effects (Bouhoutsos, Holroyd, Lerman, Forer, & Greenberg, 1983; Disch & Avery, 2001; Moggi, Brodbeck, & Hirsbrunner, 2000; Nachmani & Somer, 2007).

There will be times when you will experience feelings of attraction to a client. Such feelings are normal and all too human, and should not be acted upon. It is vital that you recognize these feelings as early as possible and take action to prevent the relationship from developing into something other than a professional one. The majority of psychologists who sexually exploit their clients are males who are older than their female clients by more than a decade, experiencing personal problems such as loneliness or marital discord, and misinterpret their client's overtures for support and acceptance as romantic or erotic (Bouhoutsos et al., 1983). Research on the characteristics of clients who are sexually exploited finds no distinguishing risk factors apart from being female (Moggi et al., 2000).

Before actual sexual intimacies are initiated, there are often subtle changes in a psychologist's behaviour that alter the professional boundaries toward more personal role expectations. You should be alert to such signs that suggest you may be starting to treat a particular client differently than others. These may include higher levels of self-disclosure including sharing your personal problems with the client, offering favours to the client such as a drive home, providing services in social rather than professional settings, not charging for services rendered, and scheduling appointments outside of regular hours or when no one else is present (Gutheil & Gabbard, 1993). If you are having a problem with how you are feeling about or treating a client, seek assistance as soon as possible. Talk to a trusted colleague or seek professional help from a qualified practitioner. Consider having your practice supervised or transferring the client to another psychologist. In almost no instance will it be in the client's or your best interest to disclose that you are having sexual feelings toward them.

SEXUAL ADVANCES FROM CLIENTS

For female psychologists, a more common problem than sexually exploiting clients is clients making sexual advances toward you, although it can obviously also happen to male psychologists. Even if it is the client who attempts to sexualize the relationship, however, it is still your responsibility to keep it professional or end it. One of the features of client sexual advances that seems to make resisting awkward is social norms regarding female and male sexuality and "normal" heterosexual relationships (Kelly, 1987). Particularly problematic are cultural beliefs that men are perpetually enthusiastic about sex and expectations that women are to passively acquiesce. This can leave female psychologists without a socially acceptable script for responding. Many report that they do not want to "hurt the client's feelings" or "harm the therapeutic relationship," for example.

The best way to maintain professional boundaries in such situations is through attending to your personal psychological well-being, acknowledging your own sexual desires, avoiding ambiguity around sexual topics, and being alert to clients' sexual overtures. Proper professional boundaries should be communicated clearly, promptly, and with a degree of assertiveness proportional to the client's insistence. The following guidelines can help you to avoid having your client assume that the professional relationship could become a sexual one:

- Pay attention to cultural differences regarding psychological intimacy, personal space, and physical contact that may lead to misunderstandings about role expectations.
- Be very judicious regarding initiating "affectionate" behaviours such as hugging or kissing, and respond respectfully yet assertively to any initiated by a client.
- Do not ask details of a client's sexual history or activity unless directly related to the purpose of the service.
- Refrain from providing more than a noncommittal "thank you" to any compliments about your appearance and do not reciprocate by complimenting the client.
- Respond, carefully, to any sexualized comment even obliquely referring to you, and to those about anyone else not directly relevant to the purpose of the service.
- Do not answer questions about your own sexual preferences, fantasies, problems, activities, or performance and instead use them as an opportunity to review role expectations.

If the client will not desist, terminate the relationship respectfully and unequivocally. Document the client's behaviour dispassionately and professionally, along with your decision and actions taken. An offer of referral to another professional can be considered, provided it is made clear that the client's attempt to establish a sexual relationship is not appropriate and the next professional is informed of the reason for the transfer.

SEXUAL INVOLVEMENT WITH FORMER CLIENTS

The issue of whether a sexual relationship with a former client is ever acceptable, even after the professional relationship has ended, is a difficult and controversial one (Akamatsu, 1988). Some have argued that psychologists must never have a sexual relationship with a person who has ever been a client because the influence the psychologist had while in the professional role may never truly dissipate, and thus the power imbalance will always persist to some extent, leaving the former client susceptible to exploitation. Others have argued that this places a unreasonable limitation on our social lives, particularly in rural settings, is disrespectful of the client's autonomy, and does not acknowledge the range of professional services psychologists provide and the corresponding degree of influence.

Professional practice standards generally strike a middle ground between these two extremes by requiring that psychologists refrain from sexual relationships with clients for at least two years after termination of professional services *or for as long as the client is vulnerable to the psychologist's influence*. This means that the onus is on you to be sure that the professional contract was clearly terminated, the emotional component of the professional bond has dissipated (this applies particularly but not exclusively to psychotherapeutic services), and your motives are not exploitative. Consultation with a trusted colleague is especially indicated in such circumstances.

Summary

Maintaining professional boundaries is based upon always acting in the best interest of the client. In exchange for doing so, psychologists receive payment either from the client or in the form of a salary or third-party payment. When another personal or professional relationship with the client includes additional expectations, either on the part of the client or the psychologist, the primary professional relationship can be jeopardized. Such situations include bartering and business relationships, giving and receiving gifts, rural practice, forensic services, teaching and supervision, self-disclosure, physical contact, and social relationships. Sexual involvement with a client is the most obvious and blatant form of boundary violation and is always unethical. It is also illegal in most instances. Sexual involvement with a former client is less straightforward, but is always unethical for as long as the client is vulnerable to exploitive influence by the psychologist.

Discussion Questions

1. In your opinion, what are the ethics of having a sexual relationship with the parent of one of your child clients? If the relationship occurred a year after termination of services, would this affect your decision? Why or why not?

2. Do you think the rule governing sexual contact with clients should be extended to include students? Why or why not?

3. What is your stance with respect to accepting gifts from clients? Explain.

4. Do you think the expectations for professional role boundaries should be different in rural settings than urban ones? Why or why not?

Your Reflective Journal

Take some time to think about important relationships in your life. In particular, think about a relationship (or relationships) in which you felt exploited or betrayed. What made these relationships special or impactful (for good or ill)? Think about a relationship in which you were the one who let the other person down. What went wrong? To what extent do residual feelings from past relationships impact your current relationships? What might you do to come to some resolution of these feelings?

Case Study

New Business Partner

Your spouse's childhood dream is about to come true with the impending purchase of an I ♥ Tarts® fast-food franchise. Together you attend a function hosted by the restaurant chain. You are introduced to the regional manager who will be working very closely with your spouse on a regular basis to oversee the restaurant's finances. Your knees go weak and the room starts to spin as you realize that the manager is a former client who sought therapy to help overcome a compulsion to embezzle from employers. Therapy was a dismal failure. The last time you saw your client was just before he left town under the cover of darkness after it was discovered that he had misappropriated funds from the company for which he was working at the time. You tell your spouse that you must have eaten too many pastries and ask to go home early.

Case Study

Custody Dispute

You have been providing psychotherapy to a young boy brought in by his mother to help him deal with being upset about his parents' acrimonious divorce. The mother currently shares custody with the boy's father and has authority to consent to her son being in therapy. Therapy has gone well and the boy has made significant progress. The mother asks you to write a letter to court supporting her request for sole custody of her son. Although you have not conducted a custody assessment of the mother or the boy, you have spent quite a lot of time speaking with her about her son's treatment and observed them together before and after sessions. You have formed a positive opinion of her as a person and a mother. Your only contact with the boy's father has been one phone call, during which he was rather unpleasant and rude to you.

Case Study

Nobody Does It Better

You are a former teacher on long-term disability benefits as a result of psychological injuries sustained when a group of students attacked you after hours in the parking lot of your school. You have been receiving psychotherapy paid for by your insurance carrier and have been assessed as being unable to return to teaching. While on disability benefits they also paid for you to complete your graduate training, after which you obtained your registration as a psychologist. You are currently still receiving benefits while you establish your practice. Your case worker from the insurance company contacts you and asks if you would be willing to provide psychological services for them to teachers who are on long-term disability. She says that with your background as a teacher, your experience with psychological disability, and your professional credentials, no one is better qualified than you.

Recommended Reading

Gabbard, G.O., Kassaw, K.A., & Perez-Garcia, G. (2011). Professional boundaries in the era of the Internet. *Academic Psychiatry, 35*, 168–74.

Gutheil, T.G., & Brodsky, A. (2008). *Preventing boundary violations in clinical practice.* New York: Guilford.

Malone, J.L., & Dyck, K.G. (2011). Professional ethics in rural and northern Canadian psychology. *Canadian Psychology, 52*, 206–14.

Pope, K.S., Sonne, J.L. & Greene, B. (2006). *What therapists don't talk about and why: Understanding taboos that hurt us and our clients.* Washington, DC: American Psychological Association.

9

Providing Services
Across Cultures

Case Study

Hearing Voices

A seventeen-year-old young man of First Nations heritage has been referred to you by his school for an assessment of his treatment needs. Over the past year, he has become increasingly withdrawn and his academic performance has been declining. He arrives with his parents and, after being told the purpose and nature of the assessment, requests to have his parents present during debriefing. He reports hearing predominantly benign voices. He says that he is unsure what the voices mean, but that they do upset him. Upon presenting your opinion to the young man and his family that all indicators point toward an incipient schizophrenic process, his parents reject this "bad news." They tell you that the voices are communications from his dead grandfather who was a powerful healer. They fear that a pathological colonial understanding of his experience will sever their son's connection with his ancestors.

Questions for consideration

1. What is your initial reaction to this situation? How will this reaction need to be taken into account when responding to this situation?

2. If some members of the family understood the boy's voices to be healthy, and some members understood them to be unhealthy, how would this affect your response?

3. To what extent is your appraisal of this situation influenced by your personal cultural worldview? How do you know?

4. What knowledge do you need to respond in a helpful way to this situation?

Perhaps it is because a decline in the Canadian birth rate, coupled with an increase in immigration, has resulted in persons who had been considered members of cultural minorities quickly becoming the numerical majority. Perhaps it is because the ready availability of information from around the globe has raised our awareness of cultures and life circumstances quite different than what we take for granted. Whatever the reason, as a profession, we have become sensitized to cultural diversity. Psychology, along with most health professions, is coming to appreciate how cultural differences impact our practices. Persons who are not members of Canada's dominant culture tend to underutilize and derive less benefit from psychological services than their majority counterparts. Indeed, commonly practiced professional services may be ineffective and even antagonistic to the goals desired by persons who do not share the majority view of what constitutes desirable behaviour and lifestyle. For these reasons, psychologists who provide services across cultures are expected to be alert to ethical hazards. The ethical psychologist recognizes that culture is central to our practice, rather than ancillary, and seeks to be sensitive to the role of culture in service provision.

Culture refers to the set of shared beliefs, values, customs, and behaviours of a group that provide norms for interactions between members (Fowers & Richardson, 1996). Note that the concept of culture applies to a broad range of groups of people. People cannot be assigned to a particular cultural group in the way that we can designate one geometric shape a triangle and another a quadrangle. We cannot say that one person belongs to a cultural group based on nationality, geographical ancestry, religious affiliation, or any other essential characteristic. Instead, all groupings of people consist of uniquely different individuals that differ from other groupings not by their essences but by average statistical differences. Indeed, there are many characteristics by which people identify themselves as belonging to a cultural group, such as ethnic heritage, age, gender, sexual orientation, and physical abilities.

The concept of a *minority* refers to a culturally defined group that experiences oppression in relation to the dominant cultural group of a society. Most importantly, minority status is a function of access to power within a society. A cultural minority is typically, though not necessarily, numerically smaller than the dominant culture. Women, for example, are considered a minority due to having restricted access to power in our society even though they have a numerical majority. Understanding the importance of adopting a cultural perspective in psychological practice requires us to accept that not everyone has equal access to power in our society. In particular, many groups have been subjected to oppression and mistreatment, and the prejudicial attitudes and behaviours that allow such violations to occur are far from extinct. Canadians have a mythology that we are race-less and racism-less. We tend to think that we don't have a problem with oppression of minorities and that it is rude to even discuss such matters (for an example of such an attitude, see Bowman, 2000). This is not the case. Access to power in our society affects all of us, whether Canadian-born of Aboriginal or European heritage, immigrant or refugee, minority or majority member.

Duties and Virtues Underlying Cross-Cultural Practice

RESPECT

Psychologists are expected to cultivate respect for cultural understandings of the human condition that diverge from their own and, in particular, an openness to divergent views of a good life. Psychologists—who as a profession tend to pride ourselves on being fair and tolerant—may inadvertently perpetuate practices that disadvantage persons from minority groups. This is because we, just like every other member of a group, internalize cultural norms of behaviour. When providing psychological services to clients, you are expected to appreciate that they will not necessarily have the same worldview as you do. This requires you to be able to tolerate the discomfort you may feel when others base their decisions on different standards than your own (Fowers & Davidov, 2006). The Code of Ethics sets an expectation that psychologists:

I.2   Not engage publicly (e.g., in public statements, presentations, research reports, or with clients) in degrading comments about others, including demeaning jokes based on such characteristics as culture, nationality, ethnicity, colour, race, religion, sex, gender, or sexual orientation.

This is the ultimate expression of respect for our clients' dignity as persons. It requires gaining knowledge of other cultures and the biases, values, and assumptions about human behaviour arising out of them. Obviously, it is not possible to become knowledgeable about every culture you might ever come into professional contact with. As an ethical psychologist you are expected to learn about the cultures of the clients you serve.

NONMALEFICENCE

Psychologists are expected to refrain from harming our clients by imposing our personal cultural expectations upon them. In order to do so, we must strive to become aware of our cultural values, assumptions, and biases about the human condition—the lessons we have learned from our own culture. It can be surprisingly difficult to do. Cultural norms help us to make sense of the world and our place in it. One consequence is that we assume that others whom we identify as belonging to our same cultural group share our circumstances, opportunities, hopes, and dreams. Psychologists tend to be tolerant and accepting and thus particularly prone to assume that our professional services are equally applicable to anyone, regardless of their cultural affiliation. This mistaken assumption is known as cultural encapsulation (Wrenn, 1962) and can render us ill-prepared to deal effectively with culturally diverse clients. Psychologists who strive to treat everyone the same, therefore, risk harming clients from other cultures whose worldviews require us to adapt our services to their needs and circumstances. Thus, the Code of Ethics expects psychologists to:

II.10   Evaluate how their own experiences, attitudes, culture, beliefs, values, social context, individual differences, and stresses influence their interactions with others, and integrate this awareness into all efforts to benefit and not harm others.

III.10   Evaluate how their personal experiences, attitudes, values, social context, individual differences, and stresses influence their activities and thinking, integrating this awareness into all attempts to be objective and unbiased in their research, service and other activities.

BENEFICENCE

In order to benefit our clients, psychologists are expected to provide services that are responsive to the expectations that arise out of worldviews different from those of our culture. An important function of cultural norms is to provide information about how to behave in order to remain a part of our group and, by extension, about who is not a part of our group. Thus, if someone is categorized as not belonging to our cultural group, we do not assume that they share the same worldview as we do. We then turn to whatever knowledge we possess about the other group as a whole. That is, we can fall into the trap of not paying attention to individual characteristics of persons who are not of our culture. This manifests itself in the expectation that all persons from a culturally diverse group are different in the same way. Sometimes these expectations are that persons of other groups are inferior—the more common usage of the concept of discrimination—but not necessarily. Psychotherapists, for example, have been found to tend toward a "positive bias" in their assessment of culturally diverse clients (Jones, 1982; Smith, 2005).

Standardized psychological interventions or assessment methods may not sufficiently address the needs of persons from minority cultures. In particular, we should be willing to involve support people from our clients' self-identified cultural group and to make referrals based on the clients' needs and wishes in relation to their culture when appropriate. This may involve referral to a psychologist or other professional who shares a common cultural identity with the client, or to a professional who is knowledgeable and skilled regarding the client's culture. It may also be appropriate to consult with an expert from your client's culture who may or may not be a psychologist, such as an elder, healer, or advocate.

Responsive failures are rarely the result of malicious intentions, but rather of "cultural blindness" that prevents us from seeing the world as our client sees it. This blinding is perpetuated by the belief that our psychological practices are morally, ethically, and politically neutral (Ibrahim, 1996). When a client does not respond positively to psychological services, it is not uncommon to see the fault as residing in the client or, at best, in a poor match between the service and client. What is typically not considered is a conflict between the cultural worldview inherent in our service and that of the client. Psychologists are thus expected to:

II.21 Strive to provide and/or obtain the best possible service for those needing and seeking psychological service. This may include, but is not limited to: selecting interventions that are relevant to the needs and characteristics of the client...; consulting with, or including in service delivery, persons relevant to the culture or belief systems of those served; [and] advocating on behalf of the client.

Relationships and Consequences Relevant to Cross-Cultural Practice

There are many different ways to think about the influence of cultural biases and ignorance on your professional practice and the salience of culture for your clients because there are many ways that we are different from one another. One way to systematically consider differences that are relevant to the Canadian context is the ADRESSING model (Hays, 1996), presented in Table 9.1.

Cultural Factor	Minority Group	Oppression
Age	Older adults	Ageism
Disability	People with disabilities	Ableism
Religion	Religious minorities	Religious intolerance
Ethnicity	Ethnic minorities	Racism
Social status	People of lower status	Classism
Sexual orientation	Gay, lesbian, and other sexual minorities	Heterosexism
Indigenous heritage	First Nations persons	Colonialism
National origin	Refugees and immigrants	Racism
Gender	Women	Sexism

Source: Adapted from "Addressing the Complexities of Culture and Gender in Counseling" by P.A. Hays, 1996, *Journal of Counseling & Development*, 74, 332–38.

Table 9.1. The ADRESSING model: Nine cultural factors, associated minority group, and oppression

AGE

Psychologists, like other health care providers, tend to have negative attitudes toward the elderly, expect less positive outcomes in psychotherapy, and do not want to provide services to them (Helms & Gee, 2003). Psychologists tend to attribute depression, anxiety, and dementia as natural consequences of aging, and not as a focus of intervention, for example (Danzinger & Welfel, 2000). On the other hand, difficulties inconsistent with stereotypes about the elderly, such as substance abuse, interpersonal difficulties, and learning disabilities are under-diagnosed, misdiagnosed, and therefore undertreated, if at all. Many psychologists, reflecting the attitudes of Canadians in general, seem to think of the elderly as not being worth the investment of time and energy relative to their limited lifespan (Lagana & Shanks, 2002).

Probably in large part due to these negative attitudes on the part of health professionals, older adults seek mental health services at a rate lower than any other adult age group (Bogner, de Vries, Maulik, & Unützer, 2009; Sareen, Cox, Afifi, Yu, & Stein, 2005). This despite the fact that rates of depressive symptoms increase with age (Alexopoulos, 2005), suicide rates are higher among older than younger people (Klinger, 1999), and older people with mental health problems respond well to treatment (Wilson, Mottram, & Vassilias, 2008).

In order to avoid discriminating against the elderly and provide effective services, psychologists are encouraged to resolve their own existential fears of mortality (Kastenbaum, 1963), and seek at least some training in the mental health needs of older adults (Qualls, Segal, Norman, Neiderhe, & Gallagher-Thompson, 2002).

DISABILITY

Among the disadvantages commonly faced by people with disabilities are discrimination, alienation, and barriers to independence (Soffer, McDonald, & Blanck, 2010). Often the most serious problems are not directly related to the disability itself but to reactions evoked in others (Scott, 1981). Appraisals of people with disabilities are not consistently negative, but rather tend to be either extremely positive or extremely negative (Katz, Hass, & Bailey, 1988). This attitudinal ambivalence is likely attributable to discomfort, competing responses (to assist or avoid), and the degree of anxiety about one's own vulnerability (Jureidini, 1988). While negative reactions are obviously disrespectful, overprotective helping behaviours and overestimation of limitations also restrict opportunities for people with disabilities to experience their full potential as human beings (Cornish, Gorgens, Olkin, Palombi, & Abels, 2008).

In order to provide effective and ethical services, psychologists are advised to attend to their attributions and attitudes about people with disabilities (Artman & Daniels, 2010). Negative attributions can limit therapeutic effectiveness and diagnostic accuracy, particularly when a person with a disability seeks help for problems unrelated to their disability. Psychologists often fail to ask about aspects of a client's life that are important to her or him because the presence of a disability leads us to assume that other issues are unimportant. Errors of commission occur when we assume that an issue should be important for a client because of a disability when, in reality, it is not. Overemphasis on the disability, rather than the clients' presenting issue, is a common result (Olkin, 2008). In fact, persons with disabilities seek psychotherapy, for example, to address the same issues that prompt able-bodied persons to do so (Pelletier, Rogers, & Dellario, 1985). A common instance is the avoidance of sexuality and intimate relationship issues. Persons with disabilities are often incorrectly assumed by non-disabled persons to have lost the capacity and interest for pursuing these intimacies (Diamond, 1984). Similarly, ableism negatively distorts estimates of job placement success and leads to a paternalistic bias in assessment recommendations (Kemp & Mallinckrodt, 1996).

RELIGION

Religion involves a system of beliefs, rituals, and observances organized around an integrated understanding of the world and our place in it. In fact, religious and spiritual dimensions of an individual's worldview are among the most important factors that structure experience and behaviour. Religious beliefs influence the form and especially the content of psychological distress, yet professional psychologists tend to ignore our clients' religious beliefs at best and consider them to be pathological at worst (Sevensky, 1984). This may be due in large part to a lack of professional training regarding the role of religious beliefs (Shafranske & Malony, 1990). There is a real likelihood for misinterpretation or error if these beliefs are not considered when providing services.

Ideally, psychologists should be able to take into account the interaction of our professional services with our clients' religious beliefs and practices, especially those that play significant roles in their lives. Many people grapple with spiritual issues such as the meaning of life, suffering, good versus evil, guilt, and forgiveness. Failure to take into account a client's spiritual life and religious beliefs can seriously limit psychotherapeutic effectiveness and diagnostic accuracy (Fitchett, Burton, & Sivan, 1997).

ETHNICITY

An individual's ethnicity is often imprecisely assigned by way of visible physical characteristics commonly associated with geographical ancestry, such as skin colour or facial features. The vagueness of such a categorization is usually further compounded by the use of the term *race* to categorize individuals who share common physical characteristics (Helms & Talleyrand, 1997) and to imply genetic lineage that is more accurately characterized as a "myth of common bloodlines" (Shapiro, 2010). True ethnicity is one's subjective identification with a group on the basis of presumed (and usually claimed) commonalities that confer a sense of belonging and pride. These typically include some combination of language, history, civic nationalism, geographic region of origin, customs, religion, physical appearance, and ancestry (Markus, 2008).

A few of the predominant values from a Euro-North American cultural ethnicity that are particularly relevant to psychological practice are an emphasis on the individual, an action-oriented approach to problem solving, the Protestant work ethic, the scientific method, and rigid time schedules (Axelson, 1993). Such values are not universally held, however, and a mismatch between those you assume and those of your client can result in inferior or even harmful service delivery. Some psychotherapies, for example, pay relatively little attention to the client's personal history, while others rely on formulas of how certain historical or childhood events necessitate particular interventions. Still other therapies focus on rationality and the scientific method as the standard for mental health. And most approaches to psychotherapy focus on the individual as the source of difficulties in life, the target for intervention, and the standard by which success is judged. These foci very much reflect the Euro-North American worldview in which they were constructed, however, and can be at odds with that of people of other cultures. The same is true for most psychological assessment methods (Cheung, van de Vijver, & Leong, 2011).

SOCIAL STATUS

Currently, some 14 per cent of Canadians are living in poverty, with much higher rates for single-parent mother families, unattached female seniors, urban Aboriginals, and recent immigrants (National Council of Welfare, 2006). Although the overall rate of poverty has decreased somewhat in the last decade, the depth and span of income inequality has increased (National Council of Welfare, 2006). And while Canada's health care system does moderate health disparities attributable to social status when compared with the United States (Ross, Wolfson, Dunn, Berthelot, Kaplan, & Lynch, 2000), not having access to economic power in Canada is still bad for your health (Collins & Hays, 2007; Vozoris & Tarasuk, 2004). The lower one's social status, the higher one's mortality and morbidity for almost every disease category, including psychological problems such as depression, anxiety, eating disorders, learning disabilities, and substance abuse (Pope & Arthur, 2009; Raphael, 2004).

Most Canadians attribute low social status to governmental policies and unequal opportunities, rather than personal choices and actions, although higher social status Canadians are more likely to blame others for their low status (Reutter et al., 2006). As a consequence of the considerable academic hurdles that must be cleared in order to gain entry into the profession, psychologists tend to endorse middle-class values, resulting in the assumption that upward social mobility is desirable and that failing to strive for it is a sign of laziness or deviance (Liu et al., 2004). Indeed, many psychologists are uncomfortable working with socially disadvantaged clients, finding it difficult to empathize with people of low social status and tending to view them as disorganized, inarticulate, apathetic, overwhelmed, and inappropriate for most psychological services (Smith, 2005). Obviously, such attitudes interfere with the provision of helpful psychological services and should be addressed.

SEXUAL ORIENTATION

Stigmatization, oppression, and violence toward members of sexual minorities is well-documented and includes discrimination in housing, employment, and custody rights, as well as physical, verbal, and sexual harassment and assault (Herek & Garnets, 2007). In addition to such overt acts, individuals of minority sexual orientation also face marginalizing and stigmatizing social forces, such as anti-gay jokes, in a society that values sexual conformity (Garnets, Herek, & Levy, 2003; Rivers & D'Augelli, 2001). Not surprisingly, such experiences are associated with negative physical and mental health, regardless of whether individuals make public their sexual orientation (Garnets et al., 2003). Mental health consequences include anxiety, depression, substance abuse, suicidal ideation, and suicide attempts (Berg, Mimiaga, & Safren, 2008).

The profession of psychology is largely—though not uniformly—affirmative of sexual minorities. The larger culture, however, is far less so, and psychologists are not immune to the dominant cultural heteronormativity (Robinson, 1999). Psychologists are expected to reconcile their personal values with the affirmative culture of the profession in order to provide helpful services (Bieschke & Dendy, 2010). Psychologists who are willing to explore their sexual identity, and whose self-acknowledged gender attributes reflect their overall identity, are more confident working with sexual minority clients, open to learning about and applying knowledge of sexual minority issues, and willing to implement affirmative professional services (Dillon, Worthington, Soth-McNett, & Schwartz, 2008).

INDIGENOUS HERITAGE

Colonialism has left deep scars on the psyche of Canada's indigenous people (McMillan, 1995). One need only consider the legacy of our residential school system to appreciate the oppressive impact of being a Canadian of indigenous heritage (Robertson, 2006). The psychological consequences of systematic efforts to dismantle traditional indigenous life and the subsequent loss of cultural identity (York, 1990) has resulted in disproportionately high rates of domestic and physical violence, substance abuse, suicide, poor parenting, and criminal behaviour (Kirmayer, Brass, & Tait, 2000; Shepard, O'Neill, & Guenette, 2006). These problems have had a devastating intergenerational impact on Aboriginal communities in Canada (Yellow Horse Brave Heart & DeBruyn, 1998). Not surprisingly, most indigenous Canadians perceive mental health services to be inaccessible and culturally insensitive (Uchelen, Davidson, Quressette, Brasfield, & Demerais, 1997) and are more than twice as likely as majority clients to discontinue counselling after the first session (McCormick & France, 1995).

Psychologists providing services to persons of indigenous heritage often have very different academic and career expectations than they would for someone of Euro-Canadian heritage. While most, if not all, psychologists would deny that they consider persons of indigenous heritage to be inferior, the effect is the same as if it were intentional and, in many ways, more difficult to address. After all, who can argue that persons of indigenous heritage are overrepresented in Canadian prisons and underrepresented in our universities and professions? Surely these facts should be properly considered when providing professional services, the argument goes. Such beliefs have been internalized from the negative messages and characterizations from the dominant Canadian culture and form part of psychologists' worldview about indigenous Canadians. While generalizations about persons of indigenous heritage may be statistically accurate (or inaccurate —the argument is the same), failing to take proper account of individual differences and external influences is very likely to result in the provision of services that do not help, and could harm, your clients.

NATIONAL ORIGIN

Even though our immigration policies ensure that those admitted into Canada are healthier upon arrival than the Canadian-born population, immigrants experience a deterioration in health status, including mental health, over time (De Maio & Kemp, 2010). That is, immigrating to Canada is detrimental to one's health. The process of acculturation, during which a person relinquishes the cultural norms of the culture in which they were raised and adopts the norms of the dominant Canadian culture (Schwartz, Unger, Zamboanga, & Szapocznik, 2010), has a particularly important influence on the provision of psychological services (Merali, 1999). The values and assumptions about human behaviour embedded within our service delivery are crucial to our clients' struggle with the expecta-. tions of their national heritage that conflict with those of the dominant Canadian culture. A useful starting point when working with immigrant clients, therefore, is understanding the degree to which the client has acculturated to Canadian norms (Berry, 1997):

1. Traditional: holds traditional beliefs and values, and practices only traditional customs and methods of worship.
2. Marginal: partially, though not fully accepting of either their cultural heritage or mainstream Canadian culture.
3. Bi-cultural: accepts both Canadian and traditional cultures.
4. Assimilated: accepts only Canadian culture.
5. Pantraditional: assimilated into Canadian culture, and makes a conscious effort to embrace traditional ways and lost traditions.

Knowledge of how acculturated your client is allows you to be more accommodating of their expectations for professional services. If a client is highly assimilated into mainstream Canadian culture, for example, it could be harmful to press them to draw upon aspects of their traditional culture. Conversely, for the many immigrant clients who continue to embrace aspects of their traditional culture, incorporating healing practices of that culture can be very helpful.

GENDER

Women and men are thought of, treated, and live their lives as different kinds of people with different types of bodies and different roles, responsibilities, and opportunities (Ad Hoc Working Group on Women, Mental Health, Mental Illness and Addictions, 2006). This results in women and men having different access to life choices and chances, including economic activity, educational attainment, and health care (Statistics Canada, 2006). For example, women as a group have less financial security and are more likely to be employed part-time with subsequently less access to health benefit plans (National Council of Welfare, 2006). Women are also at greater risk for interpersonal victimization, including childhood abuse, sexual abuse, and intimate partner violence (Church, Pettifor, & Malone, 2006). Historically, women were delivered into treatment by their husbands or families not just because they were distressed, but also for being sexually unresponsive, lesbian, unwilling to marry, or generally nonconformist (Chesler, 1972). Even today, most of the psychiatric symptoms associated with being female are exaggerations of what society expects of the feminine, such as depression, frigidity, paranoia, psychoneurosis, self-harm, and anxiety (Larkin & Caplan, 1992). Ideals of mental health such as autonomy, individuality, and independence, however, continue to be associated with masculinity (Miller, 1986).

Men's mental health is also negatively influenced by gender role strain (O'Neil, 2008), which occurs when men's essential nature conflicts with society's expectation that they be aggressive, uncaring, and self-reliant (Levant, 2011). This results in violent behaviour, intolerance, exploitation of women, and neglect of their health (Addis & Mahalik, 2003). When men are given a psychiatric diagnosis, it tends to be one consistent with societal expectations of masculinity, such as substance abuse, brain disease, and psychopathy (Wade & Good, 2010).

As with sexual orientation, consideration and exploration of how gender expectations influence your identity is associated with greater respect for and responsiveness to your clients' actual nature and avoidance of gendered assumptions. This allows you to provide more unbiased services to your clients.

Summary

When there are differences of culture between psychologist and client, the risk of ineffective or even harmful professional service delivery increases. Cultural differences can be based on age, disability, religion, ethnicity, social status, sexual orientation, indigenous heritage, national origin, or gender. Ethical psychologists should make every effort to cultivate an attitude of openness to and respect for cultural diversity, be aware of their own cultural worldview so that they might avoid harming their clients, and become more culturally responsive so that they might benefit them. The ethical significance of culture is not the fact of difference in itself, but that we may fail to recognize how our clients' worldview may be different than our own. Psychologists are cultural beings just like any other, but our professional status requires that we protect our clients' needs and safety by being more sensitive to cultural diversity in all its forms.

Discussion Questions

1. In some societies the norms differ dramatically from what are considered universal human rights. For example, currently in some countries girls and women are denied education. Can psychologists provide services respectfully with clients who honour those values?

2. Should unintentional acts of racial discrimination be dealt with by disciplinary bodies differently than intentional acts? If not, why not? If so, identify the differences you think are important.

3. Do you think professional training or life experience is more important to psychologists' cross-cultural competence?

4. To what extent do you think it is acceptable to restrict your practice to only providing services to clients of the same cultural background as yourself, such as men/women, persons of a particular heritage, or middle-class professionals?

Your Reflective Journal

Take some time to think about who you are in relation to groups you belong to. Start by categorizing yourself on each of the following dimensions:

Age: young adult, middle-age, elderly, _____

Disability: able, disabled, _____

Religion: _____

Ethnicity: _____

Social status: lower, middle, upper class, _____

Sexual orientation: _____

Indigenous heritage: First Nation, colonial, _____
National origin: _____
Gender: female, male, _____

Now rank order these attributes from 1 to 9 based on how much it represents who you are. After you have done so, put a ✓ beside those that are a source of pride for you or that give you an advantage. Next, put an ✗ beside those that are a source of shame or that cause you difficulties.

After reflecting on your rankings and ratings, write in your journal your answers to the following questions and any others that may occur to you: How much of who I am is chosen by me, and what might I choose to discard or add? How much of who I am is chosen for me, and what might I choose to resist or accept? To what extent does my cultural self influence my being an ethical psychologist?

Case Study

Real-world Assessment

You have been hired to conduct educational assessments on behalf of a psychology firm. This firm has a practice of administering an intelligence scale to all children. You observe that most of the children undergoing assessment are of Aboriginal heritage. You know that children of Aboriginal heritage typically score lower on verbal intelligence than their non-Aboriginal peers. You propose to your supervisor/employer that you could collect local norms in order to better speak to each child's strengths and weaknesses relative to other children of similar circumstances. You are told that doing so would represent "racist" practice and would not accurately represent the child's potential to "succeed in the real world." She tells you that you are to administer the assessments according to the test's standard protocol and report the results accordingly, or start looking for another job.

Case Study

Protection from Whom?

A six-year-old student is referred to you by Social Services for an evaluation. They are considering apprehending him because his teachers have reported that he often comes to school tired and hungry. When you interview the boy and his mother, you find the boy to be in no obvious distress, although he is very shy. His mother is vague and you gradually learn that they are recent immigrants from a South American country and that her husband deserted them shortly after they arrived in Canada. He had served time in prison in their homeland where he was tortured, and the guards sexually assaulted her when she tried to visit him. It is clear that she is not doing an adequate job of taking care of her son, or herself, due to her extreme suspiciousness. She wants reassurances that you are not working for the authorities, and that her son will not be taken away from her and tortured.

① Report to Authorities

②

Case Study

The Cost of Friendship

A young man comes to see you in a student counselling centre presenting with loneliness. He has moved from another country to attend university in Canada and is having trouble making friends. His cultural tradition has highly prescribed rules and roles for dating and he is uncomfortable with the laxity of Canada's. He tells you that he wants to become more comfortable so that he can date and make friends. Over the course of two months of therapy, he reports that he is pleased with his progress and he is seeing someone in a satisfying relationship. Then, in a later session, he presents as very upset. He tells you that his parents are very angry that he is not behaving in ways consistent their cultural prescriptions. They are threatening to stop supporting him financially and to insist that he return home. He is confused and unsure what to do.

Recommended Reading

Church, E., Pettifor, J.L., & Malone, J. (2006). Evolving Canadian guidelines for therapy and counselling with women. *Feminism & Psychology, 16,* 259–71.

Pettifor, J. (2001). Are professional codes of ethics relevant for multicultural counselling? *Canadian Journal of Counselling, 35,* 26–35.

Pope, J.F., & Arthur, N. (2009). Socioeconomic status and class: A challenge for the practice of psychology in Canada. *Canadian Psychology, 50,* 55–65.

Wihak, C., & Merali, N. (2007). Adaptations of professional ethics among counselors living and working in a remote Native Canadian community. *Journal of Multicultural Counseling and Development, 35,* 169–81.

10

Promoting Social Justice

Case Study

The Disruptive Student

You are a psychologist who has been asked to assess an eight-year-old boy and then refer him for appropriate services. He has been very disruptive in class, destructive of other students' property, and once attempted to start a fire in a wastebasket. His classmates are being deprived of educational opportunities due to his troublesome behaviour and his disproportionate demands on the teacher's time, and they are at risk of physical harm. Based on your assessment, it is clear that the boy has individual needs that can only be addressed by services offered outside of his regular classroom. An in-school special education class capable of providing such services is full, however, with a waiting list many months long. Comparable services are available at a nearby private facility, and are very expensive. If you were to refer the boy to the private facility the school would be obligated by provincial regulation to provide funding. Doing so would result in depletion of the school's entire budget for such services.

Questions for consideration

1. What are your professional obligations with respect to the eight-year-old student?

2. What are your professional obligations with respect to the other students in his classroom?

3. On what basis would you weigh your obligations to the eight-year-old student against those of the other students?

4. How would your choice of action be affected if you knew that the special education class was scheduled to be discontinued?

The conventional expectations of psychologists are that we protect and promote the welfare of individuals with whom we have a professional relationship. As psychologists we also often find ourselves in situations where our actions in relation to the individuals we serve have social consequences, and our ability to help them is bounded by social constraints. Failure to recognize or properly handle these social implications can result in ethical missteps. The aims and hazards arising out of these concerns is the realm of social justice ethics.

When we speak of justice in an everyday manner, we are usually referring to moral issues having to do with individual behaviour affecting goods or property. It is, we say, unjust for people to steal from others or not to give them what they are owed. We also say it is unjust if someone expected to distribute something good, bad, or both among members of a group uses an arbitrary or unjustified basis for making the distribution. For most ethicists, however, justice is considered to be a vital quality of social institutions beyond that of the behaviour of individuals.

The concept of social justice is as old as civilization itself and was the subject of serious consideration at least as far back as the ancient Greek philosophers. Indeed, Plato and Aristotle considered societal good to be the ultimate ethical good. A just society is one in which human rights and liberties are safeguarded, material resources are equally distributed, and public involvement in decisions that affect us all is high. Of course, psychology functions as a profession within the context of society and, in fact, can be said to exist in any practical sense only because it is recognized by society as such (see Chapter 2). Professional psychologists, therefore, have responsibilities to the society in which we live and work, and by extension to all members of it. Social justice argues against a limited professional focus only on individuals and in favour of ensuring that all people have access to communal resources and are treated fairly regardless of their status within society. If as psychologists we are truly concerned with human welfare, such considerations ought to be a part of our professional activities.

One of the unique features of the Canadian Code of Ethics for Psychologists is that it sets out responsibility to society as a core ethical principle (Sinclair, 1998), and the Values Statement of Principle IV declares:

> Psychologists will do whatever they can to ensure that psychological knowledge, when used in the development of social structures and policies, will be used for beneficial purposes, and that the discipline's own structures and policies will support those beneficial purposes.

Principle IV, Responsibility to Society, although presented as subordinate to the other three ethical principles of the Code, is the only principle to make explicit reference to human welfare beyond the individual. Psychological knowledge is to be used for beneficial social purposes, as conceptualized in terms of respect for the dignity of persons, responsible caring, and integrity in relationships. Here we can see how the Code, with its basis in deontology (see Chapter 1), struggles to incorporate social justice. This is because social justice obligations are derived from relational ethics, which motivate us to act out of concern for others and consideration of social contexts and consequences. If we think of our professional ethical obligations only from the point of view of the individualistic ethics of deontology, teleology, and virtue, therefore, we risk neglecting our responsibility to society and may find ourselves behaving in a manner that causes harm.

Duties and Virtues Underlying Social Justice
JUSTICE AND BENEVOLENCE

Justice is the deontological obligation to act fairly and is difficult to understand, let alone realize, independent of benevolence (Beauchamp & Childress, 2012). In the context of professional ethics it refers to fairness and equity in the allocation of, impact of, and access to psychological services. Whereas the Code differentiates responsibility to society from respect for individuals and renders it a lesser consideration (Clark, 1993), Principle I does contain much that is representative of the ethical duty of justice. In particular, the Values Statement of Principle I articulates the belief that:

> all persons are entitled to benefit equally from the contributions of psychology and to equal quality in the processes, procedures, and services being conducted by psychologists, regardless of the person's characteristics, condition, or status.

This is consistent with Canadian legal values (see Chapter 3), whereby social institutions are expected to refrain from discrimination (see Chapter 9) and correct existing social disadvantages through the establishment of appropriate policy. By extension, individual professionals are expected to do all that is practically possible to ensure that these policies are enacted. One particular standard within the Code of Ethics is helpful in understanding our responsibility to promote social justice, whereby psychologists are expected to:

IV.6   Participate in the process of critical self-evaluation of the discipline's place in society, and in the development and implementation of structures and procedures that help the discipline to contribute to beneficial societal functioning and changes.

Benevolence, being a character trait of concern for bettering the welfare of others, draws us to an appreciation of the social context and reciprocal nature of our actions—and inactions. Realizing this virtue invariably leads to consideration of how we might influence social institutions for the good of all members of society. The duty of justice and the virtue of benevolence underlying psychologists' responsibilities toward society, therefore, can be understood as twofold: concern for all persons as individuals and concern for collective social betterment.

INTEGRITY IN RELATIONSHIPS

Most psychologists think of their ethical and professional obligations in relation to the clients that we serve. For some of us, this is manifested in behaviour toward other professionals—for example, in case conferences—that can fall rather short of the standards we uphold in the consulting room. Public trust in the discipline of psychology includes the expectation that psychologists will act fairly toward all members of society, however. Because our role as agents of desired change for our clients can clash with the preservation of existing values, conflict between ourselves and others with whom we work can, and often does, result. At such times psychologists are expected to uphold our ethical and professional obligations of openness, honesty, and respect in all of professional relationships, including relationships with other professionals, and act with integrity.

Relationships and Consequences Relevant to Social Justice

ACCESS TO SERVICES

Psychologists are often faced with circumstances whereby demand for our services exceeds our ability to provide them. Deciding how they should be distributed in a fair and just manner can be quite vexing. The basic expectation of fair access to services can be stated as *equals should be treated as equals, and unequals should be treated as unequals*. This means that persons who are equal in whatever aspects are relevant to a decision should be treated equivalently. Potentially relevant aspects include: need, effort, contribution, merit, and equal share. This theoretical ideal is seldom helpful in our real-world decision making, however, because rarely will we find agreement on which of these aspects are relevant to deciding how to apportion services (Tjeltveit, 2000). What does help is a systematic framework for deciding which aspects are relevant to which particular circumstance. In Canada, we have historically agreed that everyone has the right to equitable and just access to health care (Kluge, 1992). The framework for realizing this principle is the rule of "fair opportunity" (Daniels, 1985; Rawls, 1971). Fair opportunity obligates us to act so that no persons receive services on the basis of undeserved advantageous attributes because they are not responsible for having these attributes. It also obligates us to act so that no persons are denied services on the basis of undeserved disadvantageous attributes because they are similarly not responsible for having these attributes.

Take, for example, the issue of access to educational opportunities. Imagine a school system that offers a high-quality education to all children with basic abilities, but not to children with attributes that interfere with the realization of their basic abilities, such as poverty or minority status. This system would violate the rule of fair opportunity because children are not responsible for these disadvantageous attributes. The fair opportunity rule obligates us to provide an education suitable to their needs and indeed that maximizes their opportunities.

The issue is made difficult, however, when we attempt to realize fair opportunity within a finite budget. Our society has decided that all children should receive educational services, without allocating unlimited resources to pay for them. In the normal course of providing limited services to (essentially) unlimited individuals, therefore, need and likelihood of benefiting from the service are considered first, followed by "first come, first served" when likelihood of benefit is roughly equal for equally needy recipients (Beauchamp & Childress, 2012). In this way deontological principles are balanced with teleological consequences. Such decisions can be very difficult to enact experientially (i.e., from a relational and virtue point of view), however. In fact, they are often the cause of significant "moral distress" for psychologists (Austin et al., 2005) when we have to deny services to an individual in great need because they are unlikely to benefit from them and there are others who likely will.

SOCIAL INTERVENTIONS

The emphasis on helping individuals that is so much a part of the professional identity of psychologists puts us at risk of downplaying or disregarding the importance of societal factors. Psychologists are typically not socialized through our training to strive to change the circumstances that are the root cause of social problems or alleviating their effects. We tend to direct our services toward individual problems and solutions. Such an approach tends to be a reactive one in which clients are assisted in taking responsibility for helping themselves (Kakkad, 2005). We therefore tend to conceptualize the solutions to the challenges confronting our clients as being within their grasp if they can figure out how to make the right choices. This passive approach is not helpful, however, with the many clients for whom overcoming social impediments to achieving their personal goals is impossible via individual efforts (Maton, 2000). This is especially true for those who are marginalized or otherwise denied access to the means to make personal change (see Chapter 9). In order to properly realize the value of promoting social justice, therefore, it is necessary for psychologists to implement social interventions (Prilleltensky, 1990). In fact, many psychologists are involved in public education interventions to change societal attitudes (Nelson & Prilleltensky, 2010), with goals such as preventing eating disorders, discouraging illegal drug use, or reducing bullying, for example (Hage & Kenny, 2009).

Addressing social factors through broad-based interventions carries its own unique challenges, however. In particular, the understanding that the roots of many individual problems are situational is not consistent with what most people (not just psychologists) believe. If we seek to act on behalf of a community without knowing how all of the individuals feel about intervening communally, we risk establishing a paternalistic relationship that does not respect the dignity of the individuals involved (Pope, 1990b). By doing so we may inadvertently interfere with individuals' autonomy, thereby harming rather than helping (Walsh, 1988). Clarifying for yourself and with the members of the community the degree to which you are acting on behalf of the community and on behalf of your own agenda, however benevolent, is strongly recommended (Toporek & Williams, 2006).

A related challenge is obtaining consent (see Chapter 5) given that, even if a majority of the community welcomes a social intervention, it is impossible to incorporate the wishes and preferences of the minority who do not want the ecology of their social and individual lives disrupted (Pope, 1990b). While there are goals upon which almost everyone will agree, such as adjustment and adaptation (Cowen, 1977), the right to refuse to participate is a fundamental one in our society. Even in situations where we might intervene for everyone's good to bring about these "general agreement" goals, therefore, our ethical responsibilities for ensuring that individuals are able to be left alone are unclear. What is clear is that we are expected to establish collaborative relationships with leaders of the target community—such as school principals and civic officials—to establish goals that meet communal needs, and employ empowering interventions that foster the competence of all its members (Schwartz & Hage, 2009). The Code of Ethics thus expects psychologists to:

IV.15 Acquire an adequate knowledge of the culture, social structure, and customs of a community before beginning any major work there.

IV.16 Convey respect for and abide by prevailing community mores, social customs, and cultural expectations in their scientific and professional activities, provided that this does not contravene any of the ethical principles of this Code.

Finally, we have an obligation to ensure that our social interventions produce the outcomes intended. Broad-based interventions, in particular, are very commonly employed on the assumption that being informed about the risks of undesired behaviour or that providing general mental health service to persons "at risk" for problem behaviour will decrease the behaviour. This assumption is by no means uniformly true, however, particularly with respect to anti-social behaviours (McCord, 2003; Rhule, 2005; Werch & Owen, 2002; Wilson, Gottfredson, & Najaka, 2001). Psychologists are expected to evaluate such programs to determine if our interventions are actually beneficial and, if not, to alter or discontinue as appropriate. In some instances it may even be necessary to undo harms caused by social interventions.

MISUSE OF PSYCHOLOGICAL KNOWLEDGE

An especially tricky issue is the use to which psychological knowledge is put and the role of the individual psychologist in preventing its misuse. It is very difficult to know or influence how what we say or publish will be portrayed or used by others. In one prominent example, the well-known psychologist Martin Seligman reports having given a presentation to representatives of the US Armed Forces on how troops and personnel could use what is known about learned helplessness (Seligman, 1975) and related findings to resist torture and interrogation by their enemies. Subsequently, two psychologists employed by the Central Intelligence

Agency (CIA) apparently "reverse-engineered" his findings to refine their torture and interrogation techniques with detainees suspected of anti-US activities (US Central Intelligence Agency, 2004). Whether or not Seligman knew the CIA's intentions, and whether or not the governance of the American Psychological Association was complicit in allowing psychologists to be involved in torture (Pope, 2011b), remain open—and controversial—questions. Given the morally abhorrent nature and devastating psychological impact of torture (Brenner, 2010), however, Seligman's reputation and that of professional psychology has certainly been tarnished (Pope & Gutheil, 2009).

While psychologists are expected to correct any misrepresentations or misuses of psychological knowledge, the lengths to which we should go in order to do so is unclear. In reality, it is usually extremely difficult to influence others to retract statements already made public, revise policies already enacted, or remedy actions already taken. Nevertheless, the Code of Ethics has quite a bit to say about the issue, and advises psychologists to:

I.6   Refuse to advise, train, or supply information to anyone who, in the psychologist's judgement, will use the knowledge or skills to infringe on human rights.

I.7   Make every reasonable effort to ensure that psychological knowledge is not misused, intentionally or unintentionally, to infringe on human rights.

IV.11 Protect the skills, knowledge, and interpretations of psychology from being misused, used incompetently, or made useless (e.g., loss of security of assessment techniques) by others.

IV.25 Make themselves aware of the current social and political climate and of previous and possible future societal misuses of psychological knowledge, and exercise due discretion in communicating psychological information (e.g., research results, theoretical knowledge), in order to discourage any further misuse.

IV.27 Not contribute to nor engage in research or any other activity that contravenes international humanitarian law, such as the development of methods intended for use in the torture of persons, the development of prohibited weapons, or destruction of the environment.

How we interpret psychological knowledge can be another source of ethical concern. One set of results can support many conclusions—some benevolent, some malevolent. Which conclusion we favour will be influenced by our motives, intentions, and social context (see Chapter 4). If our actions are incongruent with ethical virtues and duties, negative consequences are likely to result. A notorious Canadian example is psychologist J. Philippe Rushton who has (mis)interpreted "racial" differences on a variety of behavioural attributes as being representative of biological reality (Rushton, 1995), a conclusion at odds with both science and ethics (see Chapter 9). Whether Ruston's intentions were purely to discover the truth or not, there is no doubt that his actions are harmful. In order to avoid such unjust consequences, the Code of Ethics states that psychologists are expected to:

IV.23 Provide thorough discussion of the limits of their data with respect to social policy, if their work touches on social policy and structure.

IV.26 Exercise particular care when reporting the results of any work regarding vulnerable groups, ensuring that results are not likely to be misinterpreted or misused in the development of social policy, attitudes, and practices (e.g., encouraging manipulation of vulnerable persons or reinforcing discrimination against any specific population).

SOCIAL ACTIVISM

The promotion of social justice is grounded in respect for the rights, dignity, and worth of all individuals. Certainly, the reduction of human suffering and furtherance of human rights are the basis of psychology's concern for society in general (Kendler, 1999). Social justice goes beyond the particular ethical obligations owed to individuals arising out of professional relationships, however, to include obligations owed to individuals collectively. Action is taken external to any particular client on behalf of client groups or society in general, although it will often involve confronting majority groups, societal systems, or cultural norms. Thus, the Code expects psychologists to:

IV.22 Speak out, in a manner consistent with the four principles of this Code, if they possess expert knowledge that bears on important societal issues being studied or discussed.

Social justice has traditionally been thought of as being the concern of policy planners and politicians, however. Indeed, the Values Statement of Principle IV states:

Those psychologists having direct involvement in the structures of the discipline, in social development, or in the theoretical or research data base that is being used (e.g., through research, expert testimony, or policy advice) have the greatest responsibility to act. Other psychologists must decide for themselves the most appropriate and beneficial use of their time and talents to help meet this collective responsibility.

Yet, psychologists who provide services to clients are in the position to listen and affirm, and also to appreciate that the private troubles of individuals are commonly the result of social processes. Indeed, much of the misery that psychologists address is the product of the exploitation and mistreatment of human beings. Many of the circumstances that prompt individuals to seek our services are the direct or indirect consequence of unjust social, economic, and political institutions (Senate of Canada, 2008). The principle of social justice obligates us to be concerned for the welfare of all human beings in society. It follows that psychologists' commitment to the welfare of others can be understood as bringing with it a responsibility to change social systems (Robinson, 1984). There are multiple avenues for social action, however, and psychologists are expected to choose for ourselves the most beneficial use of our time and abilities to help meet this collective responsibility. Knowledge may be used to influence social policy, educate the public, advocate on behalf of individuals or groups, or lobby political representatives to support a social justice cause.

If social policy and societal attitudes seriously ignore or violate the ethical principles of autonomy, beneficence, nonmaleficence, and fidelity, then we as psychologists have a responsibility to advocate for change to occur as quickly as possible. To the extent that individuals and groups without power suffer oppression in our imperfect society (see Chapter 9), psychologists have an ethical responsibility to use our knowledge and influence to contribute to social change. It is easy to see that social justice considerations pervade all of our work, and it will ever be thus. Our choice is the degree to which we intentionally engage in socially responsible activities.

To a large extent, psychologists epitomize the goals of progressive social reform to promote the well-being of all people. The reality, however, is that most of us do not spend much time thinking about such things, and even less time taking action to improve society. Terms such as *activist*, *advocacy*, *social action*, and *change agent* are far from prominent in the psychological literature or the curriculum of our professional training. Most psychologists would agree that the broad goal of improving our social systems for the benefit of all members of society is desirable. The role that psychology as a profession should play in bringing about such improvements, however, enjoys much less agreement (Prilleltensky, 1994). The role that an individual psychologist might play in particular circumstances arouses downright conflict (e.g., Smith, 2000; Suedfeld & Tetlock, 1992). Regardless of one's stance on the matter, encountering social justice issues in relation to particular individuals is unavoidable, and very likely to give rise to ethical challenges.

Even if we accept that it may be desirable for the profession to advocate openly for social change, when enacted by individual psychologists it often appears to others as a bias on our part (Brown, 1997). In general, psychologists are expected to assume an objective stance in relation to the people to whom we provide services. This means that we are entrusted to act without any agenda that opposes the status quo. If we do have social advocacy intentions and make them explicit, therefore, we are perceived as being biased and our opinions discounted or outright rejected. Then there is the issue of those in the majority who are benefiting from the existing system are very unlikely to want change. Our opinions may not be considered by the very persons whose decisions we hope to influence, therefore, and we may not continue to receive requests for our services. Professionals whose practice is uninformed by social justice ethics are thereby more likely to be in positions that impact the lives of individuals who are suffering under existing systems (Prilleltensky, 1989).

Thus, psychologists are placed in a dilemma of either covertly addressing particular social issues as they affect individuals and thereby violating our ethical obligations to avoid misrepresentation and deception, or abandoning our social justice obligations (Bazelon, 1982). Ultimately, a failure to be forthcoming about your social advocacy position, no matter how valid and noble it may be, is to risk the loss of role integrity (O'Neill, 1989) with all of the associated negative consequences for you, the profession, and the individuals involved.

When psychologists have undertaken to provide services to individuals, therefore, we are expected to balance the ethical risks associated with advocacy for particular social changes against the missed opportunity for promoting social justice. Psychologists are expected to work to ensure that the individuals we come in contact with are treated justly by the systems that impact their lives. In so doing we should be open about our intentions and act in accordance with our professional ethical duties in all of our professional activities. If we advocate on behalf of a client in order to correct larger social wrongs, we must be very careful to ensure that doing so is congruent with the client's desires and preferences. If not, the client can feel that their individual needs are being ignored or even sacrificed.

If the system within which we are providing services is unjust, psychologists are expected to seek remediation at the system level through changes to or development of policy and procedures. We can sit on policy boards and steering committees, for example, or contribute in any number of ways at a political level. In response to such situations, the Code of Ethics advises psychologists to:

IV.9   Help develop, promote, and participate in accountability processes and procedures related to their work.

IV.29   Speak out and/or act, in a manner consistent with the four principles of this Code, if the policies, practices, laws, or regulations of the social structure within which they work seriously ignore or contradict any of the principles of this Code.

The following considerations may assist you when faced with a situation that calls for social activism:

· Is my knowledge of the matter sufficiently complete and accurate?
· To what extent is this a case of individual rights as opposed to an unjust system?
· Will I be violating any implicit or explicit agreements by taking social action?
· Will I be violating any implicit or explicit agreements by not taking social action?
· What ethical duties or professional standards are relevant to this situation and the action I am considering?
· What can I realistically expect to achieve by taking social action in this particular matter?
· Am I willing to make the personal and professional sacrifices that will likely be necessary if I take action?

Summary

Social justice is concerned with the well-being of individuals by assuring that all have equal access to psychological services and with the well-being of society in order that all individuals might benefit. Obligations and challenges arising out of these values can occur at the level of the professional service relationships and our interactions with social systems. Particular ethical challenges are inherent in circumstances of access to limited services, misuse of psychological knowledge, social interventions, and social advocacy. When psychologists are faced with unjust circumstances, there are two broad courses of action. If a just system is being applied unjustly, psychologists are expected to advocate on behalf of our clients. If a system is unjust, psychologists have a responsibility to take action at a system level.

Discussion Questions

1. Do you think that psychological services should be equitably distributed among all Canadians via the public health care system in the same way that medical services are? If so, how? If not, why not?

2. What do you think is the basic level of psychological health to which all members of society are entitled? How would such a level be determined or realized?

3. To what extent do you think psychologists have an obligation to promote social change? Explain your position.

4. Should efforts to make social change be made if doing so would violate other ethical principles? If doing so would violate the law? Why or why not? What ethical system does your answer reflect?

Your Reflective Journal

For most psychologists our motivation for pursuing our careers is, at least in part, the desire to be of service for others. What is your motivation for psychology? If you had to choose between two employment opportunities, one that allowed you to be of greater service to others at a reduced income and the other that provided greater income but reduced service, which would you choose? What does this tell you about your personal sense of social justice? Take some time to write down your responses to these questions and any others that occur to you.

Case Study

A Good Night's Sleep

You are working with a client who is an engineer. The client tells you that she has been feeling fearful over the fact that her company is dumping potentially cancer-causing chemicals into the local water supply. Even though your client admits she knows that what her company is doing is wrong, she has no intention of telling anyone else about it because if the authorities knew what they were doing she would lose her job, or even be charged with committing a crime. She asks you to help her overcome her fears so that she can sleep at night and feel calmer during the day in order to perform well at her job. When you raise the issue of whether or not it might be best to inform the public of the risks to their health, the client asks about her right to confidentiality and insists that what she told you be kept private.

(1) Do nothing ; Council for Honesty

(2) Break Confidentiality ; Report

(3)

Case Study

Thriving Practice

You are a psychologist working in a small, prosperous town that is the hub of a broad geographical region that includes a large community of people of indigenous heritage. You are the only registered mental health professional within a day's drive, and your practice is thriving. Your caseload consists exclusively of highly paid executives who work for the large industrial project that is the most significant influence on the town's economy. The indigenous population is severely disadvantaged relative to the employees of the industrial project, and plagued by many mental health issues. Yet, they have access to pitifully few services. When the town's mayor asks you why you don't extend your services to include those who are most in need, you explain that you are seeing as many clients as your schedule will allow, and that you have the right to practice as you see fit.

Case Study

Banality of Evil?

As a psychologist directing a mental health clinic you report to a central administration that has continuingly asked you to find efficiencies in your clinic's service delivery. You have dutifully responded with a variety of changes. Through your effort the clinic has simplified its record-keeping requirements, increased the number of clients who receive group therapy, reduced individual therapy case loads, and streamlined the referral procedure for pharmacological consultation. Your supervisor is very pleased with your leadership, citing increases in the number of client hours billed, decreased staffing expenditures, and overall improved profitability. Your staff, however, are complaining that case notes are too sparse, clients' unique treatment needs are not being addressed, and the number of clients on medication has more than doubled.

Recommended Reading

Aubé, N. (2011). Ethical challenges for psychologists conducting humanitarian work. *Canadian Psychology, 52,* 225–29.

Forster, D. (2009). Rethinking compassion fatigue as moral stress. *Journal of Ethics in Mental Health, 4,* 1–4.

Kakkad, D. (2005). A new ethical praxis: Psychologists' emerging responsibilities in issues of social justice. *Ethics & Behavior, 15,* 293–308.

O'Neill, P. (2005). The ethics of problem definition. *Canadian Psychology, 46,* 13–20.

11

Conducting Research

Case Study

Assisted Suicide

You conducted a study on assisted suicide among persons with AIDS. It took many months of patient, gentle persistence to gain sufficient trust before anyone would talk with you. You promised potential participants that you would interview them anonymously and that you would not disclose any identifying information you might unintentionally learn. True to your word, you did not record anything that could identify anyone. The nature of your involvement was such that you got to know the people you interviewed quite well, and certainly know their first names and much of their personal circumstances. A number of people you interviewed subsequently committed suicide with the help of others who you also came to know through your research. Some time later you receive a subpoena to appear in court to give testimony in a criminal trial involving an alleged assisted suicide death. The police believe you have information pertinent to their case.

Questions for consideration

1. What individuals and/or groups are affected in this situation?
2. Are any feelings aroused in you by this situation that might influence your decision as to how to act?
3. What ethical values are in conflict in this situation?
4. What consequences could reasonably be expected to result from what you decide to do?

Research is unlike almost any other activity in which psychologists are involved because it places the interests of the participant second
to the interests of others. Indeed, human research can be defined as obtaining
information about persons for the purpose of extending our knowledge rather
than furthering their well-being. We undertake research to better the human
condition (broadly speaking), obtain material benefit (in the form of employment
advancement, salary, patent royalties, meeting educational requirements, etc.),
or simply satisfy our curiosity. Those who participate in research typically derive
no direct benefit and, in fact, are usually exposed to at least some risk of personal
harm. When we conduct research, therefore, we assume an augmented ethical
responsibility and are expected to meet stringent standards.

Since the Age of Enlightenment (during the eighteenth century) Western
society has, to varying degrees, held up science as the foremost means of enrich-
ing humanity, with those who conduct research consequently afforded social
status above the norm. Whenever researchers are revealed to have betrayed this
public trust, the resulting "moral panic" has provoked calls for stricter regulation
of research activities (Fitzgerald, 2004; van den Hoonaard, 2011). This despite the
fact that for many centuries the least valued and thereby most vulnerable members of society have been subjected to dangerous research with little remorse
(Bassiouni, Baffes, & Evrard, 1981). The example most prominent in the modern
consciousness is of course the Nazi physicians who conducted callous and
deadly experiments on captive individuals during the Second World War. At their
subsequent trial for crimes against humanity these "researchers" argued that no
international law defined illegal human experimentation (which was true) and
that medical research on unwilling subjects was common practice (which was also
true). This defence was not accepted by the court, however. Despite their rejection
of the accuseds' defence, the court was obliged to respond to the veracity of their
argument and its final judgement included a section entitled "Permissible Medical
Experimentation," which established the right of participants to voluntarily

consent to and withdraw from research. The ten points within this section came to be known as the *Nuremberg Code* (1949) and have served as a template for most subsequent ethical standards pertaining to research involving humans.

The events that have had the most direct influence on present-day North American research ethics occurred during the 1970s in the United States when various journalists exposed a number of appalling medical studies. The most prominent of these horrors were the Jewish Chronic Disease Hospital study of the effects of injecting live cancer cells into chronically ill patients without their knowledge (Katz, 1972), the Tuskegee study of untreated syphilis among economically disadvantaged black men (Jones, 1981), and the United States Energy Department's clandestine radiation experiments on unsuspecting citizens (Welsome, 1999). In response to the public outcry, political pressure was applied to strengthen the consent provisions of existing ethical codes and establish new ethical review bodies (Fitzgerald, 2004) that are still in place today.

During this same period psychological research aroused its own share of negative public reaction. Stanley Milgram's (in)famous 1963 investigation into obedience of the sort that resulted in the Nazi medical experiments—whereby participants were led to believe that they were in a study of learning in which they had to apply an electrical shock to a "pupil"—sparked considerable controversy, ostensibly due to his use of deception. Even though Milgram went to great lengths to demonstrate that the participants in his research did not experience harm (Milgram, 1964), commentators vociferously argued that such research was unethical (e.g., Baumrind, 1964; Fischer, 1968; Kaufman, 1967; Mixon, 1972). The resulting moral panic led to the buttressing of standards of informed consent for psychological studies involving deception. Psychological research also gained a negative reputation that continues to influence policy makers (Adair, 2001). Indeed, Milgram's study remains very much active and influential in the consciousness of those interested in psychological research (e.g., Burger, 2009; Perry, 2012).

More recently, public concern over biomedical—predominantly pharmaceutical—corporations suppressing, falsifying, and otherwise manipulating data for substantial monetary gain (e.g., Law, 2006; Shuchman, 2005) has provoked the latest round of revising research ethics standards.

Tri-Council Policy Statement: Ethical Conduct for Research Involving Humans

The institutionalization of the research ethics review process in Canada began at the tail end of the flurry of activity in the United States during the 1970s. In 1978, the Social Sciences and Humanities Research Council and the Medical Research Council each introduced their own voluntary guidelines for research involving human subjects that were patterned after US regulations. Concerns were being voiced about the adequacy of the guidelines—especially the fact that they were voluntary—the shortcomings of a patchwork approach, and the need to demonstrate to US funding bodies that their research ethics standards were being met (McDonald, 2009). The moral panic that appears to have provided the impetus for common enforceable standards was a series of highly publicized accounts of falsification and fabrication of data (Adair, 2001; Lytton, 1996) as well as the public clamour and subsequent legal proceedings in response to psychiatrist Ewen Cameron's "brainwashing" of patients at Montreal's Allan Memorial Institute on behalf of the US government (O'Neill, 2011). In 1994, the three federal bodies that funded research involving humans (Medical Research Council; Social Sciences and Humanities Research Council; National Science and Engineering Research Council) formed the Tri-Council Working Group with the intention of developing uniform mandatory regulations to replace the existing disparate voluntary guidelines.

A draft document produced in 1996 by the Working Group was circulated for consultation, but a consensus among researchers representing the various disciplines could not be reached. While medical researchers were generally pleased—or at least not seriously displeased—those in the social sciences and engineering were highly critical of its overwhelmingly biomedical perspective. A second document was produced in 1997 and again considerable disagreement ensued. In 1998, the *Tri-Council Policy Statement: Ethical Conduct for Research Involving Humans* (*TCPS*; Canadian Institutes of Health Research, Natural Sciences and Engineering Research Council of Canada, & Social Sciences and Humanities Research Council of Canada, 1998) was finally published. It was substantially revised from its original form, retaining only fifty of the original 130 standards, and was generally less prescriptive. Most significantly, although lacking any legal force, funding from the three councils was made dependent on researchers and institutions complying with the policy. This means that all research involving humans conducted by anyone in any way affiliated with a Canadian university (that desires federal research monies) must be approved by a research ethics board as being compliant with the *TCPS*.

Continued concerns expressed by social researchers led the Interagency Advisory Panel on Research Ethics (the body that oversees the *TCPS*) to establish a Social Sciences and Humanities Research Ethics Special Working Committee. The committee conducted a series of consultations and produced two reports highly critical of the *TCPS* and its imposition of a biomedical framework on other forms of research. When the second edition of the *TCPS* was released in December of 2010 (Canadian Institutes of Health Research, Natural Sciences and Engineering Research Council of Canada, & Social Sciences and Humanities Research Council of Canada, 2010), some of these criticisms were addressed (e.g., using "participant" instead of "subject" and clarifying consent requirements with low-risk research). Chapters were also added on qualitative research and research involving First Nations, Inuit, and Métis peoples, but it has to be concluded that the ethical standards governing research in Canada remain predominantly biomedical in focus and worldview.

Duties and Virtues Underlying Research

AUTONOMY AND RESPECT

For most psychologists, the duty of respecting the autonomy of the participants and potential participants in our research is not in any way an onerous one because it is the leading value of our profession (see Chapter 1). Thus, psychological researchers should find familiar the expectation that the autonomy of participants in our research should be preserved. Normally, therefore, potential participants should be offered the opportunity to consent or decline to participate in our research and to withdraw from participation as they wish. Thus, the CPA Code of Ethics expects psychologists to:

> I.8 Respect the right of research participants...to safeguard their own dignity.

> I.16 Seek as full and active participation as possible from others in decisions that affect them, respecting and integrating as much as possible their opinions and wishes.

BENEFICENCE AND NONMALEFICENCE

When planning and conducting a research project, psychologists are expected to first ensure that the research is likely to be of benefit—usually in the form of contributing to our knowledge base and occasionally through direct benefit to the participants. We are then to eliminate any possible harms that are not necessary to the research design and minimize or offset those that are. This is represented in the CPA Code of Ethics through directing psychologists to:

> II.1 Protect and promote the welfare of...research participants....

> II.2 Avoid doing harm to...research participants....

> II.17 Not carry out any scientific or professional activity unless the probable benefit is proportionately greater than the risk involved.

II.36   Act to minimize the impact of their research activities on research
participants' personalities, or on their physical or mental integrity.

An important corollary of this duty is that research that seeks to answer an
essentially trivial question either should not be undertaken at all or designed such
that the risks of harm are correspondingly trivial (typically wasting the participants' time or boring them).

JUSTICE

The primary implication of justice duties in research are that researchers are
expected to make all reasonable efforts to ensure that the benefits and burdens
of participation are shared equally by all members of society. This means that
those who are recruited to participate are representative of all segments of our
society, particularly with regard to the scope and objectives of the research.
Those who are expected to gain from the knowledge generated by the research
should be exposed to any risks the research entails. This speaks to the heart of
the outrage that gave rise to the Nuremberg trials where individuals judged to
be inferior were harmed in order to benefit those deemed superior. Thus, convenience sampling from populations that are easy to access or manipulate—such as
residents in an institutional setting or a prison—when the research question
is intended to apply to all members of society, for example, would violate our
duty to uphold justice.

Justice duties also compel us to expand the scope of our research to include
those who could potentially gain from it. Thus, we should strive to include groups
who may be difficult or inconvenient to recruit, in order that they may benefit
from research results. This does not mean that psychologists wanting to answer
a research question about a particular segment of society—such as why men
commit more crimes than women, for example—are expected to expand the
scope their research.

With respect to justice duties in research, the Code of Ethics expects us to:

I.11   Seek to design research...activities in such a way that they contribute
to the fair distribution of benefits to individuals and groups, and that
they do not unfairly exclude those who are vulnerable or might be
disadvantaged.

IV.20 Be sensitive to the needs, current issues, and problems of society,
when determining research questions to be asked.

FIDELITY AND INTEGRITY

Fidelity involves both maintaining honesty in our relationships with participants and more generally in relationship to society at large through accurately, truthfully, and openly handling our research data and reporting our findings. Fidelity and integrity are necessary so that we might maintain society's trust in the benefits and usefulness of research (Council of Canadian Academies, 2010).

The Code thus expects psychologists to:

III.5 Accurately represent their own and their colleagues' activities, functions, contributions, and likely or actual outcomes of their activities (including research results) in all spoken, written, or printed communication. This includes, but is not limited to...research reports.

III.10 Evaluate how their personal experiences, attitudes, values, social context, individual differences, stresses, and specific training influence their activities and thinking, integrating this awareness into all attempts to be objective and unbiased in their research.

Indeed, as a condition of applying for or receiving funding from any of the three federal councils that fund research in Canada, researchers are required to grant permission to disclose any serious breach of the TCPS (Canadian Institutes of Health Research, Natural Sciences and Engineering Research Council of Canada, & Social Sciences and Humanities Research Council of Canada, 2011). The councils can thereby make public the researcher's name, the nature of the breach, the institution where the researcher was employed at the time of the breach, and the institution where the researcher is currently employed.

Relationships and Consequences Relevant to Research

CONSENT

In most respects, consent does not pose any particular difficulties in the research context and psychologists are expected to uphold the same duties as when providing services to clients. Consent is expected to be voluntary, informed, understood, and ongoing, and should normally precede data collection. Thus, the Code of Ethics advises to psychologists to:

I.20 Obtain informed consent for all research activities that involve obtrusive measures, invasion of privacy, more than minimal risk of harm, or any attempt to change the behaviour of research participants.

I.28   Not proceed with any research activity, if consent is given under any condition of coercion, undue pressure, or undue reward.

III.32 Not offer rewards sufficient to motivate an individual or group to participate in an activity that has possible or known risks to themselves or others.

Under the *TCPS*, exceptions can be made whereby data that was collected in an ethical manner primarily for some other use (such as the provision of health care or education) may be accessed for secondary use in research without consent only if the information is not personally identifiable. Examples include rates of psychological disorders or developmental learning trends. If researchers seek secondary use of data that contains personally identifiable information, they must satisfy their Research Ethics Board that seeking consent is impossible or impracticable, the information is essential to the study, the participants will not be harmed, and any agreements under which the data was collected will be honoured.

Of particular concern to psychologists is the issue of deception in research (Pascual-Leone, Singh, & Scoboria, 2010). Incomplete disclosure or temporarily leading research participants to believe that a research project has a purpose other than its actual purpose is sometimes necessary to obtain valid results when full disclosure would be expected to influence the responses of the research participants. Although research that uses deception can lead to beneficial knowledge, we are expected to weigh the benefits of incomplete disclosure against the research participant's right to self-determination and the threat to the public's trust in psychology. Psychologists have an obligation, therefore, to avoid the use of deception whenever possible and to attempt to offset any resulting harm by properly debriefing participants. The Code correspondingly devotes considerable attention to the issue and expects psychologists to:

III.23 Not engage in incomplete disclosure, or in temporarily leading research participants to believe that a research project or some aspect of it has a different purpose, if there are alternative procedures available or if the negative effects cannot be predicted or offset.

III.24 Not engage in incomplete disclosure, or in temporarily leading research participants to believe that a research project or some aspect of it has a different purpose, if it would interfere with the person's understanding of facts that clearly might influence a decision to give adequately informed consent (e.g., withholding information about the level of risk, discomfort, or inconvenience).

III.25 Use the minimum necessary incomplete disclosure or temporary leading of research participants to believe that a research project or some aspect of it has a different purpose, when such research procedures are used.

If the use of incomplete disclosure meets these standards, we are expected to debrief participants following their involvement so that they understand the nature of the study, particularly with regard to the necessity of deception in order to obtain scientifically valid findings, and work to regain any trust that may have been lost. Such debriefing should take place as soon as possible and efforts made to correct any resulting harm. Importantly, participants must be given the option of removing their data provided doing so will not compromise the validity of the research design and thereby negate the contribution of the other research participants.

PRIVACY AND CONFIDENTIALITY

Privacy concerns in research arise out of the risk of harm from identification of participants and intentional or unintentional disclosure of personal information. Much of the potential harms of psychological research are related to violations of a person's privacy. Thus, the Code of Ethics expects psychologists to:

I.39   Record only that private information necessary...for the goals of the particular research study being conducted.

I.40   Respect the right of research participants...to reasonable personal privacy.

I.41   Collect, store, handle, and transfer all private information, whether written or unwritten (e.g., communication during service provision, written records, e-mail or fax communication, computer files, video-tapes), in a way that attends to the needs for privacy and security. This would include having adequate plans for records in circumstances of one's own serious illness, termination of employment, or death.

In practice, this obligates us to collect only that information that is necessary to obtain valid results and to ensure that data is de-identified as soon as reasonably possible. This is typically a straightforward task in quantitative research. Qualitative research, however, often makes anonymity difficult, if not impossible in some cases, and researchers are expected to clarify the unique limits to privacy when obtaining consent from potential participants.

CHILDREN AND VULNERABLE PERSONS

Ever since the publication of the *Nuremberg Code* in 1949, laws, ethics codes, and practice standards have emphasized the need for special protection of children and vulnerable persons against abuse or exploitation in research. The foundational premise is that anyone who is unable to give consent should not be subjected to *any* invasive or potentially harmful activity that is not intended to benefit them. This is an inflexible and uncompromising rule. No one is justified in harming anyone who is unable to give consent, regardless of the good that might come to others. Even a child's or dependent adult's guardian cannot give consent on their behalf to participate in research that will not directly benefit them.

Of course, both the *Nuremberg Code* and the TCPS were developed in response to invasive medical research. Most of the research undertaken by psychologists is non-invasive and only exposes participants to the sort of risks normally encountered in everyday life. Asking children or dependent adults to indicate a preference or complete a puzzle would hardly be expected to harm them in any way. With this in mind, the Code of Ethics expects psychologists to:

I.32   Not use persons of diminished capacity to give informed consent in research studies, if the research involved may be carried out equally well with persons who have a fuller capacity to give informed consent.

I.34   Carry out informed consent processes with those persons who are legally responsible or appointed to give informed consent on behalf of persons not competent to consent on their own behalf, seeking to ensure respect for any previously expressed preferences of persons not competent to consent.

I.35   Seek willing and adequately informed participation from any person of diminished capacity to give informed consent, and proceed without this assent only if the service or research activity is considered to be of direct benefit to that person.

It is not only diminished capacity to consent that renders an individual vulnerable to exploitation in research. Persons who are in situations or relationships of

unequal power are also vulnerable to pressure to submit to research. This applies
most particularly to individuals in the role of student, soldier, prisoner, or patient.
In these circumstances, great care must be taken to ensure that consent is given
voluntarily and that the research involves only minimal risk. The requirement for
free consent requires us to refrain from conducting invasive or potentially harmful
research in contexts with authoritarian structures such as prisons. Therefore, the
Code of Ethics requires psychologists to:

I.28   Not proceed with any research activity, if consent is given under any
       condition of coercion, undue pressure, or undue reward.

I.36   Be particularly cautious in establishing the freedom of consent of any
       person who is in a dependent relationship to the psychologist (e.g.,
       student, employee). This may include, but is not limited to, offering
       that person an alternative activity to fulfill their educational or employ-
       ment goals, or offering a range of research studies or experience
       opportunities from which the person can select, none of which is
       so onerous as to be coercive.

CONFLICTS OF INTEREST

Strictly speaking, conflicts of interest are unavoidable in research. Everyone who
undertakes research does so in order to obtain some sort of benefit, either material in the form of salary or advancement, or personal in the form of recognition or
curiosity. Thus, every research study is at risk of being biased. We may introduce
bias—consciously or unconsciously—in such aspects as participant recruitment,
data collection, data analysis, and results interpretation. Psychological research
is especially prone to publishing only positive results and discouraging the reporting of negative findings—so much so that over 90 per cent of the psychological
research that is published contains statistically significant positive results, which
is statistically impossible (Yong, 2012).

Financial conflicts of interest are of particular concern for post-secondary
institutions that have become increasingly reliant on monies from businesses that
expect a return on their dollars and researchers seeking to profit from patents
and royalties (Krimsky, Rothenberg, Stott, & Kyle, 1996). Financial conflicts are
so prevalent that the TCPS devotes an entire chapter to them. In fact, 15 per cent
of researchers report changing the design, methodology, or results of a study in
response to pressure from a funding source (Martinson, Anderson, & de Vries,
2005). Additionally, 60 per cent report direct knowledge of another researcher
who has fabricated or falsified data (Titus, Wells, & Rhoades, 2008). If such biases

come to dominate the research enterprise, psychological knowledge will be rendered invalid and lose credibility. With respect to conflict of interest in research, the Code of Ethics expects psychologists to:

So close

III.19 Carry out, present, and discuss research in a way that is consistent with a commitment to honest, open inquiry, and to clear communication of any research aims, sponsorship, social context, personal values, or financial interests that might affect or appear to affect the research.

AUTHORSHIP

The issue of appropriate credit for authorship is a frequent source of acrimony among researchers and is one of the most common complaints made by academic researchers to ethics boards. In principle, the expectations are clear, and the Code of Ethics advises us to:

So close

III.7 Take credit only for the work and ideas that they have actually done or generated, and give credit for work done or ideas contributed by others (including students), in proportion to their contribution.

In practice, personal ambition and pressures to publish often complicate the issue. If possible, agreements should be clarified well ahead of publication. The research and publication process is typically a fluid one, however, which makes such agreements difficult as the relative importance of each potential author's contribution fluctuates. The first author should be the individual who developed the research design, contributed to the writing of the manuscript, and accepts responsibility for final approval of the document. Co-authors should have contributed to the writing of the manuscript and be listed in order of their contribution to the research design or analysis of the data. If the extent of contribution among co-authors is equal, they should be listed alphabetically. In the case of publications arising out of a student's doctoral research, the student should *always* be first author because the awarding of the doctoral degree is predicated on the student having made a contribution to the field of inquiry and must therefore have developed the research design, written the dissertation, and been responsible for its final form.

A more difficult issue is the practice of assigning authorship on research papers to people who have made no contribution. This is usually done in order to gain favour with powerful people, such as chairs of academic departments, to help get an article published by including someone with an established reputation, or in arrangements whereby researchers put each other's name on a publication so that they both receive more credit than they deserve (Bennett & Taylor, 2003). It should be obvious that all such actions are improper.

REPORTING RESULTS

While it might be said that if you talk to two psychologists you will get three opinions, a consensus certainly exists that researchers must not falsify their results. The essential nature of science is that knowledge is incrementally built on the verifiable measurement of phenomena. If research results cannot be trusted, the entire scientific enterprise collapses. Thus, the reporting of research results involves potential harms to society—as opposed to strictly the participants themselves—in the form of cynicism, mistrust, and misinformation. Recent high profile cases include Harvard psychologist Marc Hauser falsifying data purporting to show that monkeys have important capacities for language, which has brought into question his other research on—ironically—the origins of morality (Johnson, 2010, 2011) and Dutch psychologist Diederik Stapel manipulating and fabricating data in at least thirty publications published in such esteemed journals as *Nature* and *Science* (Callaway, 2011). If the public ceases to trust research findings, then tax-supported funding will likely decline (as we are currently experiencing) and societal decisions will tend to be based on non-scientific sources of information (as we are also experiencing). The Code of Ethics therefore advises psychologists to:

So Close

III.9 Not suppress disconfirming evidence of their own and their colleagues' findings and views, acknowledging alternative hypotheses and explanations.

So close

III.11 Take care to communicate as completely and objectively as possible, and to clearly differentiate facts, opinions, theories, hypotheses, and ideas, when communicating knowledge, findings, and views.

III.12 Present instructional information accurately, avoiding bias in the selection and presentation of information, and publicly acknowledge any personal values or bias that influence the selection and presentation of information.

Summary

Scientists have historically been held in high esteem by Western society, and whenever they blatantly betray the public's trust, the resulting outrage has prompted tighter regulations of research activities. Although our Code of Ethics has much to say about research, psychologists who undertake research are also expected to abide by the *Tri-Council Policy Statement: Ethical Conduct for Research Involving Humans.* Fortunately, both are founded on the ethical duties of Respect for Persons, Concern for Welfare, and justice. Although not covered in the *Tri-Council Policy Statement*, the duty of fidelity (i.e., Integrity in Relationships) is central to avoiding the most common forms of scientific misconduct. Relationships and consequences relevant to research include consent (particularly when employing deception), privacy and confidentiality, children and vulnerable persons, conflicts of interest, authorship, and reporting results.

Discussion Questions

1. Do you think researchers should abide by the same ethical principles that apply to practitioners? Why or why not? Should additional ethical concepts, such as academic freedom, apply? Explain.

2. To what extent do you think that intellectual property rights undermine openness in scientific inquiry? Explain.

3. What is the difference between an actual and apparent conflict of interest and is the distinction important in the research context?

4. Do you think that animals should be protected by the Canadian Code of Ethics for Psychologists? Why or why not?

Your Reflective Journal

What are your thoughts about yourself as a researcher? How has your experience—or lack thereof—with research influenced your sense of sharing the values of a researcher? Have you experienced unethical researchers or heard stories of same? How has this influenced your attitude toward research ethics? Do you hold researchers to a higher, lower, or equal ethical standard than practitioners? Can you imagine conducting research in which you are value neutral or without any vested interest? Take some time to consider these and any other questions about research ethics that are important for you.

Case Study

So Close

You have just completed collecting your thesis data after many long months and numerous obstacles. In fact, it has taken you so long to recruit participants that you are perilously close to your program's deadline for completion, leaving you no time for further recruitment efforts. When you finally analyze your data, you find that your results are close to meeting statistical significance, but are nonetheless non-significant. Upon conducting additional analyses, you find that your sample size is insufficient to identify the effect you were testing for, even if it did exist. If you were to refrain from reporting the secondary analyses and instead write up your results as supporting your hypothesis, no one is likely to be the wiser.

- leave of secondary results to support Hyp.

- Do ~~nothing~~ ~~fill info~~

= Ask for extension to get it right

= Write rprt as is with its non significant findings.

- ~~finding~~ sample size

Case Study

Safe Youth

You want to conduct a study of condom use among adolescents. You plan to include measures of attitudes and beliefs about sexuality as well as questions about sexual activity, drug use, sports participation, gender identity, and sexual orientation. Participants are to be recruited at shopping malls near large high schools. No personally identifying information will be requested, although you will ask them their age. Potential participants will be told the nature of the research and completing the survey will be accepted as evidence of consent. No inducements or coercion will be used.

Case Study

Proposal with Potential

You have been asked to review a grant application and, as per standard practice, have agreed to maintain the confidentiality of what you review. The research design of the study is so flawed that it would not provide results of any value whatsoever. As such, you couldn't possibly recommend the research be funded as proposed. The research idea is a very clever one, however, and if the study were to be conducted using a valid design, could make a highly valuable contribution to the field. Taking the time and trouble to provide sufficient feedback to the grant applicant to make the study viable would essentially entail rewriting the entire methodology yourself, which you are quite capable of doing. In fact, you are considering revising the method and conducting the study yourself.

① Deny Grant leave alone

② Rewrite methodology wt dude in collaboration

③ Rewrite as own idea

④ Provide feedback and with him confidentiality!

Recommended Reading

Adair, J.G. (2001). Ethics of psychological research: New policies; continuing issues; new concerns. *Canadian Psychology, 42*, 25–37.

Haverkamp, B.E. (2005). Ethical perspectives on qualitative research in applied psychology. *Journal of Counseling Psychology, 52*, 146–55.

Marshall, D.T. (2000). *The law of human experimentation.* Toronto: Butterworths.

O'Neill, P. (2011). The evolution of research ethics in Canada: Current developments. *Canadian Psychology, 52*, 180–84.

References

A.C. v. Manitoba (Director of Child and Family Services) [2009], 2 S.C.R. 181.

Ackerley, G.D., Burnell, J., Holder, D.C., & Kurdek, L.A. (1988). Burnout among licensed psychologists. *Professional Psychology: Research and Practice, 19*, 624–31.

Ad Hoc Working Group on Women, Mental Health, Mental Illness and Addictions. (2006). *Women, mental health and mental illness and addiction in Canada: An overview.* Ottawa: Health Canada.

Adair, J.G. (2001). Ethics of psychological research: New policies; continuing issues; new concerns. *Canadian Psychology, 42*, 25–37.

Addis, M.E., & Mahalik, J.R. (2003). Men, masculinity, and the contexts of help seeking. *American Psychologist, 58*, 5–14.

Adelman, H.S., Lusk, R., Alvarez, V., & Acosta, N.K. (1985). Competence of minors to understand, evaluate, and communicate about their psycho-educational problems. *Professional Psychology: Research and Practice, 16*, 426–34.

Akamatsu, T.J. (1988). Intimate relationships with former clients: National survey of attitudes and behavior among practitioners. *Professional Psychology: Research and Practice, 19*, 454–58.

Alexopoulos, G. (2005). Depression in the elderly. *The Lancet, 365*, 1961–70.

Ambady, N., LaPlante, D., Nguyen, T., Rosenthal, R., Chaumeton, N., & Levinson, W. (2002). Surgeons' tone of voice: A clue to malpractice history. *Surgery, 132*, 5–9.

Anderson, S.K., & Kitchener, K.S. (1998). Nonsexual posttherapy relationships: A conceptual framework to assess ethical risks. *Professional Psychology: Research and Practice, 29*, 91–99.

Artman, L.K., & Daniels, J.A. (2010). Disability and psychotherapy practice: Cultural competence and practical tips. *Professional Psychology: Research and Practice, 41*, 442–48.

Association of State and Provincial Psychology Boards. (2005). *ASPPB Code of Conduct.* Peachtree City, GA: Author. Available at www.asppb.org.

Austin, W., Bergum, V. & Dossetor, J.B. (2003). Relational ethics: An action ethic as foundation for health care. In V. Tshudin. (Ed.), *Approaches to ethics* (pp. 45–52). Woburn, MA: Butterworth-Heinemann.

Austin, W., Bergum, V., Nuttgens, S., & Peternelj-Taylor, C. (2006). A re-visioning of boundaries in professional helping relationships: Exploring other metaphors. *Ethics & Behavior*, 16, 77–94.

Austin, W., Rankel, M., Kagan, L., Bergum, V., & Lemermeyer, G. (2005). To stay or to go, to speak or stay silent, to act or not to act: Moral distress as experienced by psychologists. *Ethics & Behavior*, 15, 197–212.

Axelson, J.A. (1993). *Counseling and development in a multicultural society* (2nd ed.). Pacific Grove, CA: Brooks/Cole.

Bandura, A. (2002). Selective moral disengagement in the exercise of moral agency. *Journal of Moral Education*, 31, 101–19.

Bassiouni, M.C., Baffes, T.G., & Evrard, J.T. (1981). An appraisal of human experimentation in international law and practice: The need for international regulation of human experimentation. *Journal of Criminal Law & Criminology*, 72, 1597–666.

Baumrind, D. (1964). Some thoughts on the ethics of research: After reading Milgram's "Behavioral Study of Obedience." *American Psychologist*, 19, 421–23.

Bazelon, D.L. (1982). Veils, values, and social responsibility. *American Psychologist*, 37, 115–21.

Beauchamp, T.L., & Childress, J.F. (2012). *Principles of biomedical ethics*. Oxford, UK: Oxford University Press.

Beckman, H.B., Markakis, K.M., Suchman, A.L., & Frankel, R.M. (1994). The doctor-patient relationship and malpractice. Lessons from plaintiff depositions. *Archives of Internal Medicine*, 154, 1365–70.

Bendixen, L.D., Schraw, G., & Dunkle, M.E. (1998). Epistemic beliefs and moral reasoning. *The Journal of Psychology*, 132, 187–200.

Bennett, D.M., & Taylor, D. McD. (2003). Unethical practices in authorship of scientific papers. *Emergency Medicine*, 15, 263–70.

Berg, M.B., Mimiaga, M.J. & Safren, S.A. (2008). Mental health concerns of gay and bisexual men seeking mental health services. *Journal of Homosexuality*, 54, 293–306.

Bergum, V., & Dossetor, J. (2005). *Relational ethics: The full meaning of respect*. Hagerstown, MD: University Publishing Group.

Berry, J. (1997). Immigration, acculturation, and adaptation. *Applied Psychology: An International Review*, 46, 5–68.

Betan, E.J., & Stanton, A.L. (1999). Fostering ethical willingness: Integrating emotional and contextual awareness with rational analysis. *Professional Psychology: Research & Practice*, 30, 295–301.

Bieschke, K.J., & Dendy, A.K. (2010). Using the ethical acculturation model as a framework for attaining competence to work with clients who identify as sexual minorities. *Professional Psychology: Research and Practice*, 41, 429–31.

Bogner, H.R., de Vries, H.F., Maulik, P.K., & Unützer, J. (2009). Mental health services use: Baltimore epidemiological catchment area follow-up. *American Journal of Geriatric Psychiatry*, 17, 706–15.

Bois, J.S.A. (1948). The certification of psychologists in Canada. *Canadian Journal of Psychology*, 2, 1–13.

Bonitz, V. (2008). Use of physical touch in the "talking cure": A journey to the outskirts of psychotherapy. *Psychotherapy: Theory, Research, Practice, Training*, 45, 391–404.

Bouhoutsos, J., Holroyd, J., Lerman, H., Forer, B.R., & Greenberg, M. (1983). Sexual intimacy between psychotherapists and patients. *Professional Psychology: Research and Practice*, 14, 185–96.

Bowman, M.L. (2000). The diversity of diversity: Canadian-American differences and their implications for clinical training and APA accreditation. *Canadian Psychology, 41*, 230–43.

Boychyn v. Abbey (2001), O.J. No. 4503.

Brabeck, M.M. (2000). *Practicing feminist ethics in psychology.* Washington, DC: American Psychological Association.

Bram, A.D. (1995). The physically ill or dying psychotherapist: A review of ethical and clinical considerations. *Psychotherapy, 32*, 568–80.

Brenner, G.H. (2010). The expected psychiatric impact of detention in Guantanamo Bay, Cuba, and related considerations. *Journal of Trauma & Dissociation, 11*, 469–87.

Brezis, M., Israel, S., Weinstein-Birenshtock, A., Pogoda, P., Sharon, A., & Tauber, R. (2008). Quality of informed consent for invasive procedures. *International Journal for Quality in Health Care, 20*, 352–57.

Brown, L.S. (1997). The private practice of subversion: Psychology as *tikkun olam. American Psychologist, 52*, 449–62.

Burger, J.M. (2009). Replicating Milgram: Would people still obey today? *American Psychologist, 64*, 1–11.

Cacioppo, J.T. (2002). Social neuroscience: Understanding the pieces fosters understanding the whole and vice versa. *American Psychologist, 57*, 819–31.

Callaway, E. (2011). Report finds massive fraud at Dutch universities. *Nature, 479*, 15.

Canadian Institutes of Health Research, Natural Sciences and Engineering Research Council of Canada, & Social Sciences and Humanities Research Council of Canada. (1998). *Tri-council policy statement: ethical conduct for research involving humans* (with 2000, 2002, 2005 amendments). Ottawa: Public Works and Government Services Canada.

Canadian Institutes of Health Research, Natural Sciences and Engineering Research Council of Canada, & Social Sciences and Humanities Research Council of Canada. (2010). *Tri-council policy statement: ethical conduct for research involving humans* (2nd ed.). Ottawa: Public Works and Government Services Canada.

Canadian Institutes of Health Research, Natural Sciences and Engineering Research Council of Canada, & Social Sciences and Humanities Research Council of Canada. (2011). *Tri-agency research integrity policy.* Ottawa: Public Works and Government Services Canada.

Canadian Psychological Association. (1986). *CPA policy for agreement between the Canadian Psychological Association and provincial/territorial regulatory bodies and voluntary associations with respect to the investigation and adjudication of complaints regarding professional conduct.* Ottawa: Author.

Canadian Psychological Association. (1990). *Rules and procedures for dealing with ethical complaints.* Ottawa: Author.

Canadian Psychological Association. (2000). *Canadian code of ethics for psychologists* (3rd ed.). Ottawa: Author.

Canadian Psychological Association. (2001a). *Practice guidelines for providers of psychological services.* Ottawa: Author.

Canadian Psychological Association. (2001b). *Guidelines for non-discriminatory practice.* Ottawa: Author.

Canadian Psychological Association. (2007a). *Guidelines for ethical psychological practice with women.* Ottawa: Author.

Canadian Psychological Association. (2007b). *Guidelines for professional practice for school psychologists in Canada.* Ottawa: Author.

Canadian Psychological Association. (2009). *Ethical decision making in supervision: Teaching, research, practice, and administration.* Ottawa: Author.

Carnahan v. Coates (1990), 47 B.C.L.R. (2d) 127.

Cassileth, B.R., Zupkis, R.V., Sutton-Smith, K., & March, V. (1980). Informed consent— Why are its goals imperfectly realized? *New England Journal of Medicine, 302,* 896–900.

Castonguay, L.G., Boswell, J.F., Constantino, M.J., Goldfried, M.R., & Hill, C.E. (2010). Training implications of harmful effects of psychological treatments. *American Psychologist, 65,* 34–49.

Charter of Rights and Freedoms, 46 (as amended) Part I of the Constitution Act, 1982, being schedule B of the Canada Act 1982 (U.K.) 1982, c.11.

Chesler, P. (1972). *Women and madness.* Garden City, NY: Doubleday.

Cheung, F.M., van de Vijver, F.J., & Leong, F.T.L. (2011). Toward a new approach to the study of personality in culture. *American Psychologist, 66,* 593–603.

Church, E., Pettifor, J.L., Malone, J. (2006). Evolving Canadian guidelines for therapy and counselling with women. *Feminism & Psychology, 16,* 259–71.

Clark, C.R. (1993). Social responsibility ethics: Doing right, doing good, doing well. *Ethics & Behavior, 3,* 303–27.

Collins, P.A., & Hays, M.V. (2007). Twenty years since Ottawa and Epp: Researchers' reflections on challenges, gains and future prospects for reducing health inequities in Canada. *Health Promotion International, 22,* 337–45.

Cornish, J.A.E., Gorgens, K., Olkin, R., Palombi, B.J., & Abels, A.V. (2008). Perspectives on ethical practice with people who have disabilities. *Professional Psychology: Research & Practice, 39,* 488–97.

Cottone, R.R. & Claus, R.E. (2000). Ethical decision-making models: A review of the literature. *Journal of Counseling & Development, 78,* 275–83.

Council of Canadian Academies. (2010). *Honesty, accountability and trust: Fostering research integrity in Canada/Expert Panel on Research Integrity.* Ottawa: Author.

Cowen, E.L. (1977). Baby steps toward primary prevention. *American Journal of Community Psychology, 5,* 1–22.

Cox, D., La Caze, M., & Levine, M.P. (2003). *Integrity and the fragile self.* Burlington, VT: Ashgate.

Craig, C.D., & Sprang, G. (2010). Compassion satisfaction, compassion fatigue, and burnout in a national sample of trauma treatment therapists. *Anxiety, Stress and Coping, 23,* 319–39.

Craigie, J. (2011). Thinking and feeling: Moral deliberation in a dual-process framework. *Philosophical Psychology, 24,* 53–71.

Criminal Code of Canada, R.S.C. c.C–46 (1985).

Crits v. Sylvester (1956), 1 D.L.R. (2d) 502.

Daniels, A.S., & Walter, D.A. (2002). Current issues in continuing education for contemporary behavioral health practice. *Administration and Policy in Mental Health, 29,* 359–76.

Daniels, N. (1985). *Just health care.* Cambridge: Cambridge University Press.

Danzinger, P.R., & Welfel, E.R. (2000). Age, gender and health bias in counselors: An empirical analysis. *Journal of Applied Mental Health Counseling, 22,* 135–49.

Davis, D., O'Brien, M.T., Freemantle, N., Wolf, F.M., Mazmanian, P., & Taylor-Vaisey, A. (1999). Impact of formal continuing medical education: Do conferences, workshops, rounds, and other traditional continuing education activities change physician behavior or health care outcomes? *Journal of the American Medical Association, 282,* 867–74.

De Maio, F.G., & Kemp, E. (2010). The deterioration of health status among immigrants to Canada. *Global Public Health, 5,* 462–78.

Diamond, M. (1984). Sexuality and the handicapped. In R.P. Marinelli & A.E. Dell Orto (Eds.), *The psychological and social impact of physical disability* (2nd ed., pp. 207–19). New York: Springer.

Dillon, F.R., Worthington, R.L., Soth-McNett, A.M., & Schwartz, S.J. (2008). Gender and sexual identity-based predictors of lesbian, gay, and bisexual affirmative counseling self-efficacy. *Professional Psychology: Research & Practice, 39,* 353–60.

Disch, E., & Avery, N. (2001). Sex in the consulting room, the examining room, and the sacristy: Survivors of sexual abuse by professionals. *American Journal of Orthopsychiatry, 71,* 204–17.

Dunbar, J. (1998). A critical history of CPA's various codes of ethics for psychologists. *Canadian Psychology, 39,* 177–86.

Eisel v. Board of Education, 324 Md. 376, 597 A.2d 447 (Md. Ct. App. 1991).

Evans, D.R. (2011). Law, standards, and ethics in the practice of psychology. In D.R. Evans (Ed.), *The law, standards, and ethics in the practice of psychology* (3rd ed., pp. 1–19). Toronto: Carswell.

Farber, B.A., & Heifetz, L.J. (1982). The process and dimensions of burnout in psycho-therapists. *Professional Psychology, 13,* 293–301.

Farberman, R.K. (1997). Public attitudes about psychologists and mental health care: Research to guide the American Psychological Association public education campaign. *Professional Psychology: Research and Practice, 28,* 128–36.

Fielding, S.L. (1999). *The Practice of uncertainty: Voices of physicians and patients in medical malpractice claims.* Westport, CT: Auburn House.

Figley, C.R. (2002). Compassion fatigue: Psychotherapists' chronic lack of self care. *Journal of Clinical Psychology, 58,* 1433–41.

Fischer, C.T. (1968). Ethical issues in the use of human subjects. *American Psychologist, 23,* 532.

Fischer, K.W., Stein, Z., & Heikkinen, K. (2009). Narrow assessments misrepresent development and misguide policy: Comment on Steinberg, Cauffman, Woolard, Graham, and Banich. *American Psychologist, 64,* 595–600.

Fisher, C.D. (2004). Ethical issues in therapy: Therapist self-disclosure of sexual feelings. *Ethics & Behavior, 14,* 105–21.

Fitchett, G., Burton, L.A., & Sivan, A.B. (1997). The religious needs and resources of psychiatric patients. *Journal of Nervous and Mental Disease, 185,* 320–26.

Fitzgerald, M.H. (2004). Punctuated equilibrium, moral panics and the ethics review process. *Journal of Academic Ethics, 2*, 315–38.

Fontigny, N. (1996). When yes really means yes: The law of informed consent in Canada revisited. *Health Law Review, 4*, 17–22.

Fowers, B.J., & Davidov, B.J. (2006). The virtue of multiculturalism: Personal transformation, character, and openness to the other. *American Psychologist, 61*, 581–94.

Fowers, B.J., & Richardson, F.C. (1996). Why is multiculturalism good? *American Psychologist, 51*, 609–21.

Gabbard, G.O., Kassaw, K.A., & Perez-Garcia, G. (2011). Professional boundaries in the era of the Internet. *Academic Psychiatry, 35*, 168–74.

Garland, J.C. (2011). Regulation of psychology in Newfoundland and Labrador: 1985 to present. In D.R. Evans (Ed.), *The law, standards, and ethics in the practice of psychology* (3rd ed., pp. 57–81). Toronto: Carswell.

Garnets, L.D., Herek, G.M., & Levy, B. (2003). Violence and victimization of lesbians and gay men: Mental health consequences. In L.D. Garnets & D.C. Kimmel (Eds.), *Psychological perspectives on lesbian, gay, and bisexual experiences* (pp. 188–206). New York: Columbia University Press.

Glaser, R.D., & Thorpe, J.S. (1986). Unethical intimacy: A survey of sexual contact and advances between psychology educators and female graduate students. *American Psychologist, 41*, 43–51.

Gottlieb, M.C., Robinson, K., & Younggren, J.N. (2007). Multiple relations in supervision: Guidance for administrators, supervisors, and students. *Professional Psychology: Research and Practice, 38*, 241–47.

Government of Canada. (1994). *Agreement on internal trade.* Ottawa: Author.

Government of Canada. (2009). *Agreement on internal trade, ninth amendment.* Ottawa: Author.

Grisso, T., & Vierling, I. (1978). Minors' consent to treatment: A developmental perspective. *Professional Psychology, 9*, 412–37.

Gutheil, T.G., & Gabbard, G.O. (1993). The concept of boundaries in clinical practice: Theoretical and risk-management dimensions. *American Journal of Psychiatry, 150*, 188–96.

Guy, J.D., Poelstra, P.L., & Stark, M.J. (1989). Personal distress and therapeutic effectiveness: National survey of psychologists practicing psychotherapy. *Professional Psychology: Research and Practice, 20*, 48–50.

Guy, J.D., & Souder, J.K. (1986). Impact of therapists' illness or accident on psychotherapeutic practice: Review and discussion. *Professional Psychology: Research and Practice, 17*, 509–13.

Hass, L.J., & Malouff, J.L. (1995). *Keeping up the good work: A practitioner's guide to mental health ethics* (2nd ed.). Sarasota, FL: Professional Resource Press.

Haas, L.J., Malouf, J.L., & Mayerson, N.H. (1988). Personal and professional characteristics as factors in psychologists' ethical decision making. *Professional Psychology: Research and Practice, 19*, 35–42.

Hage, S.M., & Kenny, M.E. (2009). Promoting a social justice approach to prevention: Future directions for training, practice, and research. *Journal of Primary Prevention, 30*, 75–87.

Hahn, W.K. (1998). Gifts in psychotherapy: An intersubjective approach to patient gifts. *Psychotherapy: Theory, Research, Practice, Training, 35*, 78–86.

Haidt, J. (2001). The emotional dog and its rational tail: A social intuitionist approach to
    moral judgment. *Psychological Review, 108*, 814–34.

Haines v. Bellissimo [1977], 18 O.R. (2d) 177.

Hamberger, L.K. (2000). Requests for complete record release: A three-step protocol.
    Psychotherapy: Theory, Research, Practice, Training, 37, 89–97.

Hays, P.A. (1996). Addressing the complexities of culture and gender in counseling.
    Journal of Counseling & Development, 74, 332–38.

Helbok, C.M., Marinelli, R.P., & Walls, R.T. (2006). National survey of ethical practices across
    rural and urban communities. *Professional Psychology: Research and Practice, 37*, 36–44.

Helms, E. & Gee, S. (2003). Attitudes of Australian therapists toward older clients:
    Educational and training imperatives. *Educational Gerontology, 29*, 657–70.

Helms, J.E., & Talleyrand, R.M. (1997). Race is not ethnicity. *American Psychologist, 52*, 1246–47.

Henretty, J.R., & Levitt, H.M. (2010). The role of therapist self-disclosure in psychotherapy:
    A qualitative review. *Clinical Psychology Review, 30*, 63–77.

Herek, G.M., & Garnets, L.D. (2007). Sexual orientation and mental health. *Annual Review
    of Clinical Psychology, 3*, 353–75.

Hickson, G.B., Clayton, E.W., Entman, S.S., Miller, C.S., Githens, P.B., Whetten-Goldstein, K.,
    & Sloan, F.A. (1994). Obstetricians' prior malpractice experience and patients' satisfaction
    with care. *Journal of the American Medical Association, 272*, 1583–87.

Holroyd, J.C., & Brodsky, A.M. (1977). Psychologists' attitudes and practices regarding erotic
    and nonerotic physical contact with patients. *American Psychologist, 32*, 843–49.

I.G. v. Rusch (1999), B.C.J. No. 2999.

Ibrahim, F.A. (1996). A multicultural perspective on principle and virtue ethics.
    Counseling Psychologist, 24, 78–85.

J.S.C. and C.H.C. v. Wren (1986), 76 A.R 115 (Alta. C.A.).

Jennings, F.L. (1992). Ethics of rural practice. *Psychotherapy in Private Practice, 10*, 85–104.

Jensen, R. (1979). Competent professional service in psychology: The real issue behind
    continuing education. *Professional Psychology, 10*, 381–89.

Johnson, C.Y. (2010, August 10). Author on leave after Harvard inquiry: Investigation
    of scientist's work finds evidence of misconduct, prompts retraction by journal.
    The Boston Globe. Retrieved from http://www.boston.com/news/education/higher/
    articles/2010/08/10/author_on_leave_after_harvard_inquiry/.

Johnson, C.Y. (2011, July 20). Embattled Harvard professor resigns. *The Boston Globe.*
    Retrieved from http://www.boston.com/news/education/higher/articles/2011/07/20/
    embattled_professor_resigns_harvard_post/.

Johnson-Greene, D. (2007). Evolving standards for informed consent: Is it time for an
    individualized and flexible approach? *Professional Psychology: Research and Practice,
    38*, 183–84.

Jones, E.E. (1982). Psychotherapists' impressions of treatment outcome as a function of race.
    Journal of Clinical Psychology, 38, 722–31.

Jones, J.H. (1981). *Bad blood: The Tuskegee syphilis experiment.* New York: Free Press.

Jureidini, J. (1988). Psychotherapeutic implications of severe physical disability. *American
    Journal of Psychotherapy, 42*, 297–307.

Kahneman, D., & Klein, G. (2009). Conditions for intuitive expertise: A failure to disagree. *American Psychologist, 64,* 515–26.

Kakkad, D. (2005). A new ethical praxis: Psychologists' emerging responsibilities in issues of social justice. *Ethics & Behavior, 15,* 293–308.

Kapp, M.B. (2006). Patient autonomy in the age of consumer-driven health care: Informed consent and informed choice. *Journal of Health & Biomedical Law, 2,* 1–31.

Kaser-Boyd, N., Adelman, H.S., & Taylor, L. (1985). Minors' ability to identify risks and benefits of therapy. *Professional Psychology: Research and Practice, 16,* 411–17.

Kaslow, N.J., Grus, C.L., Campbell, L.F., Fouad, N.A., Hatcher, R.L., & Rodolfa, E.R. (2009). Competency assessment toolkit for professional psychology. *Training and Education in Professional Psychology, 3,* S27–S45.

Kastenbaum, R. (1963). The reluctant therapist. *Geriatrics, 18,* 296–301.

Katz, I., Hass, R.G., & Bailey, J. (1988). Attitudinal ambivalence and behavior toward people with disabilities. In H.E. Yuker (Ed.), *Attitudes toward persons with disabilities* (pp. 47–57). New York: Springer.

Katz, J. (1972). *Experimentation with human beings: The authority of the investigator, subject, profession, and state in the human experimentation process.* New York: Russell Sage.

Kaufmann, H. (1967). The price of obedience and the price of knowledge. *American Psychologist, 22,* 321–22.

Keith-Spiegel, P. (1977). Violation of ethical principles due to ignorance or poor professional judgment versus willful disregard. *Professional Psychology, 8,* 288–96.

Kelly v. Hazlett (1976), 15 O.R. (2d) 290 (H.C.).

Kelly, L. (1987). The continuum of sexual violence. In J. Hanmer & M. Maynard (Eds.), *Women, violence and social control* (pp. 46–60). Basingstoke, UK: Macmillan.

Kemp, N.T., & Mallinckrodt, B. (1996). Impact of professional training on case conceptualization of clients with a disability. *Professional Psychology: Research and Practice, 27,* 378–85.

Kendler, H.H. (1999). The role of value in the world of psychology. *American Psychologist, 54,* 828–35.

Kirkland, K., Kirkland, K.L, & Reaves, R.P. (2004). On the professional use of disciplinary data. *Professional Psychology: Research and Practice, 35,* 179–84.

Kirmayer, L.J., Brass, G.M., & Tait, C.L. (2000). The mental health of Aboriginal peoples: Transformations of identity and community. *Canadian Journal of Psychiatry, 45,* 607–16.

Kitchener, K.S. (1984). Intuition, critical evaluation and ethical principles: The foundation for ethical decisions in counseling psychology. *The Counseling Psychologist, 12,* 43–55.

Klinger, J. (1999). Suicide among seniors. *Australasian Journal on Ageing, 18,* 114–18.

Kluge, E.W. (1992). *Biomedical ethics in a Canadian context.* Scarborough, ON: Prentice-Hall.

Knox, S., Dubois, R., Smith, J., Hess, S.A., & Hill, C.E. (2009). Clients' experiences giving gifts to therapists. *Psychotherapy: Theory, Research, Practice, Training, 46,* 350–61.

Koltko-Rivera, M.E. (2004). The psychology of worldviews. *Review of General Psychology, 8,* 3–58.

Koocher, G.P. (1979). Credentialing in psychology: Close encounters with competence? *American Psychologist, 34,* 696–702.

Krimsky, S., Rothenberg, L.S., Stott, P., & Kyle, G. (1996). Financial interests of authors in scientific journals: A pilot study of 14 publications. *Science and Engineering Ethics, 2*, 395–410.

Lagana, L., & Shanks, S. (2002). Mutual biases underlying the problematic relationship between older adults and mental health providers: Any solution in sight? *International Journal of Aging and Human Development, 55*, 271–95.

Laliotis, D.A., & Grayson, J.H. (1985). Psychologist heal thyself: What is available for the impaired psychologist? *American Psychologist, 40*, 84–96.

Larkin, J., & Caplan, P. (1992). The gatekeeping process of the DSM. *Canadian Journal of Community Mental Health, 11*, 17–28.

Law, J. (2006). *Big Pharma: Exposing the global healthcare agenda*. New York: Carroll & Graf.

Leigh, I.W., Smith, I.L., Bebeau, M.J., Lichtenberg, J.W., Nelson, P.D., Portnoy, S., Rubin, N.J., & Kaslow, N.J. (2007). Competency assessment models. *Professional Psychology: Research and Practice, 38*, 463–73.

Levant, R.F. (2011). Research in the psychology of men and masculinity using the gender role strain paradigm as a framework. *American Psychologist, 66*, 765–76.

Levinson, W., Roter, D.L., Mullooly, J.P., Dull, V.T., & Frankel, R.M. (1997). Physician-patient communication: The relationship with malpractice claims among primary care physicians and surgeons. *Journal of the American Medical Association, 277*, 553–59.

Lewis, C.C. (1981). How adolescents approach decisions: Changes over grades seven to twelve and policy implications. *Child Development, 52*, 538–44.

Lichtenberg, J.W., Portnoy, S.M., Bebeau, M.J., Leigh, I.W., Nelson, P.D., Rubin, N.J., Smith, I.L., & Kaslow, N.J. (2007). Challenges to the assessment of competence and competencies. *Professional Psychology: Research and Practice, 38*, 474–47.

Lilienfeld, S.O. (2007). Psychological treatments that cause harm. *Perspectives on Psychological Science, 2*, 53–70.

Liu, W.M., Ali, S.R., Soleck, G., Hopps, J., Dunston, K., & Pickett, T., Jr. (2004). Using social class in counseling psychology research. *Journal of Counseling Psychology, 51*, 3–18.

Lytton, H. (1996). "This is how it's always been done": The treatment of academic misconduct in Canada. *Canadian Journal of Sociology, 21*, 223–35.

Mahoney, M. (1997). Psychotherapists' personal problems and self-care patterns. *Professional Psychology: Research and Practice, 28*, 14–16.

Malone, J.L., & Dyck, K.G. (2011). Professional ethics in rural and northern Canadian psychology. *Canadian Psychology, 52*, 206–14.

Mann, L., Harmoni, R., & Power, C. (1989). Adolescent decision-making: The development of competence. *Journal of Adolescence, 12*, 265–78.

Markus, H.R. (2008). Pride, prejudice, and ambivalence: Toward a unified theory of race and ethnicity. *American Psychologist, 63*, 651–70.

Martinson, B.C., Anderson, M.S., & de Vries, R. (2005). Scientists behaving badly. *Nature, 435*, 737–38.

Maton, K.I. (2000). Making a difference: The social ecology of social transformation. *American Journal of Community Psychology, 28*, 25–57.

McCord, J. (2003). Cures that harm: Unanticipated outcomes of crime prevention programs. *Annals of the American Academy of Political and Social Science, 587*, 16–30.

McCormick, R., & France, M.H. (1995). Counselling First Nations clients on career issues: Implications for the school counsellor. *Guidance and Counselling, 10,* 27–30.

McDonald, M. (2009). From code to policy statement: Creating Canadian policy for ethical research involving humans. *Health Law Review, 17,* 12–25.

McGuire, J. (2004). Minimising harm in violence risk assessment: Practical solutions to ethical problems? *Health, Risk & Society, 6,* 327–45.

McInerney v. MacDonald (1992), 12 C.C.L.T. (2d) 255 (SCC).

McNeil-Haber, F.M. (2004). Ethical considerations in the use of nonerotic touch in psychotherapy with children. *Ethics & Behavior, 14,* 123–40.

McMillan, A.D. (1995). *Native peoples and cultures of Canada.* Vancouver: Douglas & McIntyre.

Mello, M.M., & Brennan, T.A. (2002). Deterrence of medical errors: Theory and evidence for malpractice reform. *Texas Law Review, 80,* 1595–1637.

Merali, N. (1999). Resolution of value conflicts in multicultural counselling. *Canadian Journal of Counselling, 33,* 28–36.

Milgram, S. (1963). Behavioral study of obedience. *Journal of Abnormal and Social Psychology, 67,* 371–78.

Milgram, S. (1964). Issues in the study of obedience: A reply to Baumrind. *American Psychologist, 19,* 848–52.

Miller, D.J., & Thelen, M.H. (1986). Knowledge and beliefs about confidentiality in psychotherapy. *Professional Psychology: Research and Practice, 17,* 15–19.

Miller, J.B. (1986). *Toward a new psychology of women* (2nd ed.). Boston: Beacon.

Minuchin, S. (1974). *Families and family therapy.* Cambridge, MA: Harvard University Press.

Minuchin, S., Montalvo, B., Guerney, B., Rosman, B., & Schumer, F. (1967). *Families of the slums: An exploration of their structure and treatment.* New York: Basic Books.

Mixon, D. (1972). Instead of deception. *Journal for the Theory of Social Behavior, 2,* 145–77.

Moggi, F., Brodbeck, J., & Hirsbrunner, H.-P. (2000). Therapist-patient sexual involvement: Risk factors and consequences. *Clinical Psychology and Psychotherapy, 7,* 54–60.

Murstein, B.I., & Fontaine, P.A. (1993). The public's knowledge about psychologists and other mental health professionals. *American Psychologist, 48,* 839–45.

N.V. v. Blank (1988), O.J. No. 2544.

Nachmani, I., & Somer, E. (2007). Women sexually victimized in psychotherapy speak out: The dynamics and outcome of therapist-client sex. *Women & Therapy, 30,* 1–17.

National Council of Welfare. (2006). *Poverty profile 2002 and 2003.* Ottawa: Minister of Public Works and Government Services Canada.

Neimeyer, G.J., Taylor, J.M., & Wear, D.M. (2009). Continuing education in psychology: Outcomes, evaluations, and mandates. *Professional Psychology: Research and Practice, 40,* 617–24.

Nelson G., & Prilleltensky, I. (2010). *Community psychology: In pursuit of liberation and well-being.* New York: Palgrave Macmillan.

Norko, M.A., & Baranoski, M.V. (2005). The state of contemporary risk assessment research. *Canadian Journal of Psychiatry, 50,* 18–26.

Nuremberg Code. (1949). *Trials of war criminals before the Nuremberg military tribunals under control council law,* No. 10, Vol. 2, pp. 181–82. Washington, DC: US Government Printing Office.

Ochsner, K.N., & Lieberman, M.D. (2001). The emergence of social cognitive neuroscience. *American Psychologist, 56,* 717–34.

Olkin, R. (2007). Disability-affirmative therapy and case formulation: A template for understanding disability in a clinical context. *Counseling & Human Development, 39,* 1–20.

O'Neil, J.M. (2008). Summarizing 25 years of research on men's gender role conflict using the Gender Role Conflict Scale: New research paradigms and clinical implications. *The Counseling Psychologist, 36,* 358–445.

O'Neill, P. (1989). Responsible to whom? Responsible for what? Some ethical issues in community intervention. *American Journal of Community Psychology, 17,* 323–41.

O'Neill, P. (1998). *Negotiating consent in psychotherapy.* New York: New York University Press.

O'Neill, P. (2011). The evolution of research ethics in Canada: Current developments. *Canadian Psychology, 52,* 180–84.

O'Neill, P., & Hern, R. (1991). A systems approach to ethical problems. *Ethics & Behavior, 1,* 129–43.

Orchowski, L.M., Spickard, B.A., & McNamara, J.R. (2006). Cinema and the valuing of psychotherapy: Implications for clinical practice. *Professional Psychology: Research and Practice, 37,* 506–14.

Overholser, J.C., & Fine, M.A. (1990). Defining the boundaries of professional competence: Managing subtle cases of clinical incompetence. *Professional Psychology: Research and Practice, 21,* 462–69.

Owen, P.R., & Zwahr-Castro, J. (2007). Boundary issues in academia: Student perceptions of faculty–student boundary crossings. *Ethics & Behavior, 17,* 117–29.

P.H.P. v. Hillingdon London Borough (1998), E.W.J. No. 2953.

Pascual-Leone, A., Singh, T., & Scoboria, A. (2010). Using deception ethically: Practical research guidelines for researchers and reviewers. *Canadian Psychology, 51,* 241–48.

Pelletier, J.R., Rogers, E.S., & Dellario, D.J. (1985). Barriers to the provision of mental health services to individuals with severe physical disability. *Journal of Counseling Psychology, 32,* 422–30.

Perry, G. (2012). *Behind the shock machine: The untold story of the notorious Milgram psychology experiments.* Victoria, Australia: Scribe.

Pettifor, J.L., & Sawchuk, T. (2006). Psychologists' perceptions of ethically troubling incidents across international borders. *International Journal of Psychology, 41,* 216–25.

Pope, J.F., & Arthur, N. (2009). Socioeconomic status and class: A challenge for the practice of psychology in Canada. *Canadian Psychology, 50,* 55–65.

Pope, K.S. (1990a). Therapist-patient sexual involvement: A review of the research. *Clinical Psychology Review, 10,* 477–90.

Pope, K.S. (1990b). Identifying and implementing ethical standards for primary prevention. *Prevention in Human Services, 8,* 43–64.

Pope, K.S. (2011a). Are the American Psychological Association's detainee interrogation policies ethical and effective? Key claims, documents, and results. *The Journal of Psychology, 219,* 150–58.

Pope, K.S. (2011b). Psychologists and detainee interrogations: Key decisions, opportunities lost, and lessons learned. *Annual Review of Clinical Psychology, 7,* 459–81.

Pope, K.S., & Gutheil, T.G. (2009). Psychologists abandon the Nuremberg ethic: Concerns for detainee interrogations. *International Journal of Law and Psychiatry, 32,* 161–66.

Pope, K.S., Levenson, H., & Schover, L.R. (1979). Sexual intimacy in psychology training: Results and implications of a national survey. *American Psychologist, 34,* 682–89.

Prilleltensky, I. (1989). Psychology and the status quo. *American Psychologist, 44,* 795–802.

Prilleltensky, I. (1990). Enhancing the social ethics of psychology: Toward a psychology at the service of social change. *Canadian Psychology, 31,* 310–19.

Prilleltensky, I. (1994). Empowerment in mainstream psychology: Legitimacy, obstacles, and possibilities. *Canadian Psychology, 35,* 358–75.

Qualls, S.H., Segal, D., Norman, S., Neiderhe, G., & Gallagher-Thompson, D. (2002). Psychologists in practice with older adults: Current patterns, sources of training and need for further education. *Professional Psychology: Research and Practice, 33,* 435–42.

R. v. R. (K.A.) (1993), 121 N.S.R. (2d) 242.

R.G. v. Christison (1996), S.J. No. 702.

Raphael, D. (2004). *Social determinants of health: Canadian perspectives.* Toronto: Canadian Scholars' Press.

Raquepaw, J., & Miller, R.S. (1989). Psychotherapist burnout: A componential analysis. *Professional Psychology: Research and Practice, 20,* 32–36.

Rawls, J. (1971). *A theory of justice.* Cambridge, MA: Harvard University Press.

Reibl v. Hughes (1980), 14 C.C.L.T. 1 (S.C.C.).

Rest, J.R. (1984). Research on moral development: Implications for training counseling psychologists. *The Counseling Psychologist, 12,* 19–29.

Rest, J.R., & Narváez, D. (1994). *Moral development in the professions: Psychology and applied ethics.* Hillsdale, NJ: Erlbaum.

Reutter, L.I., Veenstra, G., Stewart, M.J., Raphael, D., Love, R., Makwarimba, E., & McMurray, S. (2006). Public attributions for poverty in Canada. *Canadian Review of Sociology & Anthropology, 43,* 1–22.

Reynolds, S. (2006). A neurocognitive model of the ethical decision-making process: Implications for study and practice. *Journal of Applied Psychology, 91,* 737–48.

Rhule, D.M. (2005). Take care to do no harm: Harmful interventions for youth problem behavior. *Professional Psychology: Research and Practice, 36,* 618–25.

Rice, M.E., Harris, G.T., & Quinsey, V.L. (2002). The appraisal of violence risk. *Current Opinion in Psychiatry, 15,* 589–93.

Rivers, I., & D'Augelli, A.R. (2001). The victimization of gay, lesbian, and bisexual youths. In A.R. D'Augelli & C.J. Patterson (Eds.), *Lesbian, gay, and bisexual identities and youth: Psychological perspectives* (pp. 199–223). New York: Oxford University Press.

Robertson, L.H. (2006). The residential school experience: Syndrome or historic trauma. *Pimatisiwin: A Journal of Aboriginal and Indigenous Community Health, 4,* 1–28.

Robinson, D.N. (1984). Ethics and advocacy. *American Psychologist, 39,* 787–93.

Robinson, T.L. (1999). The intersections of dominant discourses across race, gender, and other identities. *Journal of Counseling & Development, 77,* 73–79.

Rogerson, M.D., Gottlieb, M.C., Handelsman, M.H., Knapp, S., & Youngren, J. (2011). Nonrational processes in ethical decision making. *American Psychologist, 66,* 614–23.

Rosenberg, A., & Heimberg, R.G. (2009). Ethical issues in mentoring doctoral students in clinical psychology. *Cognitive and behavioral practice*, 16, 181–90.

Ross, N.A., Wolfson, M.C., Dunn, J.R., Berthelot, J.M., Kaplan, G.A., & Lynch, J.W. (2000). Relation between income inequality and mortality in Canada and in the United States: Cross sectional assessment using census data and vital statistics. *British Medical Journal*, 320, 898–902.

Rozovsky, L.E. (2003). *The Canadian law of consent to treatment* (3rd ed.). Toronto: Butterworths.

Rupert, P.A., & Holmes, D.L. (1997). Dual relationships in higher education: Professional and institutional guidelines. *Journal of Higher Education*, 68, 660–78.

Rushton, J.P. (1995). *Race, evolution, and behavior: A life history perspective*. New Brunswick, NJ: Transaction.

Ryan, R.M., & Deci, E.L. (2000). Self-determination theory and the facilitation of intrinsic motivation, social development, and well-being. *American Psychologist*, 55, 68–78.

S.T. v. Gaskell (1997), O.J. No. 2029.

Sareen, J., Cox, B.J., Afifi, T.O., Yu, B.N., & Stein, M.B. (2005). Mental health service use in a nationally representative Canadian survey. *Canadian Journal of Psychiatry*, 50, 753–61.

Schachter, D., Kleinman, I., & Harvey, W. (2005). Informed consent and adolescents. *Canadian Journal of Psychiatry*, 50, 534–40.

Schlesinger, A. (1949). *The vital center: The politics of freedom*. Boston: Houghton Mifflin.

Schwartz, J.P., & Hage, S.M. (2009). Prevention: Ethics, responsibility, and commitment to public well-being. In M.E. Kenny, A.M. Horne, P. Orpinas, & L.E. Reese (Eds.), *Realizing social justice: The challenge of preventive interventions* (pp. 123–40). Washington, DC: American Psychological Association.

Schwartz, S.J., Unger, J.B., Zamboanga, B.L, & Szapocznik, J. (2010). Rethinking the concept of acculturation: Implications for theory and research. *American Psychologist*, 65, 237–51.

Scott, D.S. (1981). Living with a physical handicap. In J.A. Downey, G. Riedel, & A.H. Kutscher (Eds.), *Bereavement of physical disability: Recommitment to life, health and function* (pp. 148–50). New York: Arno Press.

Seitz, J., & O'Neill, P. (1996). Ethical decision-making and the code of ethics of the Canadian Psychological Association. *Canadian Psychology*, 37, 23–30.

Seligman, M.E.P. (1975). *Helplessness: On depression, development, and death*. San Francisco: Freeman.

Senate of Canada. (2008). *Population health policy: Issues and options. Fourth report of the Subcommittee on Population Health of the Standing Senate Committee on Social Affairs, Science and Technology*. Ottawa: Author. Available at www.parl.gc.ca.

Seto, M.C. (1995). Sex with therapy clients: Its prevalence, potential consequences, and implications for psychology training. *Canadian Psychology*, 36, 70–86.

Sevensky, R. (1984). Religion, psychology, and mental health. *American Journal of Psychotherapy*, 38, 73–86.

Shafranske, E., & Malony, H.N. (1990). Clinical psychologists' religious and spiritual orientations and their practice of psychotherapy. *Psychotherapy*, 27, 72–78.

Shapiro, D.L. (2010). Relational identity theory: A systematic approach for transforming the emotional dimension of conflict. *American Psychologist*, 65, 634–45.

Shepard, B., O'Neill, L., & Guenette, F. (2006). Counselling with First Nations women: Considerations of oppression and renewal. *International Journal for the Advancement of Counselling, 28,* 227–40.

Shepard, M. (1971). *The love treatment: Sexual intimacy between patients and psychotherapists.* New York: Wyden.

Shuchman, M. (2005). *The drug trial: Nancy Olivieri and the science scandal that rocked the Hospital for Sick Children.* Toronto: Random House.

Shurnas, P.S., & Coughlin, M.J. (2003). Recall of the risks of forefoot surgery after informed consent. *Foot & Ankle International, 24,* 904–8.

Sinclair, C. (1993). Codes of ethics and standards of practice. In K.S. Dobson & D.J.D. Dobson (Eds.), *Professional Psychology in Canada* (pp. 167–200). Toronto: Hogrefe & Huber.

Sinclair, C. (1998). Nine unique features of the Canadian Code of Ethics for Psychologists. *Canadian Psychology, 39,* 167–76.

Sinclair, C. (2011). The evolution of the Canadian Code of Ethics over the years (1986–2011). *Canadian Psychology, 52,* 152–61.

Sinclair, C., & Pettifor, J.L. (2001). *Companion manual to the Canadian code of ethics for psychologists,* 3rd ed. Ottawa: Canadian Psychological Association.

Sinclair, C., Poizner, S., Gilmour-Barrett, K., & Randall, D. (1987). The development of a code of ethics for psychologists. *Canadian Psychology, 28,* 1–8.

Sinclair, C., Simon, N.P., & Pettifor, J.L. (1996). The history of ethical codes and licensure. In L.J. Bass, S.T. DeMers, J.R.P. Ogloff, C. Peterson, J.L. Pettifor, R.P. Reaves, T. Retfalvi, N.P. Simon, C. Sinclair, & R.M. Tipton (Eds.), *Professional conduct and discipline in psychology* (pp. 1–15). Washington, DC: American Psychological Association.

Smith, D. & Fitzpatrick, M. (1995). Patient-therapist boundary issues: An integrative review of theory and research. *Professional Psychology: Research and Practice, 26,* 499–506.

Smith, L. (2005). Psychotherapy, classism, and the poor: Conspicuous by their absence. *American Psychologist, 60,* 687–96.

Smith, M.B. (2000). Values, politics, and psychology. *American Psychologist, 55,* 1151–52.

Smith, T.S., McGuire, J.M., Abbott, D.W. & Blau, B.I. (1991). Clinical ethical decision making: An investigation of the rationales used to justify doing less than one believes one should. *Professional Psychology: Research and Practice, 22,* 235–39.

Smith v. Jones [1999], 1 S.C.R. 455.

Snell v. Farrell (1990), 72 D.L.R. (4th) 289.

Soffer, M., McDonald, K.E., & Blanck, P. (2010). Poverty among adults with disabilities: Barriers to promoting asset accumulation in individual development accounts. *American Journal of Community Psychology, 46,* 376–85.

Stark, C. (2011). The application of the *Canadian Code of Ethics for Psychologists* to teaching: Mandatory self-disclosure and alternatives in psychology courses. *Canadian Psychology, 52,* 192–97.

Statistics Canada. (2006). *Women in Canada: A gender-based statistical report* (5th ed.). Ottawa: Author.

Steinberg, L., Cauffman, E., Woolard, J., Graham, S., & Banich, M. (2009). Are adolescents less mature than adults? Minors' access to abortion, the juvenile death penalty, and the alleged APA "flip-flop." *American Psychologist, 64,* 583–94.

Stewart v. Noone (1992), B.C.J. No. 1017.

Suedfeld, P., & Tetlock, P.E. (1992). Psychologists as policy advocates: The roots of controversy. In P. Suedfeld & P.E. Tetlock (Eds.), *Psychology and social policy* (pp. 1–30). New York: Hemisphere.

Tarasoff v. Regents of the University of California, 17 Cal.3d 425, 551 P.2d 334 (1976).

Thomas, J.T. (2010). *The ethics of supervision and consultation: Practical guidance for mental health professionals.* Washington, DC: American Psychological Association.

Thoreson, R., Miller, M., & Krauskopf, C. (1989). The distressed psychologist: Prevalence and treatment considerations. *Professional Psychology: Research and Practice, 20,* 153–58.

Titus, S.L., Wells, J.A., & Rhoades, L.J. (2008). Repairing research integrity. *Nature, 453,* 980–82.

Tjeltveit, A.C. (2000). There is more to ethics than codes of professional ethics: Social ethics, theoretical ethics, and managed care. *The Counseling Psychologist, 28,* 242–52.

Toporek, R.L., & Williams, R.A. (2006). Ethics and professional issues related to the practice of social justice in counseling psychology. In R.L. Toporek, L.H. Gerstein, N.A. Fouad, G. Roysircar, & T. Isreal (Eds.), *Handbook for social justice in counseling psychology* (pp. 17–34). Thousand Oaks, CA: SAGE.

Truscott, D. (1993). The psychotherapist's duty to protect: An annotated bibliography. *Journal of Psychiatry & Law, 21,* 221–44.

Truscott, D. (2006). Ethical and legal issues for supervisors and supervisees. *College of Alberta Psychologists Monitor, 25,* 2–3.

Truscott, D. (2011). Professionalism and boundaries in psychotherapy. *College of Alberta Psychologists Monitor, 38,* 1, 6–9.

Truscott, D., & Crook, K.H. (1993). *Tarasoff* in the Canadian context: *Wenden* and the duty to protect. *Canadian Journal of Psychiatry, 38,* 84–89.

Truscott, D., & Evans, J. (2001). Responding to dangerous clients. In E.R. Welfel & E. Ingersoll (Eds.), *The mental health desk reference: A sourcebook for counselors and therapists* (pp. 271–76). New York: Wiley.

Truscott, D., & Evans, J. (2009). Protecting others from homicide and serious harm. In J. Werth, E.R. Welfel, & A. Benjamin (Eds.), *The duty to protect: Ethical, legal, and professional considerations in risk assessment and intervention* (pp. 61–77). Washington, DC: American Psychological Association.

Uchelen, C.P., Davidson, S.F., Quressette, S.V.A., Brasfield, C.R., & Demerais, L.H. (1997). What makes us strong: Urban aboriginal perspectives on wellness and strength. *Canadian Journal of Community Mental Health, 16,* 37–50.

Unger, R.K., Draper, R.D., & Pendergrass, M.L. (1986). Personal epistemology and personal experience. *Journal of Social Issues, 42,* 67–79.

US Central Intelligence Agency. (2004). *Memorandum to the DOJ Command Center, Office of Legal Counsel, U.S. Dep. Justice: Background Paper on CIA's Combined Use of Interrogation Techniques, Dec. 30.*

van den Hoonaard, W.C. (2011). *Seduction of ethics: Transforming the social sciences.* Toronto: University of Toronto Press.

Van Horne, B.A. (2004). Psychology licensing board disciplinary actions: The realities. *Professional Psychology: Research and Practice, 35,* 170–78.

VandeCreek, L., Miars, R.D., & Herzog, C.E. (1987). Client anticipations and preferences for confidentiality of records. *Journal of Counseling Psychology, 34,* 62–67.

Vogel, D.L., Gentile, D.A., & Kaplan, S.A. (2008). The influence of television on willingness to seek therapy. *Journal of Clinical Psychology, 64,* 276–95.

Vozoris, N., & Tarasuk, V. (2004). The health of Canadians on welfare. *Canadian Journal of Public Health, 95,* 115–20.

Wade, J.C., & Good, G.E. (2010). Moving toward mainstream: Perspectives on enhancing therapy with men. *Psychotherapy: Theory, Research, Practice, Training, 47,* 273–75.

Walsh, R.T. (1988). The dark side of our moon: The iatrogenic aspects of professional psychology. *Journal of Community Psychology, 16,* 244–48.

Walters, D. (1995). Mandatory reporting of child abuse: Legal, ethical and clinical implications within a Canadian context. *Canadian Psychology, 36,* 163–82.

Wampold, B.E., Imel, Z.E., & Miller, S.D. (2009). Barriers to the dissemination of empirically supported treatments: Matching messages to the evidence. *The Behavior Therapist, 32,* 144–55.

Weithorn, L.A., & Campbell, S.B. (1982). The competency of children and adolescents to make informed treatment decisions. *Child Development, 53,* 1589–98.

Welsome, E. (1999). *The plutonium files: America's secret medical experiments in the cold war.* New York: Delta.

Wenden v. Trikha (1991), 8 C.C.L.T. (2d) 138 (Alta. Q.B.); aff'd. (1993) 14 C.C.L.T. (2d) 225.

Werch, C.E., & Owen, D.M. (2002). Iatrogenic effects of alcohol and drug prevention programs. *Journal of Studies on Alcohol, 63,* 581–90.

Werth, J.L., Hastings, S.L., & Riding-Malon, R. (2010). Ethical challenges of practicing in rural areas. *Journal of Clinical Psychology, 66,* 537–48.

Williams, J., Hadjistavropoulos, T., Malloy, D.C., Gagon, M., Sharpe, D., & Fuchs-Lacelle, S. (2012). A mixed methods investigation of the effects of ranking ethical principles on decision making: Implications for the Canadian Code of Ethics for Psychologists. *Canadian Psychology, 53,* 204–16.

Wilson, D.B., Gottfredson, D.C., & Najaka, S.S. (2001). School-based prevention of problem behaviors: A meta-analysis. *Journal of Quantitative Criminology, 17,* 247–72.

Wilson, K., Mottram, P.G., & Vassilas, C.A. (2008). Psychotherapeutic treatments for older depressed people. *Cochrane Database of Systematic Reviews,* Issue 1. Art. No.: CD004853.

Wolfe, M. (1978). Childhood and privacy. In I. Altman & J.R. Wohlwill (Eds.), *Human behavior and environment: Advances in theory and research* (Vol. 3, pp. 175–222). New York: Plenum.

Wrenn, C.G. (1962). The culturally encapsulated counselor. *Harvard Educational Review, 32,* 444–49.

Wright, M.J. (1974). CPA: The first ten years. *Canadian Psychologist, 15,* 112–31.

Yellow Horse Brave Heart, M., & DeBruyn, L.M. (1998). The American Indian holocaust: Healing historical unresolved grief. *American Indian and Alaska Native Mental Health Research, 8,* 56–79.

Yong, E. (2012). Replication studies: Bad copy. *Nature, 489,* 298–300.

York, G. (1990). *The dispossessed: Life and death in Native Canada.* London: Vintage.

Young v. Bella [2006], 1 S.C.R. 108, 2006 SCC 3.

Youth Criminal Justice Act, 2002, C1.

Zakrzewski, R.F. (2006). A national survey of American Psychological Association student affiliates' involvement and ethical training in psychology educator-student sexual relationships. *Professional Psychology: Research and Practice, 37,* 724–30.

Index